A God-Given Talent

A God-Given Talent
Peter J. Brust, Architect
His Work and Legacy
1906-2006

by

Anna M. Passante

ElexDay Publications
Milwaukee, Wisconsin

© 2006 by Anna M. Passante
All rights reserved. No part of this book may be reproduced or transmitted in any form or by any means, electronic or mechanical, including photocopying, recording, or by any information storage and retrieval system without written permission from the publisher, except for the inclusion of brief quotations in a review.

Printed in the United States of America
Library of Congress Control Number: 2006926749
All non-credited photographs were either photographed by Anna M. Passante, reproduced from family photographs, or reproduced from her personal postcard collection.

Cover designed by Anna M. Passante

Publisher's Cataloging-In-Publication Data
(Prepared by The Donohue Group, Inc.)

Passante, Anna Marie.
  A God-given talent : Peter J. Brust, architect : his work and legacy, 1906-2006 / by Anna M. Passante.

  p. : ill. ; cm.

  Includes bibliographical references and index.
  ISBN: 0-9785641-0-3

1. Brust, Peter J. 2. Architects--Wisconsin--Biography. 3. Architecture--Wisconsin--20th century. I. Title.

NA737.B78 P37 2006
720.92 2006926749

ElexDay Publications
3207 South Indiana Avenue
Milwaukee, Wisconsin 53207

10 9 8 7 6 5 4 3 2 1

Dedication

This book is dedicated to three people: the late Peter Brust; my late sister, Marilyn; and the late Bishop Leo Brust, known to many as a walking encyclopedia.

Acknowledgments

This book would not have been possible without the kindness of strangers. These strangers, whether it was by phone, email, or snail mail, provided me with information and photographs that I wouldn't have been able to obtain elsewhere. I would like to thank these strangers, as well as other organizations and individuals who provided me with information. I give many thanks to the following:

- Melanie Fox of the U.S. Bank of Fond du Lac, banking staff at St. Francis Bank in Milwaukee, and Judy Greene of the M & I Bank of Stevens Point.
- A number of ecclesiastical organizations, including Sister Jeremy Quinn of the Congregation of St. Agnes of Fond du Lac; Father Melvin Wierzbicki of the Pulaski Franciscans; Sister Bernice Haase, Sister Corrine Dais, and Sister Connie of the School Sisters of St. Francis, Milwaukee; Sister Yvonne Haase of the Sisters of St. Francis of Assisi, St. Francis; Sister Mary Joella Cunnane of the Sisters of Our Lady of Mercy Convent, Chicago; Sister Johanna Hastings of the Dominican Sisters of Perpetual Rosary, Milwaukee; Sister Diane Kenel of the Dominican Sisters, Racine; St. Paul's Catholic Church, Combined Locks; St. Louis Catholic Church, Caledonia; and St. James Lutheran Church, Marinette.
- A number of health organizations, including Beaver Dam Community Hospital, Northern Wisconsin Center, and Winnebago Mental Health Institute.
- The library staffs of the University of Wisconsin-La Crosse Library, Marquette University Library, Monroe Clinic Medical Library, Alexander Hamilton High School Library, and Salzmann Library of the St. Francis Seminary. Also, the Wisconsin city libraries of Monroe, Manitowoc, Appleton, Sheboygan, and Jefferson.
- Many Wisconsin historical preservation organizations, including Milwaukee County Historical Society, Wisconsin State Historical Society, Appleton County Historical Society, Dodge Center Historical Society, Hartland Historical Society, Bay View Historical Society, St. Francis Historical Society, Washington County Historical Society, Sheboygan County Historical Society, and the Milwaukee Historic Preservation Commission.
- Many individuals, including Patsy Brust Koenings, David Brust, Marion Chester Read, Ron Winkler, and Charlotte Zaleski who is a descendant of John Baptist Brost.
- Numerous organizations and businesses, including St. Catherine's Residence, Park Falls Chamber of Commerce, Half Nuts Company, Sylvan Lodge, and the Girl Scouts of Milwaukee Area.

I would also like to give thanks to the following:
- Zimmerman Design Group for permission to use photographs and information from their archives. Special thanks go to Joanne Powell of Zimmerman Design Group who worked with me scanning hundreds of photographs from their archives. These original photographs of the work of the firms of Brust & Philipp and Peter Brust, Architect, truly enriched this book.
- Tim Cary of the Archdiocese of Milwaukee Resource Center at Cousin's Center for all of his help. Many hours were spent at the resource center locating information on the many churches designed by the firms of Brust & Philipp, Peter Brust-Architect, and Brust & Brust.
- Thomas Eschweiler who facilitates the Wisconsin Architectural Archive located at the downtown Milwaukee Public Library. Mr. Eschweiler kindly allowed me to photograph architectural drawings that are included in this book.
- The librarians in the Milwaukee Public Library Humanities Department for their help in locating reference materials and photographs that were needed to complete this book.
- My son, Robb Passante, who is a graphic artist, for reviewing and correcting the typesetting of this book and for creating the digital files before it went to press.
- My daughter, Michelle Passante, for her careful proofreading and editing of this book.

Table of Contents

Introduction

Chapter 1 Brust Family History and Peter Brust's Early Years 1

Chapter 2 Brust & Philipp   Residential Commissions   1906-1926..................31

Chapter 3 Brust & Philipp   Ecclesiastical Commissions   1906-1926..................95

Chapter 4 Brust & Philipp   Business Commissions   1906-1926..................135

Chapter 5 Brust & Philip   Medical, Public, Memorial, Recreation, and Theater Commissions, 1906-1926..................173

Chapter 6 Brust & Philipp   Planned Communities   1906-1926..................203

Chapter 7 Peter Brust, Architect..................1927-1937..................213

Chapter 8 Brust & Brust..................1938-1946..................223

Chapter 9 Legacy..................1947-2006..................235

Afterword..................263

Appendix 1: Illinois Application..................264

Appendix 2: Brust Family Memories..................265

Appendix 3: Brust Family Tree..................272

Appendix 4: Brust Ancestors: Where They Rest..................273

Appendix 5: Unknown Photographs..................277

Selected Bibliography..................281

Index..................287

Introduction

Most genealogists seek the proverbial skeleton in the closet, or perhaps they seek an ancestor who was lucky enough to have experienced the Andy Warhol fifteen minutes of fame. The need to discover the unique ancestor may account for the endless hours of researching a multitude of documents only to uncover a minuscule amount of information. But beware genealogists, for one exciting minuscule fact can send one off in an unexpected direction! A simple family tree project can precede a book project that becomes an obsession for its creator.

While doing the Brust family tree, I became acquainted with the work of Peter Brust, the architect, and his two architect sons, John and Paul. Although architecture is an admirable profession, the fact that Peter, John, and Paul were architects did not overly impress me. However, on a visit to the Milwaukee Historic Preservation office, I viewed a file on Peter, John, and Paul Brust. Even though the file was slim, I was impressed that all three were important enough, in the architectural world, to have a file at the Milwaukee Historic Preservation office. My pursuit of minuscule facts had begun.

This book tells the story of Peter Brust and the evolution of a company, Brust & Philipp, over a period of 100 years. Started in 1906, business partners have come and gone. The company, founded by Peter Brust and Richard Philipp, is now the Zimmerman Design Group. This book is dedicated to Peter Brust with the hope that the legacy, begun with Brust & Philipp, will be continued through the firm of Zimmerman Design Group for many years to come. It has been an honor to research and document the hundreds of commissions spanning the last 100 years.

Finally, this volume was written for all the members of the Brust/Brost family. This includes my husband's family. Peter's brother, Frank, was my husband's great-grandfather. All of us can now say that we possess a relative, Peter Brust, who experienced a celebrity status of sorts and the Andy Warhol fifteen minutes of fame.

Peter J. Brust ca. 1900

Chapter 1
Brust Family History and Peter Brust's Early Years

German immigration to Wisconsin increased sharply in the 1840s and 1850s. Nationally, almost one million Germans immigrated to America during that period. Most came from the southwestern German states of Baden, Bavaria, Hesse, and Rhineland. Many were farmers who sought escape from farms that were either too small, inefficient, overly populated, or heavily mortgaged. Repeatedly, these farmers were faced with crop failures and potato blight that threatened their families with starvation.

The promise of cheap land and a higher degree of prosperity drove these German farmers to America, and Nicholas Brust and his brother, John Baptist Brost, were among them. It is unclear why Nicholas took the surname Brust and John Baptist took the surname Brost. Interestingly, Nicholas and John Baptist's father's name was Peter Joseph Prost. A document was found in the possessions of the late Bishop Leo Brust that referred to the surname mystery. According to the document, the surnames Prost, Probst, Brost, and Brust are of the same surname family, and all are found in the Alflen and Ulmen areas of Germany. A number of residents from those two areas immigrated to Wisconsin. The document also stated that the surnames Prost, Probst, Brost, and Brust all derived from the Medieval Latin word "praepositus," which is defined as "a person selected to superintend or preside over."

The two brothers arrived in America at separate times with John Baptist Brost arriving first. John Baptist, his wife, Eva, and their children, ten-year-old Nicholas Joseph, seven-year-old Lambert Joseph, three-year-old Peter, and baby Mary Francisca, left their home and immigrated to America in June 1842. An historical document from the St. John the Baptist Catholic Church in Johnsburg, Wisconsin, gives the following description of the John Baptist Brost family journey to America:

> John Baptist Brost left Ulmen [Germany] on foot with his wife, Eva Bell, and their children around June 20, 1842. Five days later they got as far as Neuwied on the Rhine River. On July 1, 1842, they set sail to America on the passenger ship, Parus, from a Holland port and arrived in the New York port on August 18, 1842. They left Albany and took an Erie Canal boat, which was drawn by horses and mules to Buffalo, New York. [At this point, they probably traveled by sailboat from Buffalo to Sheboygan.] The family eventually docked in Sheboygan and from there traveled inland by covered wagon. They traveled the Military Road, which connected the forts of Green Bay and Prairie du Chien. The road ran along the eastern shore of Lake Winnebago through Fond du Lac. From here they traveled north to Johnsburg.[1]

According to the St. John's parish booklet, by 1842, twenty-three emigrants from Ulmen, Germany, settled in Johnsburg. John Baptist Brost was one of the founders of St. John the Baptist Catholic Church in Johnsburg. A historical marker in front of the church states that Catholics gathered at Brost's home on Sundays and holy days for community prayer. When his home proved too small, Brost, along with John Fuchs and Mathias Schneider, gave five acres each as a site for a church. A log church was completed in the spring of 1843.

Christopher, Catherine, and an unidentified child stand in front of their Gothic style house, located at 1738 South St. Francis Avenue in St. Francis, Wisconsin. The house was completed in 1885. Most likely, the child in the photograph was their youngest child, Anna, who died at the age of ten of lockjaw. [See Page 269 for information about Anna's accident.]

Nicholas Brust, along with his wife, Anna, and their two children, five-year-old Christopher and seven-year-old Gertrude, sailed to America on May 26, 1843. The ship on which they sailed is unknown. Most likely, Nicholas' family followed the same path as his brother from Ulmen to Wisconsin. However, Nicholas arrived in the Milwaukee area rather than Sheboygan and settled with his family in Town of Lake.

For the trip over the Atlantic Ocean, the families were allowed to bring only the bare necessities, including only enough food to last the forty-five-day trip. A family story reveals that little Gertrude, Nicholas' daughter, was caught sharing the family's prune ration with another little girl.

Nicholas Brust settled in Town of Lake, located in the southeast corner of Milwaukee County. Nicholas bought eighty acres of land on the southeast corner of what is now South 16th Street and West Layton Avenue. The land was cleared, farmed, and was considered a model farm. Nicholas and Anna went on to have two more children, Josephine in 1844 and Mary Ann in 1849. Nicholas lived on the farm until his death in May 1868. His wife, Anna, died much later in May 1887. It appears that after the death of Nicholas, Anna lived with her married daughter Josephine Linck.

In the early years of Town of Lake, there were few schools. Nicholas' son, Christopher, took lessons from a private tutor and attended a German school on the south side of Milwaukee for thirteen days. Nicholas instilled in his children the German work ethic along with a strong religious background. Every Sunday, the Brust family traveled five miles to St. Stephen's Catholic Church by horse and buggy.

On January 28, 1869, Christopher married Catherine Biever. Catherine's father, Peter Biever, owned a farm on 10th Street and Layton Avenue that ran east and west of the railroad tracks. Shortly after they were married, Christopher and Catherine moved to the northeastern corner of Town of Lake and settled on South Huron Street near East Russell Avenue. South Huron Street is now South Ellen Street. In 1879, this area became the village of Bay View.

For sixteen years, Christopher Brust worked as a pattern maker. He was employed at the roller mills on the south side of Milwaukee and for a number of other companies, such as the White Hill Sewing Machine Company, the Wilcin Manufacturing Company, and the Filer & Stowell Company. He also worked as a cabinetmaker, carpenter, and

Catherine Biever Brust

Christopher Brust

Sitting: father and mother, Christopher and Catherine Brust ca. 1910
Standing: their children (left to right), Anna Marie "Emma" Reiman Dederichs, Joseph, Peter, Reverend Nicholas, Frank, John, and Mary Schmidling

architect. Christopher's life was noteworthy enough to be included in Jerome Watrous' book, *Memoirs of Milwaukee County*, published in 1909. The article about Christopher Brust conveys a picture of a hardworking man who worked hard to save enough money to buy land.[2]

Christopher purchased land in Town of Lake in 1880, which is now part of the city of St. Francis. He started a garden business raising vegetables to be sold at market. Christopher built his family a Gothic Revival style cottage in 1885 that still exists at 1738 East St. Francis Avenue; however, the home was extensively remodeled. The house cost a total of $2,050. [See photograph on Page 2.] After subdividing some land, Christopher left evidence of his presence by naming a street after himself. Brust Avenue begins at Oklahoma Avenue in Milwaukee, continues south through St. Francis, and ends at Layton Avenue.

Peter Brust was born on November 4, 1869, in Town of Lake, Wisconsin. He was the first of eight children born to Christopher and Catherine. Peter's early education is a bit sketchy. Fortunately, some educational information was found on a 1922 permit application that Peter submitted to practice architecture in the State of Illinois.[3]

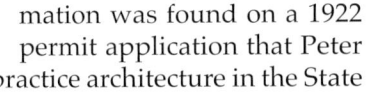
Bishop Leo Brust

According to the application, Peter attended a Town of Lake public school from 1875 to 1877, Sacred Heart Parochial School from 1878 to 1880, Pio Nono College in 1881, and a Bay View public school in 1882. [See the next page for more information on the schools Peter attended.]

By the age of fourteen, Peter was no longer attending school. It was time for him to work for his father as a carpenter in order to save money to pay for an apprenticeship with a local architectural firm. Peter's father, Christopher, encouraged his son to become an architect. He felt his son would make a better living as an architect than as a carpenter. According to the State of Illinois permit application, Peter attended some private evening mathematics classes at the Rheudes Business College and attended private evening courses for architectural engineering with an experienced engineer.

Peter's brother, Frank, followed their father into the pattern-making business as well as practicing carpentry. Another brother, Nicholas, chose the priesthood, eventually becoming a monsignor and holding the position of procurator for the St. Francis Seminary in St. Francis, Wisconsin. [See Page 6.] Later, Frank's son, Leo, would also enter the priesthood and rise to the position of auxiliary bishop of the Milwaukee Catholic Archdiocese.

Peter Brust married Olga Greulich in 1901. Olga was the daughter of Andrew Greulich and the granddaughter of August Greulich. August Greulich was prominent in Wisconsin's early political history, serving in the state's first legislature in 1848. He went on to serve as state senator in 1857 and 1858. Peter and Olga had three children, Catherine, Paul, and John. Unfortunately, Olga died on May 1, 1915, from a blood clot after minor surgery. Olga's mother, sister, and maids helped Peter raise the children after Olga's death. [See Page 264 for John Brust's childhood memories.] Peter remarried in 1921 to Charlotte (Lottie) Greulich, the sister of his first wife, Olga.

[1] Benjamin Blied, *A History of St. John the Baptist Congregation* (Johnsburg, Wisconsin: n.p., 1980), 10.
[2] Jerome A. Watrous, ed. *Memoirs of Milwaukee County* (Madison, Wisconsin: Western Historical Association, 1909), 660-661.
[3] State of Illinois Architectural Registration, (November 25, 1922).

Schools Attended by Peter Brust

Peter Brust attended elementary school in Town of Lake District #1 from 1875 to 1877 and returned to the school in 1882. The school building was affectionately known as the little red schoolhouse. It housed primary grades plus a two-year high school. The school, built in 1873, was located on South Wentworth Avenue, south of what is now Groppi's Food Store. South Wentworth Avenue was then known as Bishop Street. This brick Italianate style building served the community until Trowbridge School was built in 1894. The little red schoolhouse was razed around 1900.

Town of Lake District #1 school also known as the little red schoolhouse

Peter Brust attended Sacred Heart of Jesus School from 1878 to 1880. The parish at 3635 South Kinnickinnic Avenue in St. Francis was founded in the 1860s. The first parish school was built on the St. Francis Seminary grounds, but it was razed in 1871 to make way for the Holy Family Normal School. A new Sacred Heart School was built in 1872 near the newly constructed Sacred Heart of Jesus Catholic Church on South Kinnickinnic Avenue. By 1885, 125 families belonged to the parish. The parish was incorporated in that year, and Peter's father, Christopher, was one of the two parish trustees.

Sacred Heart of Jesus School, St. Francis

Peter Brust attended Pio Nono College in 1881. The building pictured to the right was built in 1871 and was known as the Holy Family Normal School, a teacher's college. Later, Pio Nono College moved into the building and shared space with the Holy Family Normal School. Peter attended school in this building in 1881. The building was located on what is now the Thomas More High School campus. Many years later, in 1930, Peter Brust would be the architect of the new Pio Nono building, known as Salzmann Hall. The Holy Family Normal School/Pio Nono College building was later razed.

Holy Family Normal School/Pio Nono College

The following excerpt describing Reverend Nicholas Brust comes from the book *Halcyon Days: Story of the St. Francis Seminary Milwaukee: 1856-1956*. Reverend Brust served as procurator for the St. Francis Seminary from 1921 to 1946. The procurator dealt with the financial affairs of the seminary. The excerpt reads as follows:

> Msgr. Brust is a simon-pure local product, having been born in nearby Bay View, educated in Sacred Heart parish school and at St. Francis Seminary, and having spent most of his adult years either as teacher or procurator at Pio Nono High School or the seminary.
>
> Besides depending on a combination of talent, interest, and application to his task here, he draws on a reserve of calmness, patience, and kindness under all tests which baffles others, but goes a long way in explaining the stability and success of his work. The career of Msgr. Brust touches the old and new, and represents the best ideas and procedures of both, which he has fused admirably. He is a man not likely to put any creature in the place of the Creator, with the result that everything he does follows an orderly pattern. Earthbound affairs take on real meaning because they are measured by other worldly standards. Consequently, he is able to keep order in the difficult sphere of business with all its ramifications. His philosophy of action may be described as a directive for retreating ahead, something like that of the United States Marine Corps. One of his friends delights in needling him a bit to hear him add "Voran!" to the greeting: "Immer langsam!"
>
> During the tenure of Msgr. Brust, some notable improvements were made, including the Miller gymnasium, but perhaps the more lasting memorial to his accomplishments is the transformation of the seminary grounds into a beautiful park. The change was inaugurated on a large scale in 1931 for the celebration of the diamond jubilee of the seminary. [Peter Brust performed outdoor design work for the seminary from 1930 to 1937. The total cost of the outdoor work was $18,280.] Since then the process has spread into wider areas of greenward due to the skilled operations of Peter Graf, superintendent of the grounds.[1]

[1] Rt. Rev. Msgr. Peter Leo Johnson DD, *Halcyon Days: Story of the St. Francis Seminary Milwaukee: 1856-1956* (Milwaukee, Wisconsin: The Bruce Publishing Company, 1956), 369.

This photograph of Reverend Nicholas Brust was taken in celebration of his first mass; he was ordained in 1903. The little girl standing closest to Reverend Brust is Rose Maller, granddaughter of Gertrude Brust Jordan of Caledonia, Wisconsin. Rose was Nicholas' cousin. Rose is also pictured with her sister, Helen, on Page 270.

Two of the girls standing on the right were identified. According to Sister Camille Kliebhan of the order of St. Francis of Assisi, the girl in the middle is her mother, Mary Eileen McNamara, also know as Mae. The girl on the extreme right is Coletta Phillip.

Chapter 1 – Brust Family History and Peter Brust's Early Years

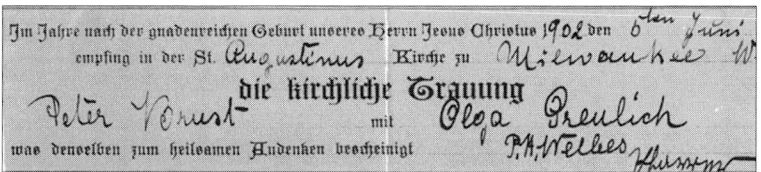

All portraits on this page are courtesy of Patsy Brust Koenings

The signatures of Peter and Olga Brust appear on this 1902 marriage license. Peter and Olga were married at St. Augustine of Hippo Catholic Church, located at 2530 South Howell Avenue in Milwaukee. Peter designed the new St. Augustine Catholic Church in 1908. (Marriage license courtesy of Patsy Brust Koenings.)

Above, Peter and Olga in their wedding portraits

Below left, Olga in her wedding gown

Below right, a portrait of Peter and Olga's children; from left to right, Paul, Catherine, and John

In 1906, Peter and Olga Brust moved to this house at 851 North 29th Street in Milwaukee. This Queen Anne style home, built in 1894, had a former address of Queen Anne Place. The North 29th Street home was part of the Concordia neighborhood, an affluent and heavily German community.

The neighborhood was named for Concordia College, a Lutheran pre-seminary school that was located in the neighborhood. It was at this home on North 29th that Peter lived with his first wife, Olga, and his second wife, Lottie, and where all three of Peter's children, Paul, Catherine, and John, were raised. Peter's son, John, mentions in his memoirs that when he lived in this house on North 29th Street, the area was at the edge of the city limits. [See Page 265 for John's memoirs about growing up at 851 North 29th Street.] The house at 851 North 29th is still at the original site.

In 1944, Peter and Lottie moved to 5044 West Washington Boulevard in Milwaukee.

Like Father, Like Son

St. Louis Catholic Church
Caledonia, Wisconsin

On February 7, 1842, Governor James D. Doty established the new town of Caledonia, Wisconsin, by carving it from the Town of Racine and Mount Pleasant. Situated in the northeast corner of Racine County, the first settlers came to the Caledonia area in the 1830s, many from the eastern United States. The Germans settled in the area in the 1840s and 1850s. The parish of St. Louis was established in Caledonia in 1848, and a church of log construction was built in 1851 on an acre of land donated by parishioner Peter Meyer. Meyer's grandson, Reverend Albert Meyer, became the Archbishop of Milwaukee in 1953.

A larger church was needed by 1859, so the parishioners voted to build a wood-framed church measuring 60 feet by 34 feet. The designing and building contract went to Christopher Brust whose sister, Gertrude, had settled in Caledonia with her husband, Casper Jordan. Christopher designed and constructed the church at a cost of $1,009, and it was completed on December 3, 1859. The church building debt was paid through subscription with all debt paid in less than two years. After fourteen years without a pastor, one was assigned in 1864.

By the turn of the twentieth century, the St. Louis parish needed a larger church. In 1901, Peter Brust designed a new church in the Romanesque Revival style with Racine cream-colored brick and Bedford sandstone trim. The cost of the new church at 13207 Hwy G was $10,000. It measured 91 feet by 43 feet and was constructed by the Elias Stollenwerk Company of Milwaukee. According to a newspaper article (*Catholic Citizen*, February 1, 1902), the church windows were of opalescent glass and ornamented with emblems and busts. The old wooden church, designed and built by Peter's father, Christopher, was put to other uses and was later razed in 1932. St. Louis Catholic Church is still an active parish in Caledonia, Wisconsin.

Above, a priest stands in front of the church that was designed by Christopher Brust in 1859. If you look closely, you can see the ladies in their Sunday hats walking behind the fence.

Left, the church designed by Peter Brust in 1901

Peter Brust Begins Employment with Ferry and Clas

Peter Brust began his career in architecture in 1890 as a draftsman with the architectural firm of Edward V. Koch & Company. After one year, Peter left Koch's employment to work for the newly established architectural firm of Ferry & Clas. At the firm of Ferry & Clas, Peter worked closely with two future business partners, Richard Philipp and Julius Heimerl. It was also during his employment with Ferry & Clas that Peter took his first tour of Europe. In 1893, he toured France by bicycle.

Architects during the 1890s learned the architectural trade by working with experienced architects. After a ten-year apprenticeship, an aspiring architect was capable of establishing his own business. Brust, Philipp, and Heimerl gained much experience and knowledge during their employment at the firm Ferry & Clas, and their work with this firm continued to influence their work for years to come. According to architectural writer Rexford Newcomb, AIA, "Taken as a whole, the work of Brust and Philipp would seem to continue in the most admirable fashion the high ideals set for architecture by their early tutors in the art, Messrs. Ferry and Clas." Newcomb went on to say, "The spirit and idealism that always infused the work of Ferry & Clas would live on in the work of the younger men."[1]

Peter Brust said the following about his time at the firm of Ferry & Clas: "Before establishing our office [Brust & Philipp], I spent twelve years in the office of Ferry & Clas where I had charge of the largest jobs going through the office."[2]

Among these large jobs were at least three jobs that were part of design competitions. The three competitions were the Tower of St. John's Cathedral, the Milwaukee Public Library and Museum, and the State

This photograph of the Ferry & Clas workroom was taken in approximately 1895 at the Ferry & Clas offices at 725-727 North Broadway Street in Milwaukee. Pictured in the photograph are Julius Heimerl, George Duse, Joseph Mc. C. Bell, Edward Main, Richard Philipp, Alfred C. Clas, Didrik Ottesen, Peter Brust, Elmer Grey, William Graves, Frank Bader, and George B. Ferry.

Historical Society in Madison. By 1900, Peter was head draftsman at the firm of Ferry & Clas.

[1] Rexford Newcomb, AIA, "The Continuity of Personal Influence as Sensed in the Work of Brust and Philipp of Milwaukee," *Western Architect* (August 1924), 87-88.
[2] State of Illinois Architectural Registration (November 25, 1922).

The Architectural Firm of Ferry & Clas

George Bowman Ferry was born in Springfield, Massachusetts, on February 7, 1851. After graduating from Springfield High School, Ferry attended the Massachusetts Institute of Technology from 1871 to 1872. In 1881, Ferry and his wife moved to Milwaukee, and in 1890, he became a senior partner in the architectural firm of Ferry & Clas. The firm of Ferry & Clas won a number of design awards at the various world fairs, including the following: the 1900 Exposition Univerelle, Paris, France; the 1901 Pan American Exposition of Buffalo, New York; and the 1904 Louisiana Purchase Exposition, St. Louis, Missouri. Well-known commissions of Ferry & Clas include the Frederick Pabst Mansion in Milwaukee, the Milwaukee Public Library and Museum, the Wisconsin Historical Society in Madison, and the tower of the Cathedral of St. John's the Evangelist in Milwaukee. The firm dissolved in 1911 after twenty plus years of partnership. Ferry died on January 29, 1918. At the time of Ferry's death, Alfred Clas described Ferry as loyal, artistic, honorable, and high-minded.

Alfred C. Clas was born in Salk City, Wisconsin, on December 26, 1859. As a young man, Clas spent two years as an apprentice to a Milwaukee architect, gaining practical instruction in building construction. In 1879, he went to Stockton, California, and spent two years working in an architectural office. Returning to Milwaukee, he entered the firm of James Douglas, a well-known architect. From 1887 to 1890, Clas practiced architecture independently, and in 1890, he teamed with George Bowman Ferry to form Ferry & Clas. After the firm of Ferry & Clas dissolved in 1911, Clas formed Clas & Clas with his son, Angelo. In 1921, the firm was reorganized as Clas, Shepherd & Clas with the addition of another son, Reuben, and Milwaukee architect, John S. Shepherd. Shepherd withdrew in 1931, and the firm was then renamed Clas & Clas, Inc. Alfred Clas was very civic minded and served on the Board of Parks Commissioners for fifteen years. A park, located at the southwest corner of the courthouse complex, was named in honor of him. Clas died in 1942.

Ferry & Clas Projects Commissioned During Peter Brust's Employment with the Firm of Ferry & Clas

The Frederick Pabst Mansion
Milwaukee, Wisconsin

Captain Frederick Pabst commissioned George Bowman Ferry in 1889 to design a new home for his family. The following year, Ferry joined with Alfred Clas to form the architectural firm of Ferry & Clas. Peter Brust was a draftsman for Ferry & Clas at this time, so he probably worked on this commission. It took two years to complete the mansion at 20th Street and West Wisconsin Avenue in Milwaukee. The Flemish Renaissance Revival style house, perched on six acres of land, was one of the most impressive homes to line Grand Avenue. The mansion featured a pressed-brick exterior trimmed in terra cotta. The Matthews Brothers Company, located at North 3rd Street & West Grand Avenue, opulently decorated the interior with custom-made furniture and woodwork. The mansion cost nearly $250,000, not including furnishings and decorating.

Frederick Pabst commissioned a gazebo to built for the 1893 World's Columbian Exposition, which was used to exhibit the Pabst Brewing Company products. After the exposition ended, Pabst moved the gazebo to his mansion on Grand Avenue, and it was attached to the dining room by a passageway. The glass-domed roof was replaced with copper.

Pabst only lived in the mansion for eleven years. He died in January 1904, and his widow, Marie, sold the mansion in 1908 to the Milwaukee Catholic Archdiocese. Very little was changed during the time that the archdiocese owned the mansion; one exception was the gazebo, which was turned into a chapel dedicated to the Virgin Mary. The mansion served as the archbishops' residence until 1974. Bishop Leo Brust, nephew of Peter Brust, lived at the mansion for a number of years.

A recent photograph of the Pabst Mansion shows the gazebo at the far right; the gazebo is now used as a gift shop.

The archdiocese sold the mansion in 1974. The new owner razed the coach house in 1977 and plans were made to raze the mansion and replace it with a parking structure. Fortunately, Wisconsin Heritage, Inc., headed by John Conlin, secured a large state grant and twenty-three mortgages to purchase the mansion. The Pabst mansion was opened to the public in May 1978, and it has since undergone extensive restoration of the interior and exterior. The mansion was featured recently on HGTV, a cable television station.

Captain Frederick Pabst

The Cathedral of St. John's the Evangelist
Milwaukee, Wisconsin

The Cathedral of St. John's the Evangelist is located at 831 North Van Buren Street and has been the seat of the Catholic Archdiocese of Milwaukee since 1847. Victor Schulte, who designed St. Mary's Catholic Church in 1847 and Holy Trinity Catholic Church in 1849, was responsible for the design of St. John's Cathedral. Dedicated in July 1853, the Cathedral reflected

A drawing that depicts the original "onion" tower on St. John's

The new tower of St. John's designed by Ferry & Clas

the German style of the Zopfstil period. The Cathedral's exterior was done in Milwaukee Cream City brick. The bulbous or onion dome tower contained three bells cast in Troy, New York; the three bells were installed in 1857. In 1858, the tower clock was honored by being designated by the Milwaukee Common Council as the official timepiece of the city.

Unfortunately, in 1880, after many years of deterioration, the City of Milwaukee ordered that the tower be repaired or removed. A decision was made to remove the tower, since no funds were available to repair or replace it. The cathedral now featured a stunted look. Fortunately, twelve years later, a generous parishioner, John Black, a former mayor of Milwaukee from 1878 to 1880, donated $10,000 in the memory of his deceased wife to rebuild the tower. However, the generous donation was not enough, and additional money was sought to finance the new tower. The Cathedral proper was also in need of renovation, so subscriptions were requested of parish members to supplement the cost of the new tower and the necessary renovation to the Cathedral. Considering that the devastating Third Ward Fire of 1892 caused financial hardship for parishioners, it is astonishing that the total of donations for the Cathedral was close to $37,000.

When the Cathedral parish was finally ready to rebuild the tower, a design competition was conducted in 1892. The architectural firm of Ferry & Clas won the commission to design the new tower. Peter Brust was a draftsman for Ferry & Clas at the time, so he probably worked on this commission.

The new tower, inspired by the work of English architect Sir Christopher Wren, was built above the original clock in two stages. The first stage contained the three bells from the original tower, and the second stage contained the dome-like roof that was crowned with a gold cross. The total cost of the tower was $16,000, and the architectural fee was $650.

Edwin C. Eldridge, the curator of the Layton Art Gallery said the following about the new tower:

> In rebuilding the tower, the architects, Messrs. Ferry and Clas, have striven to carry out the work in the spirit in which the original was executed, and this they have so admirably done that when time shall have given the same

tone to its surfaces as is peculiar to the lower part of the church, the whole edifice will have the appearance of being built at the same period.[1]

The Cathedral was placed on the National Register of Historic Places in 1977. The Cathedral was given an additional Milwaukee landmark designation through the City of Milwaukee Historic Preservation Commission. This city designation goes further than the National Register designation by protecting the Cathedral from demolition or insensitive alterations.

[1] Reverend David J. O'Hearn, *Fifty Years at Saint John's Cathedral* (Milwaukee, Wisconsin: St. John's Cathedral, 1897), 45.

The Milwaukee Public Library and Museum Milwaukee, Wisconsin

With its Neo-Renaissance revival exterior and a three-story rotunda, the Milwaukee Public Library, located at 814 West Wisconsin Avenue, is one of the most recognized and admired buildings in Milwaukee. The building was completed in 1899, but the beginnings of the Milwaukee Public Library organization date back long before then.

It all began on December 8, 1847, when the Young Men's Association met in the parlor of the United States Hotel to discuss establishing a library. This debating and literary society sought to establish a library in connection with a reading room, and on that very night the library was established. Books were purchased or donated, but only association members could use the room with paid membership. The reading room occupied a room in a building on the northwest corner of East Wisconsin Avenue and North Broadway Street. This reading room was also used as a lecture hall and was witness to notable speakers, such as Horace Greeley, Horace Mann, and James Russell Lowell.

In the 1870s, there was a national movement for free or public libraries. In 1878, the Young Men's Association, due to the lack of library funding, decided to transfer the library materials to the City of Milwaukee. An act of the Wisconsin State Legislature in March 1878 formally transferred the library and its 10,000 volumes, one-third in the German language, to the city. A board of library

Milwaukee Public Library and Museum

directors was formed, but the library remained temporarily at the Academy of Music building.

In 1890, the library directors moved the 15,000 volumes to the Library Block building at North 4th Street and Grand Avenue; Grand Avenue is now know as West Wisconsin Avenue. This building was built by John Plankinton and was later the site of J. C. Penney department store. It is now the site of the Midwest Express Center. In 1889, the Milwaukee Common Council issued bonds to pay for a new Milwaukee Public Library and Museum building. The city purchased five lots on February 24, 1890, at North 8th Street and Grand Avenue. At one time, the location was a beautiful grove named the Mozart Grove, and it was often used for summer concerts. The grove was also frequently referred to as Der Wolonsita or "seat in the clouds".[1]

During the early planning stage of the Milwaukee Public Library and Museum, the city planners expressed a desire to have two independent structures connected on the facade to give an appearance of unity. This U-shaped design was very common in library and museum facilities. A national competition was held in 1893. The majority of the designs were of classical design, influenced by the 1893 World's Columbian Exhibition.

The two competition finalists were the firms of Ferry & Clas and H.C. Koch. The library commission chose the design of the architectural firm of Ferry & Clas. The disgruntled Koch felt that the firm of Ferry & Clas illegally submitted corrected drawings after the final deadline. Despite Koch's accusations, the firm of Ferry & Clas was awarded the commission, and construction of the Italian and French design building began in 1895. Peter Brust was a draftsman for Ferry & Clas during the library construction, so he probably worked on this commission.

Blue Bedford Indiana limestone was used for the exterior, while the carved ornamentation on the exterior was done on site after the stone was set in place. Italian immigrants constructed the rotunda's hand-laid mosaic floor. The building, with a capacity for 150,000 books, was completed in 1899. The cost of the building was $780,000. The new library and museum went on to win two world prizes for its architecture. The building is currently listed on the National Register of Historic Places.

An obituary for the late George Bowman Ferry (*Milwaukee Evening Wisconsin*, January 29, 1919) related an incident regarding William Jennings Bryan's first visit to Milwaukee. As his carriage traveled up what was then called Grand Avenue, it was said that Bryan paid an unconscious tribute to Ferry by involuntarily rising from his carriage to gaze intently upon the newly completed public library and museum building.

In 1957, an addition was built to the rear of the building on West Wells Street. This addition provided much needed space to house the library's growing collection. Included in the addition were four floor levels below ground, which served as additional shelving storage areas. After the Milwaukee Public Museum moved into a separate building at North 8th Street and West Wells Street, the library remodeled the old museum spaces to house library departments.

[1] *Questions and Answers About the Milwaukee Public Library System* (Milwaukee, Wisconsin: Board of Trustees of the Milwaukee Public Library, 1953), 1.

Wisconsin Historical Society Building
Madison, Wisconsin

In 1895, two years after winning the Milwaukee Public Library and Museum design competition, the architectural firm of Ferry & Clas won another impressive design competition for the new Wisconsin Historical Society building in Madison, Wisconsin. The Wisconsin Historical Society, founded in 1846, outgrew its facility, as did the University of Wisconsin library. Reuben Gold Thwaites, the Wisconsin Historical Society's director at the time, and Charles Kendall Adams, president of the University of Wisconsin, both lobbied the state legislature for a new building that would house both of their library collections. On April 19, 1895, the legislature authorized funds and created a commission to devise a plan for the new building to be located at 816 State Street in Madison.

As with the Milwaukee Public Library and Museum project, the winning entries were narrowed down to two architectural firms, Ferry & Clas and H.C. Koch. The Historical Society awarded the commission to Ferry & Clas. Interestingly, after the commission was awarded, the design submitted by Ferry & Clas was totally scrapped. The architectural team created a new design that supposedly was heavily copied from the design submitted by H.C. Koch, especially the arrangement of the major wings. During the construction of this building, Peter Brust was employed at Ferry & Clas as a draftsman, so he probably worked on this commission.

The new Wisconsin Historical Society building was done in the Renaissance Revival style with an exterior of buff-colored Bedford limestone. The interior of the building was similar to the Milwaukee Public Library and Museum building; it was U-shaped with two separate collections housed beneath one roof. The two libraries shared a reading room that seated 240 patrons. The reading room rose two full stories and was considered the centerpiece of the building.

Construction took place from 1896 to 1900, and the building was dedicated on October 19, 1900. The final price of the building was $675,000. When the university library moved into a new facility in 1952, the Wisconsin Historical Society took over the entire building.

Wisconsin State Historical Library Building Milwaukee Public Library

Other Ferry & Clas Projects Commissioned During Peter Brust's Employment with the Firm of Ferry & Clas

First Unitarian Church
Milwaukee, Wisconsin

The First Unitarian Church at 1009 East Ogden Avenue is the oldest Unitarian church in Milwaukee. It was designed in 1892 by the architectural firm of Ferry & Clas. Peter Brust was a draftsman for Ferry & Clas at the time, so he probably worked on this commission. The exterior of the Gothic Revival style church was done in rock-faced Bedford limestone. One of the gargoyle-like faces on the west side of the church is said to represent a prominent parish member, William H. Metcalf. Metcalf donated an organ for the new church. The church was placed on the National Register of Historic Places in 1974.

Matthews Brothers Building
Milwaukee, Wisconsin

The Matthews Brothers Company building, located at North 3rd Street and West Wisconsin Avenue, flanks the entrance of the Grand Avenue Mall. The building is best known to Milwaukeeans as the former F. W. Woolworth building. The firm of Ferry & Clas designed the building in 1892. Peter Brust was a draftsman for Ferry & Clas at the time, so he probably worked on this commission. The Matthews Brothers Company was well known for its production of beautiful architectural woodwork and custom-built furniture. The company created woodwork for the House of Representatives in Washington, D. C., and made the custom-built furniture and woodwork for Captain Frederick Pabst's mansion. In 2000, the Matthews Brothers building was placed on the National Register of Historic Places.

Steinmeyer Building
Milwaukee, Wisconsin

The Steinmeyer Building, located at 1050 North Old World Third Street, is done in the Richardsonian Romanesque Revival style. The red-orange pressed-brick exterior, with terra-cotta trim, was ornamented with wrought iron. Completed in 1893, it was designed by the architectural firm of Ferry & Clas for the William Steinmeyer Company, a wholesale and retail grocery. Peter Brust was a draftsman for Ferry & Clas at the time, so he probably worked on this commission. The Steinmeyer Building now houses various retail stores and offices.

Peter Brust Leaves Ferry & Clas and Joins with Charles D. Crane Creating the Firm of Crane & Brust.

Peter Brust left the firm of Ferry & Clas in 1901 and formed a partnership with architect Charles D. Crane. The partnership lasted for only one year. [See Page 20 for biographical information about Charles D. Crane.] During 1901, the architectural firm of Crane & Brust designed a number of commissions, including the Caleb Elliot Johnson house at 2734 East Bradford Avenue on Milwaukee's northeast side.

Caleb Elliot Johnson was part of the B. J. Johnson Soap Company. When his father, Burdette Jay, died in 1902, Caleb Johnson became president of the company. The company was established in 1894 as a soap and candle manufacturer and was located on the 400 block of North Plankinton Avenue. In the 1890s, the company developed a green-colored soap, challenging the usual white-colored soap. The ingredients of the new soap included coconut oil, olive oil, and palm oil. This soap was named Palmolive and went on to become a national brand.

Caleb Elliot Johnson House

Peter Brust Takes Employment with Architects Herman J. Esser and H. C. Koch from 1902-1905

From 1902 to 1905, Peter Brust worked with two architects, Herman J. Esser and H. C. Koch. According to Milwaukee city directories, Brust worked for Esser in 1903, Koch in 1904, and Esser in 1905. The 1902 city directory lists no business address for Brust, but he probably worked for Koch and/or Esser that year. Some of Herman J. Esser's major commissions during the period of 1902 to 1905 are as follows:

The Johnson Service Company Building
Milwaukee, Wisconsin

The Johnson Service Company building, located at 507 East Michigan Street in downtown Milwaukee, is a seven-story building with limestone entrances on East Michigan Street and North Jefferson Street. The Johnson Service building, designed by Herman Esser in 1902, was one of the first reinforced concrete buildings in Milwaukee. The first half of the building collapsed while it was under construction. Fortunately, no one was hurt and the project began again. Johnson Service Company was changed to Johnson Controls in 1974. An addition was built to the east of the original building in the year 2000 and was designed by the architectural firm of Zimmerman Design Group. [See Page 259 for the Johnson Controls' Brengel Technology Building commission.]

Roman Catholic Church of the Gesu
Milwaukee, Wisconsin

H.C. Koch designed the Roman Catholic Church of the Gesu, located at 1145 West Wisconsin Avenue, in 1893. During this time, Koch was in partnership with Herman J. Esser. In 1902, Esser was commissioned to design the triple-arched portico just below the rose stained-glass window in the main entrance. Peter Brust was employed by Esser when the triple-arched portico was designed. Gesu Church was placed on the National Register of Historic Places in 1986.

Public Service Building
Milwaukee, Wisconsin

Herman J. Esser designed the Public Service Building for the Milwaukee Electric Railway and Light Company in 1903. The four-story building, located at 231 West Michigan in downtown Milwaukee, featured an exterior of limestone on the first story, with pressed-brick and cut-stone on the upper floors. The first floor was the terminal area with two waiting rooms and thirteen car tracks. It was the largest terminal of its kind in the United States. Its rails extended to Watertown to the west, Sheboygan to the north, Kenosha to the south, and Burlington and East Troy to the southwest. The last train left the terminal on June 30, 1951.

During the building restoration in 1997, the east and west train doors were replaced with replicas of the original doors, and the fifth floor, which was added during a previous renovation, was removed. The architectural firm of Zimmerman Design Group was commissioned to perform the 1997 renovation, and in 1998, the building was placed on the National Register of Historic Places. The building is now occupied by WE Energies. [See Page 260 for the WE Energies renovation commission.]

Warehouse No. 1
Milwaukee, Wisconsin

Herman Esser designed Warehouse No. 1 for Theodore L. Hansen in 1904. In the early 1890s, Hansen was in the hop and malt business; however, after the Third Ward fire of 1892, Hansen decided to go into the commercial warehouse business since there appeared to be a growing need for warehouse space. The four-story brick building, located at 126 North Jefferson, was built with a full basement, three elevators, and two firewalls. The Hansen Storage Company was incorporated on June 16, 1904.

The Hansen Storage Company headquarters occupied Warehouse No. 1 until 1974. Since then, different tenants used the building, including ComedySportz, an entertainment venue. Corcoran Place, LLC, purchased the building in 1998. The building contains 75,000 square feet of office and retail space. Capital H Group LLC, offering corporate recruiting services, recently leased 7,500 square feet of office space.

Charles D. Crane was born in Johnson's Creek, Niagara County, New York, on July 6, 1850. As a child, he and his family moved to Burlington, Wisconsin. In 1874, Crane entered the architectural firm of Edward Townsend. Townsend is well known for designing the Old Soldier's home in Woods, Wisconsin. Crane left Mix's firm in 1886, and two years later, Crane joined with Carl C. Barkenhausen to form Crane & Barkenhausen. This partnership lasted only a few years. In 1900, Crane designed his own residence at 2519 North Wahl Avenue. It is now known as the Crane-Thomas-Goll house and is part of the North Point Historic District. Crane lived in the home from 1900 to 1903. Crane joined with Peter Brust in 1901, and the partnership lasted one year. Crane went on to practice independently, and in 1906, he designed Johnston Hall, located to the east of Gesu Church on the Marquette University Campus. This Gothic style building, with Venetian features, was named for Robert A. Johnston, the founder of Johnston Biscuit Company. Johnston was a great benefactor of Marquette University. Johnston Hall is still located at its original location, and it was placed on the National Register of Historic Places in 1986. Crane later retired from architectural work and was engaged by an appraisal company. Crane died on April 7, 1928, at the age of seventy-eight.

Herman J. Esser was born in Madison, Wisconsin, on April 19, 1865. Esser graduated from Cornell University in 1888 and was apprenticed to several architectural firms in New York City. Esser designed a number of buildings in Milwaukee, including the Oneida Street Station at 108 East Wells Street in 1900. Built as a power station for the Milwaukee Electric Railway and Light Company, the exterior was done in orange pressed-brick with terra-cotta cornices. Unfortunately, the cornices were removed in 1909. When the station closed, the Wisconsin Electric Company donated the building to the Milwaukee Repertory Theater. After extensive renovation, the theater complex opened in 1997 and was later placed on the National Register of Historic Places. One of Esser's largest commissions was the 1925 remodeling of the former Gimbel's Department Store building at the southeast corner of North Plankinton and West Wisconsin Avenue. His design included the Ionic columns on the riverside of the building. He was also known for his work on the Public Service Building, the Johnson Service Company Building, and the triple-arched portico on the Church of Gesu. Peter Brust worked for Esser during the years 1902 to 1905. Esser retired in 1937 at the age of seventy-two. He died on January 17, 1957, at the advanced age of ninety-two. His son, Verner Esser, was also a Milwaukee architect.

Henry C. Koch was born in Celle, Hanover, Germany, on March 30, 1841, and immigrated with his family to Milwaukee in May 1842. After attending the Milwaukee German English Academy, Koch served as an apprentice to the architectural firm of G. W. Mygott from 1856 to 1862.

On August 18, 1862, he enlisted in the 24th Wisconsin Infantry, Company B, and served during the Civil War. With a keen interest in engineering, Koch spent his spare time drawing maps. This skill came to the attention of General Forsythe, and Koch was recommended to the engineering corps. For four years, Koch served General Sheridan as a topographical engineer.

An obituary for Koch (*Milwaukee Sentinel,* May 20, 1910) told an interesting story regarding Koch and General Sheridan. According to the story, the army under Sheridan approached the Tennessee River. Finding no bridge, they started to pitch camp. The general confronted young Koch, then only twenty-three years old, and asked him what could be done in the way of a bridge. Koch replied that he needed materials. Sheridan pointed to the troops and said, "Here are the men." Then, Sheridan pointed to a wooded area and said, "There is a forest." After 2 ☐ hours, Koch not only constructed a bridge, but the army was transferred to the other side. In a letter to Koch from Sheridan, written shortly after the war, Sheridan mentions his admiration for the maps Koch drew of the different battlefields. Sheridan was very impressed by the accuracy and details of the maps, as well as their physical attractiveness. Some of Koch's signed maps were found among Sheridan's memoirs.

Koch re-entered the office of G. W. Mygott in 1866 as a partner. The partnership dissolved in 1870 and Koch formed a partnership with Julius Hess. The partnership between Koch and Hess lasted until 1873; Koch went on to practice alone until 1878, at which point he formed the firm of H. C. Koch and Company with his brother-in-law, Paul Schnetzky. In 1887, the partnership was dissolved, and in 1890, Koch formed a new partnership with Herman J. Esser. [See previous page for biographical information on Esser.] When this partnership dissolved in 1899, Koch's son, Armand, joined his father as a partner in 1902. H. C. Koch and Company became H. C. Koch and Son in 1905. The partnership lasted until Henry's death in May 1910. Peter Brust worked for Koch during the years 1902 to 1905.

Koch is best known for the following: Calvary Church, Milwaukee (1870); Ward Memorial Theater, Woods, Wisconsin (1870s); the Ogden Building, Milwaukee (1902); the Pfister Hotel, Milwaukee (1893); Catholic Church of the Gesu, Milwaukee (1893); Milwaukee City Hall (1896); and the Wells Building, Milwaukee (1901).

Notable Men Milwaukee Public Library

Freelance Work of Peter Brust, 1895-1905

Mechanical Appliance Company & Battery Light Company
Milwaukee, Wisconsin

In 1901, the Mechanical Appliance Company began in Milwaukee with fifteen employees. The company was located in an old shoe factory at 710 Hanover Street, now the 1800 block of South 3rd Street. The company made electric motors and electrical appliances. By 1906, Louis Allis was the president of the company, and the number of employees increased to seventy-five. The company needed more space and therefore relocated to 427 East Stewart Street on the Allis' original homestead farm.

Peter Brust was hired in 1905 to design a new building for the Mechanical Appliance Company at the East Stewart Street site. The total cost of the building was $16,000. In 1922, Mechanical Appliance Company was renamed the Louis Allis Company. The Louis Allis Company later became a division of Litton Industries, Inc.

The Mechanical Appliance building designed by Brust & Philipp has been so greatly altered that it is difficult to recognize the original structure.

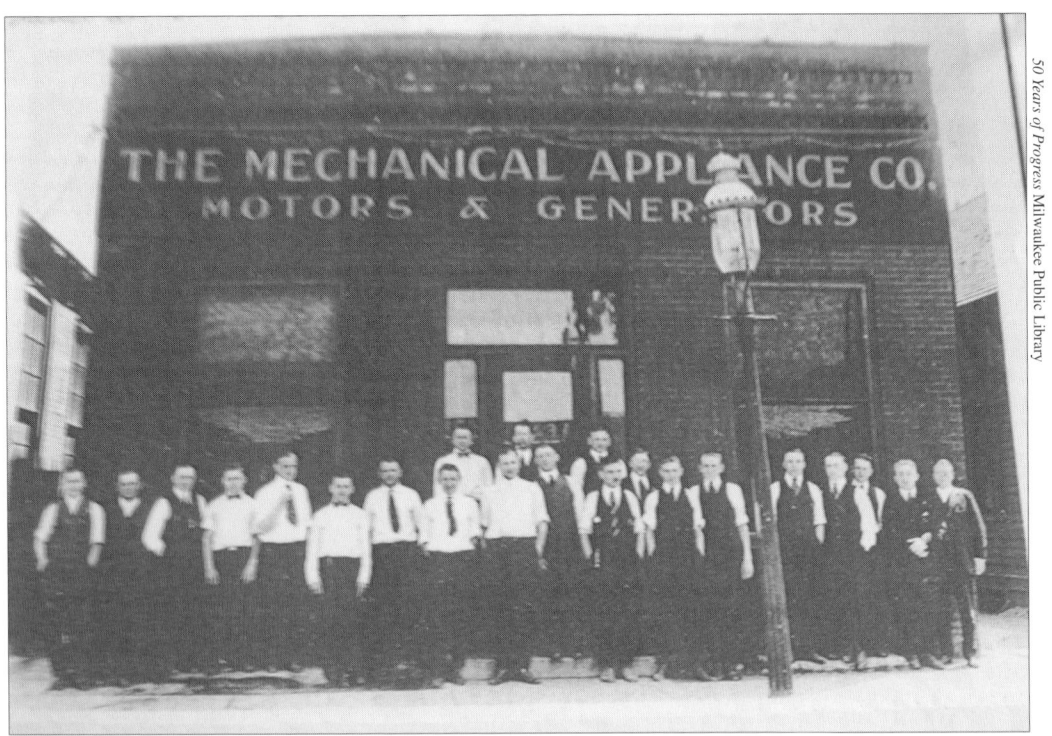

This may be the building designed by Peter Brust in 1906. The photograph was taken around 1917.

David Adler & Sons
Milwaukee, Wisconsin

Solomon Adler and his brother, David, came to America from Austria in 1848. After spending some time in New York, they came to Milwaukee and established a retail store called D. J. Adler. Soon after, they turned to manufacturing ready-made clothing for men. In 1857, Solomon retired and David took over the manufacturing business.

By 1870, sales totaled $150,000. That year, David's son, Isaac, and David's son-in-law, H. M. Mendel, joined the business. The firm's name changed to Mendel & Company, and by 1873, there were 600 employees. Solomon and David remained with the firm until 1874, with Henry Mendel staying on until 1878.

David's sons, Emmanuel and David Jr., joined the business in 1880, and the company name changed to David Adler & Sons. David Jr. later left the firm to practice as an architect, and in 1923, he designed a home for Lloyd Smith on North Terrace Avenue on Milwaukee's northeast side. The home is now the Villa Terrace Museum.

When David Adler & Sons was incorporated in 1886 the company was comprised of $250,000 in capital stock. By the 1890s, sales exceeded $1 million dollars, and the company employed 800 workers. The factory was located at North Water and East Clybourn Street.

Upon the death of David Adler Sr. in 1905, his son, Emmanuel, became the company treasurer. In 1906, the company relocated to the Third Ward at 246 North Broadway Street. The four-story building was originally designed by H.C. Koch & Company for Wellauer & Hoffmann Company. David Adler & Sons used the building on North Broadway Street for storerooms and offices. The manufacturing was done at seven factories located in various parts of the city.

Peter Brust designed factory buildings for the Adler Company in 1904; however, the location of these buildings were not found.

The firm of Brust & Philipp also designed a summer home for Emmanuel Adler on Oconomowoc Lake. [See Page 93 for the Emmanuel Adler summer home commission.]

David Adler

The drawings on this page are of the factory buildings designed by Peter Brust for the Adler Company.

Lenox Street Home Bakery
Milwaukee (Bay View), Wisconsin

Joseph Piette commissioned Peter Brust in 1898 to design him a building at 2436-2438 South Lenox Street in Milwaukee's Bay View neighborhood. The Colonial Revival style building featured a Cream City brick exterior with extensive sheet-metal work. The building contained a grocery store on the first floor and living quarters above. The carpenter was Joseph Luettgen, and the total cost of the building was $3,000. According to the *Bay View Neighborhood Historic Resources Survey*, the Piette building is exceptionally well preserved, and it is "an excellent example of the better class of commercial building built for Milwaukee's merchants at the turn of the century."[1]

Above, Michael Wierzejewski stands in the doorway of his bakery.

Top right, a recent photograph of the former bakery

The building changed hands a number of times over the years, with Richard Walsh purchasing the store in 1916. In 1922, Walsh sold it to Caspar Hach who used it as a bakery. In 1930, the store was sold to Michael Wierzejewski who ran the Lenox Street Home Bakery until his retirement in 1965. The building was eventually turned into a single-family home and remains so at the original site.

[1] *Bay View Neighborhood Historic Resources Survey*, vol. 1 (Milwaukee, Wisconsin: City of Milwaukee, 1990), 76.

Mary Schmidling House
Milwaukee (Bay View), Wisconsin

Peter Brust designed a house for his sister, Mary Brust Schmidling in 1924. The house at 3415 South Indiana Avenue is part of Milwaukee's Bay View neighborhood. Mary's father, Christopher, lived across the street, and the lot on which Mary built her home was part of her father's property. This area was part of Town of Lake until 1928, at which time the area was annexed to the City of Milwaukee.

St. Mary's Catholic Church
Juneau, Wisconsin

Immaculate Conception Catholic Church in Juneau, Wisconsin, was dedicated on June 24, 1875. Although this was the corporate title for the church, the parish was best known as St. Mary's.

The first church structure was built on Main Street in 1875 and served the parish for twenty-nine years. The frame structure measured 30 feet by 60 feet and sat 175 parishioners. The total cost of the church was $2,000. By 1885, there were thirty-five families.

The new church, built in 1903, was a large brick structure, measuring 103 feet by 44 feet. It featured a 107-foot spire, stained-glass windows, and marble-head coursing stone. Peter Brust designed the new church while he was employed at the architectural firms of H.C. Koch and Herman Esser. The cornerstone of the new church was laid on May 5, 1903, officiated by Reverend A. F. Schinner, the Vicar General; Schinner later became the Bishop of Superior.

The church was redecorated in 1911, and a new pipe organ installed. The firm of Brust, Philipp & Heimerl most likely did the 1911 redecoration, since records show that the firm did work for the parish at that time. Recently, St. Mary's Church merged with Sacred Heart Catholic Church in Horicon, Wisconsin. The old St. Mary's Church is still located on its original site on Main Street in Juneau.

Phillip Siegel House
Milwaukee (Bay View), Wisconsin

Peter Brust designed a two-family duplex for Phillip Siegel in 1899. It is unclear if Siegel lived in the house or used it as rental property. The wood-frame house measured 22 feet wide by 50 feet long by 20 feet tall. According to the building permit, the total cost of the house was estimated at $2,400. This house is located at 2513-2515 South Howell Avenue directly across from St. Augustine Catholic Church, which was designed by the firm of Brust & Philipp in 1908.

St. Mary's Nativity of Mary Catholic Church
Lomira, Wisconsin

In 1905, while in the employment of Herman Esser, Peter Brust designed St. Mary's Nativity of Mary Catholic Church in Lomira, Wisconsin. This Gothic style church, measuring 44 feet by 114 feet, was built to seat 350 people and was completed at a cost of $21,878. A church souvenir booklet described the interior as having a vaulted ceiling with molded ribs and arches. The sacristy was large and spacious. According to a newspaper article (*Lomira Review*, May 1905), Peter Brust attended the cornerstone ceremony. The article states, "Not far away stood the supervising architect, Mr. Brust of Milwaukee, keeping a discerning eye on the whole proceeding."

Unfortunately, a fire on February 11, 1988, destroyed the rear of the church from the basement up to the choir loft. Fortunately, St. Mary's was fully restored, and Archbishop Weakland rededicated the church on September 10, 1988. St. Mary's is located at 653 Milwaukee Street in Lomira and is still an active parish.

Above, an historical photograph of St. Mary's during construction

Above inset, shows four men on top of the steeple during construction

Right, a recent photograph of St. Mary's Catholic Church

Chapter 1 – Brust Family History and Peter Brust's Early Years

Frank Brust House
Milwaukee (Bay View), Wisconsin

On April 16, 1904, Frank Brust, the brother of Peter, purchased a building lot at 3375 South Illinois Avenue in Town of Lake and proceeded to build a house with the help of his father, Christopher. On October 1, 1904, Frank Brust and Matilda Dederich Brust moved into their new home on South Illinois Avenue. Due to the lack of records for this portion of Town of Lake, no building permits were found naming the architect of the home. It is likely, however, that Peter provided his brother, Frank, with a design plan. The Frank Brust home is still located at the original site but was remodeled recently. It needs to be noted that the Milwaukee assessment records list the home as being built in 1897. However, deed information and oral family history information support the 1904 date of construction.

Top right, the front view of the Frank Brust home on South Illinois Avenue

Bottom left, a side view photograph of the South Illinois Avenue house shows Frank and Matilda sitting on the lawn with their children, Raymond, William, and Ava (Florence). Two other children, Leo and Frank, were born later. Both photographs were probably taken around 1908.

Christopher Brust House
Milwaukee (Bay View), Wisconsin

When Frank Brust bought a building lot on South Illinois Avenue in 1904, his father, Christopher, entertained reservations about his son building a home in what was then considered the boonies. However, shortly after his son bought the property on South Illinois Avenue, Christopher decided to sell his property on East St. Francis Avenue and buy fifteen acres of the Steward farm property just adjacent to Frank's property. Christopher built the house pictured here at 3406 South Indiana Avenue. Assessment records show that the house was built in 1900; however, it was most likely built around 1909. Unfortunately, the deeds on file at the court house begin in the 1920s.

No records were found that name the architect, but most likely Christopher's son, Peter, helped design the home. According to Christopher's grandson, John, a frame barn was at the rear of the property where Christopher did his woodworking. The home is located at the same site but is now a two-family home.

27

St. Mary's Institute (St. Mary's Academy) St. Francis, Wisconsin

Mother Thecla of the Sisters of St. Francis of Assisi commissioned Peter Brust in 1904 to design St. Mary's Institute. Located at 3211 South Lake Drive in St. Francis, the Colonial Revival style building contained square footage of 18,712. The lower section of the exterior was done in Lannon stone, with the upper section done in brick. The total cost of the building was $45,273. The building housed a high school for girls and a dormitory for out-of-town resident students. St. Mary's was dedicated to the Virgin Mary.

The nearby St. Francis Seminary was against the plan for a female high school so close to their seminary. A provincial council finally gave their approval for the Institute, and it was completed and dedicated on the Feast of the Presentation of the Virgin Mary on November 21, 1904. The school's mission was the formation of true Christian young women through spiritual and scholastic training for each student. The school's enrollment in 1904 was sixty-nine young women; however, the first graduating class of 1909 consisted of only five candidates.

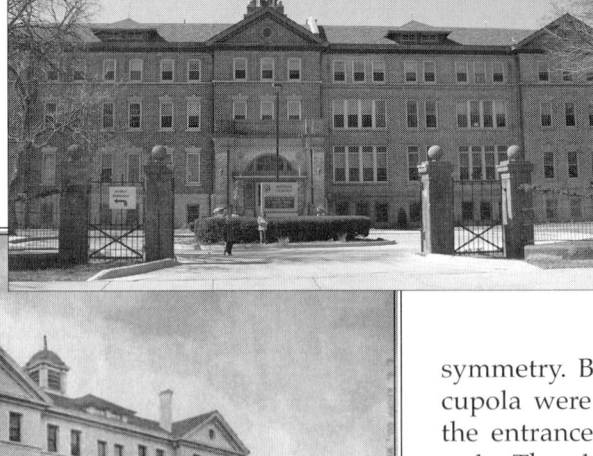

Above, the inscription above the entrance of the 1904 building reads "St. Mary's Institute."

Right, a contemporary view shows the 1904 building with the 1921 Loretto Hall addition on the right.

Later, two additions were done to the school. Loretto Hall was done on the north end in 1921, and Rosary Hall was done on the south end in 1930. Both additions were done by the architectural firm of Brielmaier & Sons. When Loretto Hall was added, remodeling was done to the original 1904 building for the sake of symmetry. Both the main entrance and the cupola were moved farther to the north so the entrance would be centered on the facade. The old 1904 entrance read St. Mary's Institute, but the new 1921 entrance read St. Mary's Academy.

In 1930, Cardinal Stritch College used the ca. 1904 building, along with Loretto Hall, for classrooms and dormitory space. Due to low enrollment, St. Mary's Academy closed in 1991. The building is now part of the Marion Center that rents space to non-profit organizations.

A postcard showing the rear view of St. Mary's Institute around 1910

St. Francis Seminary Sisters' House/Infirmary
St. Francis, Wisconsin

Beginning in the 1850s, the Sisters of St. Francis of Assisi provided domestic service to the St. Francis Seminary located at 3257 South Lake Drive in St. Francis. In 1868, the Sisters were asked to add to their domestic work the duty of nursing the sick clergy and students. When the north wing of the main seminary building was completed on December 21, 1868, the first official infirmary, as well as a pharmacy, opened on the second floor. Sister Seraphine O'Brien was assigned as nurse and attended the sick for eighteen years. Sister O'Brien also dispensed pills and potions from the pharmacy. Students were also treated for their illnesses in their dormitories or apartments.

The decades of 1880 and 1890 were difficult ones for the nursing Sisters, as their students experienced an unusual amount of communicable diseases such as diphtheria, influenza, smallpox, and scarlet fever. At times, students were sent home or classes were suspended in order to control the spread of disease.

On December 15, 1879, due to a diphtheria outbreak at the seminary, students were sent home for an early Christmas break. When school started up again, the school was forced to close down on January 10, 1880, because of the great number of incidents of the flu. School resumed on February 1 of that year. The following description comes from the book *Halcyon Days*:

> More than fifty students were laid up at that time, and although one dormitory had been turned into a hospital, space was lacking for the adequate care of the sick. The decision to allow students to leave for home seems to have had an invigorating effect on some of the ailing, because on the day following only twenty-four sick remained at the seminary.[1]

A smallpox epidemic broke out in Milwaukee in 1902. Most of the seminary students were sent to their homes, with five of the students being isolated in the Brother's House. This smallpox scare probably sped up the building of the new infirmary building.

Peter Brust designed this new infirmary building in 1902. The building also served as a residence for the Sisters who worked at the seminary. The Sisters lived on the left side of the building, and the infirmary was on the right. The Colonial Revival style

Salzmann Library

building opened on November 18, 1902, and was described as follows:

> The new infirmary building was finished and made ready for use. That evening the first patients took up their quarters in the new building, which, owing to its spacious apartments and its seclusion, is considered a very valuable improvement over the previous infirmary accommodations.[2]

The building is now known as Meyer Hall. Most recently, it contained individual apartments occupied by retired priests.

---

[1] Rt. Rev. Msgr. Peter Leo Johnson, *Halcyon Days: Story of the St. Francis Seminary Milwaukee: 1856-1956* (Milwaukee, Wisconsin: The Bruce Publishing Company, 1956), 347.

[2] *Diamond Jubilee of St. Francis Seminary, 1856-1931* (Milwaukee, Wisconsin: Husting Printing Co., [1931?]), 39.

PRIVACY IN THE HOME.

Mr. Brust Speaks of Domestic Architecture and Accompanying Problems.

THE NEED OF LAWN AND GARDEN

Undesirability of House Alignment with Street—Large Porch a Good Feature.

"Domestic Architecture, Sanitation, Ventilation and Interior Decoration" formed the subject of the address delivered this afternoon by Peter Brust before the South Side Woman's Club at the south division high school.

Mr. Brust, in his address, laid perhaps more stress upon the feature of privacy in the home than upon any other particular point. He deprecated the setting of all the houses in a street upon a uniform line and advocated that some of the houses be set back much farther from the street, giving a good lawn in front, enclosed with a hedge or a wall of brick or stone, closed with a wrought-iron gate. This he said, is the English fashion, while on the continent the houses were built close to the street, and the entire width of the back part of the lot utilized as lawn and garden.

In either case, the house should be so placed as to give the family a bit of outdoor life, which may be enjoyed fully, without intrusion by the observation of passersby. If the lawn be arranged at the back of the house, there should be a large porch connecting the house with the grounds. The front entrance should have at least a porch sufficient to shelter from the rain any person who may be waiting at the door. Walks and gardens close to the house should be formal, while naturalistic walks and gardens may be indulged in as one works away from the house towards the works of nature.

The meeting of the club this afternoon was open to both men and women. The programme for the afternoon was under the charge of Mrs. A. J. F[...]nermann.

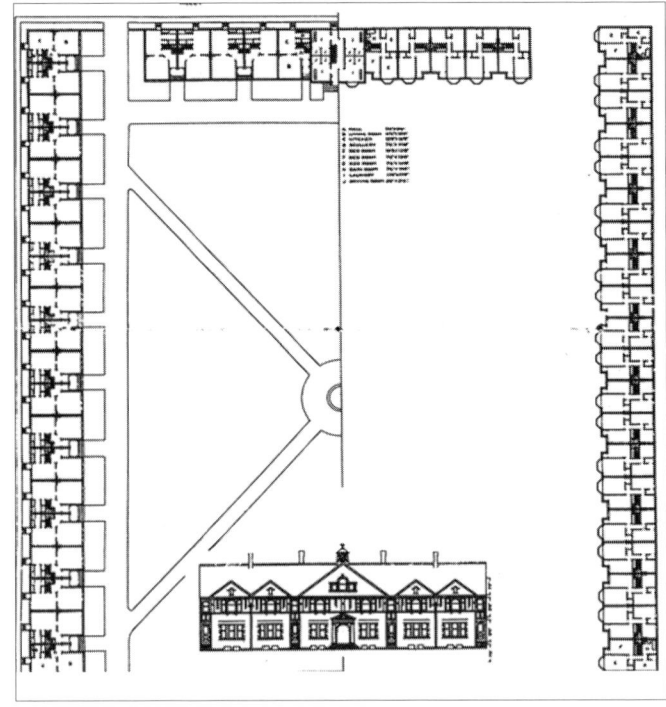

Top and above, Peter Brust submitted these architectural plans for the Shattuck Prize Competition for Artisan's Homes. These drawings were published in the November 1898 issue of *American Architect and Building News*.

Left, an article featuring Peter Brust was published in the *Evening Wisconsin* on 10 February 1903.

Chapter 2
Brust & Philipp–Residential Commissions, 1906-1926

Julius Heimerl

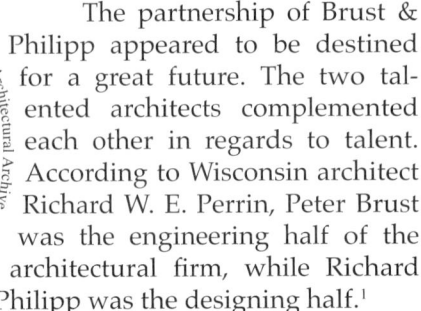

Richard Philipp

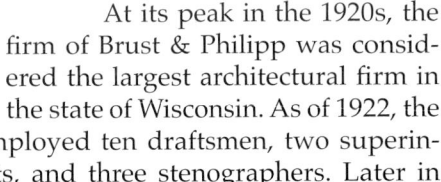

Peter Brust

After ten years of working in a number of architectural firms, Peter Brust decided in 1906 that it was time to go out on his own and form his own firm. While working side by side at Ferry & Clas, Peter Brust and Richard Philipp sensed at that time a meeting of the minds. This realization lead the two architects to collaborate together and form the firm of Brust & Philipp.

Julius Heimerl, who also worked with Brust and Philipp at Ferry & Clas, joined the firm in 1911, thus creating the firm of Brust, Philipp & Heimerl. However, the architectural firm of Brust, Philipp & Heimerl lasted only until 1913 when Heimerl left the firm.

It is important to note that a biographical article on Peter Brust in the June 1963 issue of *Wisconsin Architect* states that Heimerl was a partner in the firm of Brust & Philipp from 1906 to 1912. However, Milwaukee city directories do not list Heimerl's name in connection with Brust and Philipp until 1911. Also, building permits taken out by the firm from the time period of 1906 to 1910 do not list Heimerl. It could be speculated that Heimerl worked with Brust & Philipp on a part-time basis between 1906 and 1911.

The partnership of Brust & Philipp appeared to be destined for a great future. The two talented architects complemented each other in regards to talent. According to Wisconsin architect Richard W. E. Perrin, Peter Brust was the engineering half of the architectural firm, while Richard Philipp was the designing half.[1]

At its peak in the 1920s, the firm of Brust & Philipp was considered the largest architectural firm in the state of Wisconsin. As of 1922, the firm employed ten draftsmen, two superintendents, and three stenographers. Later in that decade, the firm would grow to employ thirty men. From 1906 to 1914, the Brust & Philipp architectural office was at 82 Wisconsin Avenue; the address changed to 206 East Wisconsin Avenue, and that building was later razed. From 1915 to 1926, their office was located at 405 Broadway Street; the address changed to 709 North Broadway Street, and the building was later razed.

The success of the firm of Brust & Philipp was not only measured by its physical growth but also by the professional recognition of the firm on a national level. Rexford Newcomb, a writer for the periodical *Western Architect*, spoke of Peter Brust and Richard Philipp in glowing terms. In an article about Brust and Philipp, Newcomb expressed his admiration for their ability to infuse their personalities into their work. Personality, Newcomb felt, was the single greatest quality that an artist could bring to his or her work. Evidence of this, according to Newcomb, was found in the Riverbend residence that the firm of Brust & Philipp designed in Kohler, Wisconsin, for Walter J. Kohler. The designers, Newcomb said, blended well the form, color, and texture of the design. In Newcomb's estimation, the design presented a "wonderful example of the intimate association of varied materials with perfect balance so far as texture and color…"[2]

Along with personality, Rexford expressed his belief that Brust and Philipp's feeling for the selected materials contributed to the artistic nature of their designs. In order to be a true artist of architecture, Newcomb felt that the artist needed to understand and to value the natural origin of the materials. The firm of Brust & Philipp not only knew the difference between the different species of wood and stone, but they intimately knew the unique texture and visual aspects of each species; this ability, according to Newcomb, made them rare designers. As craftsmen, these men not only embraced the physical characteristics of the materials, but they also appreciated and possessed a feel for the true spirit of the materials. Along with appreciation, both designers understood the uniqueness of each material and understood the physical capabilities and limitations of each material. The ability to handle materials with feeling and to use them appropriately showed creative spirit and genius; this ability, according to Newcomb, is a God-given talent.[3]

Newcomb went on to say that Brust and Philipp's handling and crafting of these various materials in a natural way showed an understanding of the form and function of building materials. This sense of naturalism resulted in designs that beautifully blended together stone, wood, glass, and metal. Honesty of materials was crucial to the firm of Brust & Philipp in the designing process. Designers of the earlier Victorian Gilded Age took materials and made them something that they were not. The firm of Brust & Philipp did not expect the materials to be something that they were not or expect the materials to do something that they could not do. Unlike the Victorian Age designers, they would not allow terra cotta to pass as cut stone, concrete would not be disguised with brick veneer, and wood trim would not be substituted for carved stone.

In an article in a September 1916 issue of *American Architect*, architectural writer Ralph Tanning agreed with the philosophy regarding the honest use of material. Rare designers, according to Tanning, executed buildings with an honest expression of materials. "Concrete is just as an honest a material as granite," Tanning stated, "but concrete could never truly be granite." Tile and plaster could also produce pleasing proportions and be as brilliant as marble, but the tile and plaster could never truly be marble. Tanning concluded, "If the material is good and its construction honest, beauty of form and ornateness of decoration may be readily secured by study of proportion, scale and expression."[4] Brust and Philipp were rare designers who also believed in such a philosophy and executed it successfully.

This watercolor was done by Peter Brust. The date at the bottom right hand corner reads 1893. This painting was inspired by churches Peter saw as he bicycled through France in 1893. The painting is courtesy of Patsy Brust Koenings.

Residential commissions

The residential designs of the firm of Brust & Philipp were overwhelmingly influenced by the Old English architecture. Many of the residences designed by the firm on Milwaukee's northeast side were Tudor inspired. Other Wisconsin residences designed by Brust & Philipp, such as the Lamoreux Mansion in Beaver Dam and Riverbend in Kohler, are also done in the Tudor Revival style. This English influence on house design was felt across America from the 1880s into the 1940s. In Milwaukee, the Tudor craze was at its peak during the 1920s and 1930s.

It was in the late nineteenth century and early twentieth century that the well-educated and wealthy sector of American society began the tradition of doing the Grand Tour of Europe. Inspired by the romantic English manor houses, they sought American architects that could build them homes in America that would evoke the sense of late-medieval England. Many picture books were published about English history and added to the craze for everything English.

Architects were expected to tour Europe to prepare themselves for this onslaught of English-inspired commissions. Richard Philipp took his first trip to Europe in 1899 while in the employment of Ferry & Clas; he traveled to Europe twice more before 1906. Peter Brust visited Europe for the first time in 1893. He also went to Europe in 1905 with a group of Milwaukee architects, Richard Philipp probably being one of them. During these tours, the architects purchased prepared architectural drawings and photographs. Cameras in hand, they also took their own photographs and created their own drawings.

Any half-timbered house, be it Elizabethan, Jacobean, or Tudor, were put in the category of Tudor Revival. These Anglo-American style homes were loosely based on the Tudor homes of old England. The firm of Brust & Philipp didn't intent to bring medieval England to Milwaukee architecture, but rather to bring the best of the English tradition and infuse them into their designs. Rexford Newcomb saw Brust & Philipp as being "grounded in the Tudor design."[5] Both Brust & Philipp acquired a great deal of knowledge about the style, and this knowledge was suffused into their work. Their designs were practical and logical with simple lines and massing. True craftsmanship was evident in their use of color and texture. Newcomb described Philipp as a colorist. Philipp was known to say that nothing affected him more than color, "especially the vari-hued Wisconsin granites, a wealth of which the state possesses."[6]

Wealthy Americans began the Tudor Revival style craze, but soon the middle class desired this style. Suburban Tudors were smaller versions and were designed by either architects or builders who used house pattern books such as Sears and Aladdin. The wealthy could afford the genuine building materials while the middle class needed to settle for imitation materials. The brickwork and half-timber houses were costly to build, so lower cost materials were sought as substitutes. Since heavy oak timber was cost prohibitive, veneered wood was used for the timbers, and plaster was put over hollow clay tile or concrete block to simulate the stucco exterior. Asbestos and composition shingles came on the market, and they looked much like the slate shingles. Glazed terra-cotta tiles substituted for the clay roof tiles, and PermaStone imitated rubble masonry on the Cotswold style cottages.

Lucky are those who own one of the Tudor Revival style homes designed by gifted architects such as Peter Brust and Richard Philipp. Preservationists now see these homes as an important but threatened part of our American architectural history. Although replacement materials can be difficult to find, these well-built, comfortable homes, in the opinion of preservationists, need to be preserved.

[1] Shirley du Fresne McArthur, *North Point Historic Districts-Milwaukee* (Milwaukee, Wisconsin: North Point Historical Society, 1981), 98.
[2] Rexford Newcomb, AIA, "Craftsmanship in Architecture," *The Western Architect* (July 1925), 71-72.
[3] Newcomb, "Craftsmanship in Architecture," 71-72.
[4] Ralph Tanning, "The Consideration of Materials in Architectural Design," *American Architect* (September 6, 1916), 343-345.
[5] Rexford Newcomb, AIA ,"Continuity of Personal Influence as Sensed in the Work of Brust and Philipp, of Milwaukee," *The Western Architect* (July 1925), 87-88.
[6] Newcomb, "Continuity of Personal Influence as Sensed in the Work of Brust and Philipp, of Milwaukee," 87-88.

Richard Philipp

Richard Philipp was born in Mayville, Wisconsin, on August 2, 1874, to Julius and Anne Sophie (Melcher) Philipp. Julius arrived in America from Berlin, Germany, in 1843 and was a cabinetmaker by trade. Julius moved his family from Mayville to Milwaukee when Richard was fifteen years old. After graduating from East Side High School, Richard became apprenticed to the architectural firm of Ferry & Clas. He was employed there for ten years before being promoted to chief designer in 1902.

It was during his employment with Ferry & Clas that Philipp took his first tour of Europe in 1899, followed by two more tours before 1906. Bicycling through the European countryside, Philipp was so impressed with the architecture that he incorporated what he saw in his own design work. Philipp brought back photographs and drawings from Europe and created three scrapbooks, each representing a different type of architecture, French, English, and Italian. These scrapbooks are still in existence.

The ladies' magazine, *House Beautiful*, sponsored a house design contest in 1898. A $50 prize was offered for a house design in which the cost of construction could not exceed $3,000. Philipp won the $50 prize with his cottage design called Halcyon.[1] Halcyon means tranquil and idyllic. The first story of the cottage was brick and the second was of shingles. The contest judges felt that Philipp showed skill and good taste in his design.

In a 1986 issue of *House Beautiful*, Philipp's Halcyon house design of 1898 was compared to the small house design contest winner of 1986. The author describes Philipp's *Halcyon* design as being ahead of its time.[2] Many of Philipp's design elements are standard design elements in today's house designs. The article mentions that Philipp broke away from the traditional front veranda and designed a back porch off the living room that would give a view of the backyard rather than the street. Philipp also grouped together three or more windows to allow for a brighter interior. Wider doorways were featured in the Halcyon house that gave the layout of the house a sense of openness. Also, Philipp included a first-floor bathroom along with the usual second-floor bathroom that served the three bedrooms. Bookcases, china cupboards, and window seat nooks were de-

signed to save space; these space-saving designs are now standard in house design.

Philipp formed an architectural firm in 1906 with Peter Brust with whom he worked at the architectural firm of Ferry & Clas. Julius Heimerl joined them in 1911 to form Brust, Philipp & Heimerl. When Heimerl left the firm in 1913, the name reverted back to Brust & Philipp.

Philipp was elected a fellow in the American Institute of Architecture in 1925 and served as president of the Wisconsin Chapter

A drawing of Richard Philipp's Halcyon house

in 1937. After collaborating on many projects, the firm of Brust & Philipp disbanded in 1926, with Peter Brust and Richard Philipp going into independent practices. During his independent practice, Philipp was commissioned in the 1930s to design homes for Alfred Lester Slocum at 2675 North Terrace Avenue, Milwaukee; Edith M. Smith at 2808 North Shepard Avenue, Milwaukee; Mrs. W. H. Alford, Kenosha; and E. S. Sensenbrenner, Lake Winnebago. Richard Philipp was considered a pioneer in his use of Lannon stone as an exterior building material. He is credited with introducing the material to the Milwaukee area.

Philipp married Ella Smith, a pianist and teacher in 1923. She died in 1953. In October 1956, Philipp was involved in an automobile accident that left him with a fractured leg and head injuries. Due to the accident, Philipp became semi-retired, keeping an office on 756 North Milwaukee Street. He resided in a remodeled farmhouse in Genesee in Waukesha County. He died in March 1959 at the age of eighty-four.

[1] "Prize Competition," *The House Beautiful* (August 1898), 75-79.
[2] Marion Gough "Best Small Houses 1898 and 1986," *The House Beautiful* (November 1986), 60-61.

Brust & Philipp Residential Commissions Located in the Milwaukee North Point Historic District

Sanford M. Cohen House
Milwaukee, Wisconsin

The architectural firm of Brust & Philipp designed a residence for Mrs. Sanford Cohen at 2750 North Shepard Avenue in 1909. The house was a fine example of the Tudor Revival style with its steeply-pitched roof, prominent gables, and distinctive chimney. The front entrance was very unique, similar to the Isidore Heller house at Big Cedar Lake, also designed by Brust & Philipp. [See Page 89 for Isidore Heller house.] The exterior of the Cohen home was brick, with a Lannon stone chimney and foundation. Roughcast plaster and timber were used in the gables, and the house was trimmed in Bedford stone.

Sanford Cohen's father, Jonas Cohen, came to Milwaukee from Germany in 1866. He established Cohen Brothers & Company, a men's clothing factory in 1870. Sanford M. Cohen later served as the treasurer for the company. The company's factory and offices were located on North Broadway Street in downtown Milwaukee.

The exterior of the Cohen house was done in the Tudor Revival style; however, the above photograph shows a Colonial Revival style interior.

Charles D. Hays House
Milwaukee, Wisconsin

Charles D. Hays commissioned the architectural firm of Brust & Philipp in 1909 to design a Colonial Revival/Georgian style home, located at 2712 East Bradford Avenue. The exterior featured multi-colored brick with Ionic columns. Charles D. Hays was the owner of Sidenberg & Hays, a coat manufacturing company located on North Water Street in downtown Milwaukee.

Walter Kasten House
Milwaukee, Wisconsin

A Colonial Revival style home was designed by the architectural firm of Brust & Philipp for Walter Kasten in 1908. The residence at 2550 North Terrace Avenue featured a red brick exterior with Ionic columns. The keystones and stringcourses were done in limestone. Walter Kasten spent most of his professional career in banking. At sixteen years old, he was hired by the Wisconsin National Bank as a messenger. Kasten then moved up to teller, and finally served as an auditor and cashier. When Wisconsin National Bank and 1st National Bank merged, Kasten became vice president, and in 1930, he became the president of the bank. In 1916, the new owner of the Kasten house, Mrs. John Elser, commissioned the firm of Brust & Philipp to design a breakfast room and a garage addition. Walter's grandson, Robert Walter Kasten Jr., served in the U.S. Senate from 1981 to 1993.

Thomas H. Gill House
Milwaukee, Wisconsin

The architectural firm of Brust & Philipp designed a Colonial Revival style house for Thomas Henry Gill in 1906. Located at 2104 East Lafayette Place, the house featured bay windows, a columned front, and side porches.

Gill practiced law in Madison, Wisconsin, from 1879 to 1887. In 1887, he took a position as a claim agent for the Wisconsin Central Railroad. Gill married Laura Alice Leuts of Milwaukee on June 30, 1904. Laura graduated from the University of Wisconsin in Madison in 1899. The couple raised two sons and one daughter.

In 1908, Gill opened a private corporate law practice in Milwaukee. Arthur Barry and Henry Mahoney practiced with Gill until 1916. Gill also served as trustee for the Northwestern Mutual Life Insurance Company. He retired from active law practice in 1933 and died in 1940. After Gill's death, his son, William, razed the house on East Lafayette Place and built two duplexes on the property. His mother lived in one of the duplexes until 1945. The duplexes still remain at the site.

Front view of the Gill house

The interior of the Gill house included oak woodwork and wainscot in the entry hall. The oriental type rug and stair runner reflected the Colonial Revival style. Portieres framed the doorway leading from the hall into the living room. Note the leaded stained-glass windows in the living room.

Side view of the Gill house

William E. Wehr House
Milwaukee, Wisconsin

William E. Wehr founded the Wehr Steel Company in 1910 with his brother, Edward R. Wehr. William served as president of the company, located at South 45th Street and West Gordon Street in West Allis. The Wehr Steel Company manufactured steel castings. William was also the secretary/treasurer of Dings Magnetic Separator Company. His father, Henry, operated a German café on the Milwaukee River on the site of the former Gimbels/Marshall Fields department store building at the corner of North Plankinton Street and West Wisconsin Avenue.

The architectural firm of Brust & Philipp designed William Wehr's home at 2134 North Terrace Avenue in 1922. The exterior of the Spanish Eclectic style house was done in Milwaukee Cream City brick; the brick was laid in a Flemish bond pattern. The home featured an Italian influenced cupola and rounded arched windows. The double-gabled roof was done in brown barrel tiles. The Spanish Eclectic style, sometimes known as the Mediterranean style, borrowed elements from Italian and Spanish architecture and became very popular in the 1920s. The Cream City brick exterior of the Wehr house was later painted.

The interior photographs on this page highlight a number of Mediterranean style elements such as the twisted newel post and arched doorways. The furniture reflected the Mediterranean style and the portieres were trimmed in Spanish style lace.

Sarah Stern Weil House
Milwaukee, Wisconsin

The architectural firm of Brust, Philipp & Heimerl designed the Sarah Stern Weil house in 1912, located at 2515 North Terrace Avenue. This English Tudor Revival style cottage featured an exterior of stucco with wood trim, a front gable, a hipped roof, and a prominent chimney. The multi-paned windows were of leaded glass.

Sarah Weil was the widow of Benjamin M. Weil Sr. who was a successful and prominent real estate businessman. Weil came to Milwaukee with his wife from Baltimore in 1870 to set up a real estate business. Benjamin was also the president of Milwaukee Gas Light Company. Sarah was known for her involvement in charitable causes and was a trustee for Mt. Sinai Hospital. Benjamin Weil Sr. died in 1901. Sarah died in 1941 at the advanced age of ninety-two. The Weil house was featured in an issue of *American Architect* on March 1, 1916.

Benjamin Weil

The interior of the home featured a number of English Tudor Revival style elements. The dining room, along with the living room, featured dark oak Jacobean furniture. The dining room featured a parged ceiling, which is plasterwork done in decorative designs. The beamed ceilings in the other two rooms were purely decorative, not structural.

Abraham L. Frisch House
Milwaukee, Wisconsin

Abraham L. Frisch commissioned the architectural firm of Brust & Philipp to design a Tudor Revival style home, located at 2607 North Wahl Street. The house was completed in 1908 and featured a rose-brown brick exterior with limestone trim. Abraham's father, Joseph, left Austria in 1849 and immigrated to New York. Joseph left New York for Milwaukee in 1854 and went into the wholesale liquor and wine business with Otto Biersbach. The J. P. Frisch & Company was established in 1872. Abraham Frisch later carried on the business with his brother-in-law, Jacob H. Newman, the husband of Abraham's older sister, Jennie. The Abraham Frisch family lived in the home until 1926.

Euclid P. Worden House
Milwaukee, Wisconsin

The Tudor Revival style home of Euclid P. Worden, located at 2637 North Summit Avenue, was designed by the architectural firm of Brust & Philipp in 1908. The house exterior reflected many of the Tudor Revival style elements, such as the half-timbered front gables, the stucco upper story, the lower brick level, and bay windows. Worden was the chief engineer for the F. M. Prescott Steam Pump Company in West Allis, Wisconsin. [See Page 152 for the Prescott Company commission.]

Edwin S. Mack House
Milwaukee, Wisconsin

Milwaukee attorney Edwin S. Mack commissioned the architectural firm of Brust & Philipp in 1906 to design his Colonial Revival home at 2215 North Lake Drive. It was reported by some researchers that Richard Philipp was responsible for the Mack design; however, the blueprints for the home are located in the Brust & Philipp files at the Wisconsin Architectural Archives. Most likely, Philipp was working on the commission when the firm of Brust & Philipp was founded in 1906.

The Colonial Revival home featured a front parapet gable. The porch roof featured a curved underside with two sets of Ionic columns. The two dormers flanking the front gable were designed to duplicate the underside curve of the front porch roof.

After attending college, Mack worked for the law firm of Finches, Lynde & Miller. Later, he became a senior partner with the firm of Miller, Mack & Fairchild of which George Peckham Miller was a partner. Mack also authored a local history book, *The Founding of Milwaukee*. Edwin Mack died in 1942, and his wife lived in the house until 1945.

The Mack house was decorated in the typical Colonial Revival style with a wingback chair, an Empire style table, and a settee.

William Ferdinand Luick House
Milwaukee, Wisconsin

During the 1920s, the Luick Ice Cream Company was one of the largest and best-equipped ice cream manufacturers in the United States. William Luick believed in quality control and made a habit of taste-testing the ice cream seeking the right flavor and texture to maintain his high quality standards. [See Page 164 for the Luick Ice Cream Garage commission.]

William Luick hired the architectural firm of Brust & Philipp in 1922 to design him a new residence in the English Cotswold style. Brust & Philipp previously designed a home for Luick at 3036 North Marietta Avenue in 1913. [See Page 51 for the North Marietta Avenue home.] Luick wanted his new home at 2601 North Wahl Avenue to reflect the dairymen's houses that he visited in the Cotswold area of England. For the exterior, the Cotswold design utilized Lannon stone and stucco, leaded stained-glass windows, and stone and marble windowsills. The

interior walls were done in textured stucco with workmen using the hand-palm method. The living rooms, with their ten-foot ceilings, boasted beautiful ornamental plaster decoration and a stone coat of arms over the living room fireplace.

Architectural writer Rexford Newcomb was so impressed with the materials used for the Luick house and for other residences designed by Brust & Philipp, that he said the following:

> The materials in these structures take their places as naturally and gracefully as they do in Nature itself with the result that such a beautiful example of the William F. Luick residence appears perfectly "at home" in its setting. Here stone, stucco, slate, wood, glass, and metal do their work so gracefully and beautifully as to inspire one immediately with their "naturalness" and appropriateness of treatment...In examining the stylistic inspiration of such an example as the William F. Luick residence, one immediately senses the influence of English precedent but what is perhaps more conspicuous are the deep measure of personality and the fine American spirit that the structure reflects. It is by no means a "bit of Old England" set down in Milwaukee; it is the best of English tradition...[1]

William Luick lived in the home until his death in 1956. The next owners were Viola and William Egan who lived there from 1956 to 1974, followed by Kenneth and Carol Schermerhorn from 1974 to 1977. In 1975, the house was dubbed the Schermerhorn's Castle when it was used for a Milwaukee Symphony fundraiser. For the fundraiser, the mansion was redecorated by local designers and opened to the public as the Symphony Show House. The home remains at the same location on North Wahl Avenue.

[1] Rexford Newcomb, AIA, "Craftsmanship in Architecture," *The Western Architect* (July 1925), 71-72.

The interior of the Luick house reflected the English style and was furnished with Jacobean style furniture. The windows are leaded glass with stained-glass inserts. The Gothic vault-like dining room ceiling was done in decorative plaster.

Albert F. Gallun Mansion
Milwaukee, Wisconsin

Monuments serve many purposes and come in many shapes and forms. Some monuments celebrate an event, while some celebrate the accomplishments of individuals or a group of people. The thirty-six room, fortress-like mansion, built for Albert F. Gallun, is a monument to the accomplishments of the Gallun Tannery dynasty and a tribute to the pioneer spirit of the Gallun family. Despite a devastating fire and the subsequent neglect of the mansion that nearly resulted in demolition, this mansion still stands proud.

Albert F. Gallun was the son of August F. Gallun, an immigrant from Osterweick, Hartz, Germany, who came to Milwaukee and founded the Gallun Tannery. [See Pages 161-162 for the Gallun Company commissions.] Albert married Hedwig Mann in 1896, and they raised four children: Elinor, Albert Jr., Gladys, and Edwin.

Ferry & Clas designed a home for Albert Gallun in 1897 at 2014 East Lafayette Place overlooking Lake Michigan. At that time, Peter Brust was employed at the firm

The basement gameroom

of Ferry & Clas. Later, in 1911, the firm of Brust, Philipp & Heimerl was hired by Gallun to design a garage for his East Lafayette Place home.

As the owner of a successful tannery business, Gallun desired a larger home for his family, so he purchased a lot at 3000 East Newberry Street in the newly developed Prospect Hill subdivision. Three streets-- Marietta, Newberry, and Lake--bordered the lot on three sides. In 1914, Gallun commissioned the architectural firm of Brust & Philipp to design him a new home on this East Newberry Boulevard property.

The house was designed in a U-shape; this design provided a courtyard for privacy. A high wrought-iron fence surrounded the house and provided additional privacy.

The fortress-like walls of this English Tudor style mansion were eighteen inches thick and contained what was considered fireproof hollow tile. This tile was covered with a heavy layer of limestone.

The mansion reflected the style of an English Tudor manor and featured a roof of Vermont green slate, an exterior of Lannon stone laid in a random ashlar pattern, and gray Indiana limestone trim. Wrought ironwork artist, Cyril Colnik, a native of Trieben, Austria, did the ironwork. The total cost of the house was $100,000.

Albert's wife died in 1932, and Albert died in 1938. The mansion passed to his daughter, Elinor, and her husband, John Pritzlaff of the Pritzlaff Hardware Company family. In 1953, after her husband died, Elinor donated the mansion to the University of Wisconsin-Milwaukee; however, Elinor remained in the house for another eight years.

It was in October 1970 that the university opened the mansion to the public. Unfortunately, within months of the opening, the mansion suffered a devastating fire. Due to disputes involving the fire insurance claims, the mansion stood vacant for a number of years and began to deteriorate. The mansion was finally sold in 1972 to two lawyers who, with a developer, sought a variance to build an apartment building on the lot. Neighbors protested and the plan was blocked. The Gallun Mansion, slated for demolition on August 8, 1973, was given a reprieve when John Conlin bought the home with plans to keep it as a single-family residence.

Besides saving the Gallun Mansion from demolition, John Conlin was also instrumental in saving the Pabst Mansion from demolition in 1977. After 377 replacement windows and 400 replacement light fixtures, the Gallun Mansion is again a tribute to the Gallun dynasty and to the tradition of solid craftsmanship demonstrated by the firm of Brust & Philipp. The residence is part of the Newberry Boulevard Historic District, which was designated in 1994.

Mrs. Adelade Grau House
Milwaukee, Wisconsin

On June 26th, 1912, a building permit was issued to Mrs. Adelade Grau for a new home to be built at 2317 East Newberry Boulevard on Milwaukee's northeast side. The firm of Brust, Philipp & Heimerl designed this Tudor Revival style home. The estimated cost was $15,629. The exterior of the house was done in a tan brick on the lower section and stucco on the upper section.

Unfortunately, Mrs. Grau, the widow of Charles Grau, died in September 1912 at the age of sixty-two. Her son, Hugo, his wife, Clara, and their son Cyril moved into the house when it was completed. Hugo Grau worked for the 1st National Bank as a teller and a clerk. According to census records, Charles Grau was the son of August M. Grau Sr. Charles' brother, August M. Grau, Jr., was the founder of the National Distilling Company that would later become the Red Star Yeast Company. [See Page 59 for the August Grau Jr. commission.]

E. A. Schroeter House
Milwaukee, Wisconsin

E. A. Schroeter commissioned the architectural firm of Brust & Philipp to design his home, located at 3264 North Hackett Avenue. According to a 1916 building permit, the estimated cost of the house and garage was $12,000. The firm of Brust & Philipp also designed a warehouse for Schroeter near North 5th Street and West Juneau Avenue in 1916. [See Page 169 for the Schroeter Warehouse commission.]

J. Nullmann House
Milwaukee, Wisconsin

The J. Nullmann House, located at 2756 North Maryland Avenue, was designed in 1906 by the architectural firm of Brust & Philipp. According to a building permit, the estimated cost of the duplex was $4,000. No records were found for the J. Nullmann commission in the Brust & Philipp archival records. Also, J. Nullmann was not listed in the Milwaukee city directories.

Other East Side Milwaukee Commissions

Louis Allis House
Milwaukee, Wisconsin

The architectural firm of Brust, Philipp & Heimerl designed a home for Louis Allis in 1912. Allis was the president of the Mechanical Appliance Company that was founded in 1903 and renamed the Louis Allis Company in 1922. The Allis home, located at 547 Juneau Place, was west of Juneau Park in the older, less fashionable section of town. The area is now known as Yankee Hill. The more fashionable area was the new Lake Park district on Milwaukee's northeast side.

The house on Juneau Place was designed in the Colonial Revival style with three full floors of living space, plus a roof garden. The roofline featured a balustrade, with a matching balustrade on the second-story porch. The third floor contained the billiard room. A dumb waiter serviced all three floors, running from the kitchen to the roof garden where many guests were entertained. The cost of the mansion was $25,000.

The family eventually moved to the Town of Granville, a rural area located on the far northwest side of Milwaukee County. In this country setting, Allis was able to actively pursue the newly popularized sport of golf. The house on Juneau Place was sold to the City of Milwaukee in 1927 and was razed when Juneau Park was expanded.

The interior of the Allis house reflected the Colonial Revival style. The woodwork was painted in a light tone and patterned oriental rugs accented the dark-stained hardwood floors. The furniture was inspired by the Colonial Revival style, as was the electric-light ceiling fixture. Simple lace curtains framed the windows, and the walls appeared to be covered in a textured wallcovering. The mantel was in the Colonial Revival style and was inset with Arts & Crafts type tiles.

Toni Zinn House
Milwaukee, Wisconsin

The architectural firm of Brust & Philipp was hired by Toni Zinn in 1907 to design a Tudor Revival style home at 3275 North Hackett Avenue. The masonry was done by Paul Riesen's Sons Company. Shortly after it was completed, the house underwent alterations that were also designed by the firm of Brust & Philipp. The alterations added a sleeping porch to the rear of the home. The sleeping porch can be viewed in the photo at the left. The firm of Brust & Philipp also designed Toni Zinn a summer home, Apple Green Lodge, on Pewaukee Lake. [See Page 91 for the Zinn summerhouse commission.]

Toni Zinn was the wife of Walter Zinn who was the president of Milwaukee Western Malt Company. Walter's grandfather, Adolph C. Zinn, established Zinn Malting Company in 1874 in the old Schlitz Brewery building at North 5th Street and West Juneau Avenue. American Malting Company absorbed Zinn Malt Company in 1893. Walter's father, Albert, organized the Milwaukee Western Malt Company in 1903 and became president of the company.

Adolph C. Zinn

Right, the living room featured a parged ceiling of decorative plaster. The furniture was in the English Jacobean style.

William F. Luick House
Milwaukee, Wisconsin

*I*ce cream maker, William Ferdinand Luick hired the architectural firm of Brust, Philipp & Heimerl in 1912 to design an English Tudor revival home at 3036 North Marietta Avenue. According to a building permit, the estimated cost of the home was $15,000 with an architectural fee of $671. The firm of Brust, Philipp & Heimerl also designed a garage for Luick on the North Marietta Avenue property at an estimated cost of $1,200.

In 1922, the firm of Brust & Phillip designed Luick another English style home a block away on North Wahl Avenue. [See Pages 45-46 for the North Wahl Avenue commission.]

William Akin House
Milwaukee, Wisconsin

*T*he Colonial Revival style home of William Akin, located at 3043 North Summit Avenue, was designed by the architectural firm of Brust & Philipp in 1910. The red brick home featured a front entrance accentuated by a decorative pediment supported by four Ionic classical columns. The double hung windows, multi-paned in the upper and lower sashes, were trimmed with limestone keystones.

George Peckham Miller House
Milwaukee, Wisconsin

Upon their return from their honeymoon trip, George Peckham Miller and his wife, Laura A. Chapman Miller, moved into their newly built residence at 1060 East Juneau Avenue in Milwaukee. The mansion was a wedding present from Laura's father, T. A. Chapman, owner of the T. A. Chapman Department Store. The mansion would be home to Laura and George Miller for all of their married life. Laura Chapman met Miller when he was hired to do some legal work for her father. Miller proposed marriage to Laura in 1893 at her father's mansion on North Marshall Street in Milwaukee, and the proposal was accepted. The newlyweds' new home on East Juneau Avenue boasted a two-story ballroom and a Victorian tower.

Miller's grandfather, Judge Andrew Galbraith Miller, of Scotch-Irish heritage, immigrated to America in 1838. Judge Miller was appointed territorial judge in November 1838, succeeding Judge Frazer. Judge Miller took on the responsibility of 8,000 cases shortly after his arrival on the job.

In 1877, George Peckham Miller graduated from Pennsylvania College in Gettysburg, Pennsylvania. He planned to work for Alexander Mitchell in Mitchell's Milwaukee bank, but since Mitchell's bank building was not yet completed, Miller decided to attend school in Germany. While there, he studied law and graduated with a law degree in 1879. In 1881, Miller practiced law in Milwaukee and became a clerk in the office of Finches, Lynde & Miller of which his father, B. K. Miller, was a member. When his father-in-law died in 1892, Miller became the president of the T. A. Chapman Company. By 1906, the firm of Finches, Lynde & Miller was known as Miller, Mack & Fairchild.

Miller, well known for his environmental concerns, was especially concerned about the raw sewage being dumped by the tanneries into the Milwaukee River. Elected in 1913 as the president of the Milwaukee Sewage Commission, Miller served as a member until his death in 1931. He was credited with the development of Milogranite, a fertilizer created from sewage wastes. The cost to develop this fertilizer was $25 million. Miller died in 1939.

Included in the Zimmerman Design Group archives is a group of photographs taken of a bedroom located in the George P. Miller mansion on East Juneau Avenue. The four pictures depict what was probably a remodeling project designed by the architectural firm of Brust & Philipp. It is unclear when the remodel was done, but it was most likely done around 1920. According to Miller's granddaughter, Marion Chester Read, the furniture in these photo-

graphs was exhibited in the English Room at the Villa Terrace Museum in Milwaukee.

The mansion at 1060 East Juneau Avenue remains at the same location and is home to the Wisconsin Conservatory and Junior League of Milwaukee. Miller's daughter, Alice Miller Chester, founded the Junior League.

George Peckam Miller

The interior photographs on this page and the previous page depict the remodeling done by the firm of Brust & Philipp for the George Peckham Miller home on East Juneau Avenue.

Below right, Brust & Philipp did not design this house on East Juneau Avenue; rather, the firm designed an interior remodel sometime around 1920.

Julia and Ralph Friend House
Milwaukee, Wisconsin

The architectural firm of Brust & Philipp designed an English Tudor style house for Ralph and Julia Friend in 1908. Located at 3008 East Linnwood Avenue, the steeply-pitched roof, bays, and stucco exterior truly represented the Tudor Revival style. The Paul Riesen's Sons Company did the masonry on this house project.

Ralph's father was involved in the wholesale clothing company of Henry Friend & Brothers. The company was later incorporated as Friend Brothers Clothing Company.

Ralph experienced an interesting life. At the age of sixteen, he traveled to Colorado and then settled in Cheyenne, Wyoming, where he took up cattle raising in Laramie County. He sold his ranch in 1883 to the Milwaukee & Wyoming Investment Company, which was headed at the time by Milwaukee railroad magnate and financier, Alexander Mitchell.

Ralph continued living in Wyoming by the Green River until 1903. In that year, Friend returned to Milwaukee and engaged in the brokerage business as an investment broker and as partner in the Charles Schley Company.

On April 30, 1903, Ralph Friend was married to Mrs. Julia C. Weide Kipp. From 1919 to 1924, Ralph Friend was the president of The Western Iron Stores Company.

Front view of the Friend house

Rear view of the Friend house

Northwest Side Milwaukee Commissions

Stephan J. Casper House
Milwaukee, Wisconsin

Stephan J. Casper was the owner of Western Bottler's Supply Company and president/treasurer of Western Glass and China Company. The Western Glass and China Company sold lunchroom equipment to hotels, restaurants, cafeterias, and clubs.

Casper was married to the daughter of John Schroeder, owner of the J.S. Lumber Company. Casper commissioned the architectural firm of Brust & Philipp to design a home, located at 3607 West Highland Boulevard. Completed in 1910, the total cost of the Foursquare style house was $5,000. The Casper home still remains at that site and is now part of the Concordia Historic District.

Charles I. Ziegler House
Milwaukee, Wisconsin

The Charles I. Ziegler home, located at 740 North 34th Street, was designed in 1912 by the architectural firm of Brust, Philipp & Heimerl. Ziegler was the secretary/treasurer of the George Ziegler Company, a confectionery. [See Pages 166-167 for the George Ziegler Company commission.] According to a building permit, the architectural fee paid to the architectural firm was $707, and the estimated cost of the building was $15,200. A recent photograph of the Colonial Revival style home shows an oriel bay located on the right side of the house, a neoclassical dormer above the front entry, and keystones above the windows.

Gustav Wollaeger Jr. House
Milwaukee, Wisconsin

Gustav Wollaeger Jr. was the son of Gustav Wollaeger Sr., a Christian minister who came to America in 1858 as a German missionary. His mission was to administer to the religious needs of the recently arrived German immigrants. In 1867, Gustav Sr. gave up his missionary work and went to work for the Pritzlaff Hardware Company in Milwaukee. In 1870, while in the employment of Pritzlaff Hardware, Gustav Sr. established the Concordia Fire Insurance Company.

At the age of seventeen, Gustav Jr. entered Harvard University where he graduated with a Bachelor of Arts degree in 1895. He then entered the University of Wisconsin law school and graduated in 1897. After being admitted to the Wisconsin Bar Association, he practiced law until 1906. It was at this time that he entered his father's business, the Concordia Fire Insurance Company. Gustav Jr. became president of the Concordia Fire Insurance Company in 1910 and served in that capacity until his death in 1921.

In 1909, Gustav Jr. commissioned the architectural firm of Brust & Philipp to design an English Tudor style home, located at 3126 West Highland Avenue. The entry porch, the parapet gables, and prominent bays reflected the Tudor Revival style. The home on Highland Avenue was razed in 1934. The location is part of the Highland Boulevard Historic District.

This 1919 drawing shows the garage designed by the firm of Brust & Philipp for Wollaeger's West Highland Avenue house. In the photograph at the top of this page, a corner of the garage is visible behind the house.

Robert John Kieckhefer House
Milwaukee, Wisconsin

The architectural firm of Brust & Philipp was commissioned in 1910 to design a home for Robert John Kieckhefer. The home, located at 736 North 31st Street, was done in the Tudor Revival style and featured a prominent chimney and a steeply-pitched roof.

Kieckhefer founded the Kieckhefer Box Company in 1899 and eventually sold the company to his brothers in 1915.

The American Lace Paper Company, of Glendale, Wisconsin, was founded by Kieckhefer in 1916. One of the largest of its kind in the country, the American Lace Company produced paper specialties. Kieckhefer remained active with this firm until his death in 1961.

After the firm of Brust & Philipp dissolved in 1929, Robert John Kieckhefer hired Richard Philipp to design him a French Norman style home in Brookfield, Wisconsin. The Brookfield home was later razed when the property was purchased by Misericordia Hospital.

The Kieckhefer house on North 31st Street is still located at the original site. It is now part of the Concordia Historic District.

The Tudor Revival style interior of the Kieckhefer house featured tall wainscot with an arched doorway. The beamed ceiling and the multi-paned, leaded-glass windows were also of the Tudor Revival style.

Francis A. Vaughn House
Milwaukee, Wisconsin

Francis A. Vaughn commissioned the architectural firm of Brust & Philipp

in 1919 to design a home at 951 North 31st Street. The style of the house was Colonial Revival with an exterior of clapboard and shingles.

The building permit issued on March 14, 1919, estimated the total cost of the building at $6,000. The Vaughn family lived in another house on this site that was built in 1898 and designed by H.C. Koch. According to the 1919 building permit, the 1898 house was razed to make room for the 1919 house. It is unclear why the home was razed, since the home was only twenty-one years old at the time.

Vaughn was the president of the Francis A. Vaughn Company, an engineering consulting firm. His intense interest in aviation enabled him to became the chairman of the National Aeronautic Association. This association drafted the first air laws for the state of Wisconsin. The Vaughn house is still located at the original site and is now part of the Concordia Historic District.

Walter A. Zinn Apartment Building
Milwaukee, Wisconsin

An apartment building was designed in 1909 by the architectural firm of

Brust & Philipp for Walter A. Zinn. Located at 953 North 10th Street, the building was done in the Tudor Revival style. The side gables were parapet gables, with no overhanging eaves; these gables reflected the late medieval period.

Zinn was the president of the Milwaukee Western Malt Company. His grandfather, Adolph C. Zinn, was also in the malt business and established Zinn Malting Company in 1874 in the old Schlitz Beer building at North 5th Street and West Juneau Avenue. In 1893, American Malting Company absorbed the Zinn Malt Company.

The firm of Brust & Philipp also designed Zinn's home on North Hackett Street in Milwaukee; his lake home, Apple Green Lodge, on Pewaukee Lake; and a store/apartment building at North 4th Street and West Juneau Avenue in Milwaukee. All of these commissions are included in this book. The apartment building pictured here was razed.

August M. Grau Observatory
Milwaukee, Wisconsin

August Grau Jr.'s family were early settlers of Wisconsin. His father, August Grau Sr., came to Milwaukee in 1840 and established a meat market and a distillery. He founded the firm of August Grau & Sons in the 1860s.

After his father's death in 1878, August Jr. joined the firm of William Bergenthal Company. Later, he became connected with the National Distilling Company, and by 1896, August Jr. was the president of the company with August Bergenthal as secretary. This firm would later become the Red Star Yeast Company. The National Distilling Company building was burned to the ground during the 1892 Third Ward fire but was rebuilt the following year.

August Jr. married Miss Christina Klaus of Green Bay in 1880. In 1881, their son, Phillip, was born. After the death of Christina, August Jr. married Clara Wehr.

The architectural firm of Brust, Philipp & Heimerl was commissioned in 1910 to build August Grau Jr. an observatory for his home at 3110 Grand Avenue. The total cost of the observatory was $831.

When Grau died, his obituary (*Milwaukee Sentinel*, August 7, 1922) mentions the observatory: "His home was well know to astronomers where many evenings were spent in research of the skies." Mrs. Clara Grau moved from the home shortly after her husband's death.

Unfortunately, the Grau house, like so many of the Grand Avenue mansions, was turned into a multi-family dwelling in the 1960s and was later razed. No pictures or drawings of the house or observatory were located, and the building permits no longer exist. [See Page 47 for the Mrs. Adelade Grau house commission. Adelade's husband, Charles, was the brother of August Grau Jr.]

August M. Grau Jr.

No photographs or architectural drawings are available

Albert R. Schmidt House
Milwaukee, Wisconsin

Albert R. Schmidt was the president and treasurer of the A. R. Schmidt Electric Company. In 1907, the architectural firm of Brust & Philipp was commissioned to design Schmidt a home at 3211 West Juneau Avenue, originally known as 3209 Chestnut Street. The Tudor Revival style home, with an exterior of brick and stucco, cost a total of $5,500. Brust & Philipp archival records indicate that the architectural firm probably designed a building for the A. R. Schmidt Electric Company in 1928, located at 50th Street and West State Street in Milwaukee. The building site is now vacant and no building permit records are available.

Commissions in Milwaukee's Bay View Neighborhood

East Rusk Avenue Homes
Milwaukee (Bay View), Wisconsin

The architectural firm of Brust & Philipp designed three homes on East Rusk Avenue in the Milwaukee neighborhood of Bay View. It appears that the architectural firm provided architectural plans to two different building contractors. The contractors built the homes and then sold them to private owners.

The wood frame home at 2028 East Rusk Avenue was designed in 1909 for the W. H. Shenners Company. The carpenter was Fred F. Giese. According to a building permit, the estimated cost of the house was $3,000.

In 1911, Brust & Philipp designed more two homes at 2016 and 2022 East Rust Avenue. Both are very similar to the home at 2028 East Rusk Avenue. According to building permits, the estimated cost of the twin wood-frame homes was $2,250 each. Brust & Philipp designed the twin homes for the Home Construction Company. The Weber Building Contractors did the carpentry. The building permit acknowledges only Brust and Philipp as the architects, so it appears that Julius Heimerl did not join the firm until later that year.

All three homes remain at their original locations.

2016 East Rusk Avenue

2028 East Rusk Avenue

2022 East Rusk Avenue

Shorewood Commissions

Charles F. Smith House
Shorewood, Wisconsin

The Charles F. Smith house was designed by the architectural firm of Brust & Philipp in 1922. The red brick home, located at 2618 East Shorewood Avenue, featured a prominent chimney and multi-pane windows that reflected the Colonial Revival style.

William H. Munkwitz House,
Shorewood, Wisconsin

William H. Munkwitz commissioned the architectural firm of Brust & Philipp in 1923 to design his Shorewood home. The Mediterranean style home, located at 4037 North Lake Drive, was done in the Mediterranean style. The exterior was done in brown brick with a red-tiled hipped roof. The Mediterranean style borrowed elements from Italian and Spanish architecture and was very popular in the 1920s.

Mrs. Anna R. Heinemann House
Shorewood, Wisconsin

In 1857, at the age of eighteen, George H. Heinemann, left Cassel, Germany, to enter the employment of the Milwaukee firm of Booth & Company, a wholesaler and retailer of hats and caps. When Mr. Salsman retired, Heinemann became a partner with Cyrus D. Booth, and the firm became known as Booth & Heinemann. In 1879, Booth retired and the firm became George H. Heinemann & Company. The company manufactured felt hats, summer straw hats, caps, gloves, mittens, and fur goods, including buffalo. The hat factory was located on Clybourn Street in Milwaukee. The company did well in 1881, grossing $400,000.

Along with investing in his own hat company, Heinemann invested in other business ventures, including real estate, finance companies, banks, and fire insurance companies. Heinemann joined Northwestern Straw Works, serving as president for five years. In 1894, Heinemann organized National Straw Works, but due to health problems, he retired shortly after the founding of the company. George H. Heinemann died on August 3, 1906, at his lake home on Cedar Lake in Washington County, Wisconsin. His wife, Anna R., and their son, Albert, survived him. The George H. Heinemann Manufacturing Company was sold the following year and dissolved in 1919.

On November 9, 1917, Anna purchased land at 4400 North Lake Drive, in

Shorewood. She hired the architectural firm of Brust & Philipp to design a home for her in the Tudor Revival style with Cotswold features. The bays and the prominent tower are elements of this Tudor style.

Anna R. Heinemann died on August 7, 1928, and probably lived at the North Lake Drive home until her death. David Brust, son of John Brust and grandson of Peter Brust, now owns the Heinemann house. Over the years, some remodeling was done, including the addition of a garage built onto the front of the house. The Heinemann house was featured in the August 1924 issue of *Western Architect*.

Heinemann living room

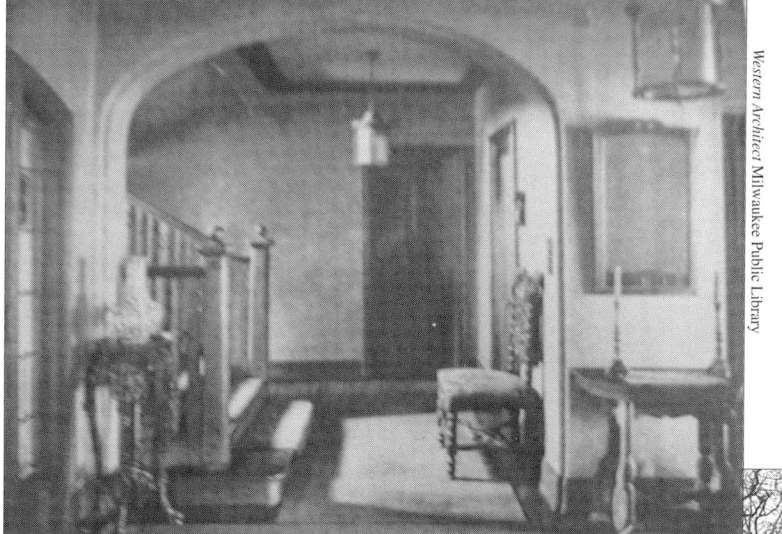

Entrance hall of the Heinemann house

A recent photograph of the Heinemann house

William Kaumheimer House
Shorewood, Wisconsin

Attorney William Kaumheimer commissioned the architectural firm of Brust & Philipp in 1922 to design his Shorewood home, located at 4025 North Lake Drive. The Colonial Revival style home featured a red brick and white-stucco exterior.

Kaumheimer worked for Benjamin M. Weil's real estate office in 1882. Kaumheimer also attended the Milwaukee Law School, now known as Marquette Law School, on a part-time basis. After earning his degree in 1895, he joined the law firm of Kaumheimer & Kaumheimer. In 1918, he became senior partner in Kaumheimer & Kenny. He served as president of the Milwaukee Bar Association in 1920.

The interior of the Kaumheimer house reflected the Colonial Revival style.

Harry S. Johnston House
Shorewood, Wisconsin

The Harry S. Johnston house was designed by the architectural firm of Brust & Philipp in 1926. Located at 3515 North Lake Drive in Shorewood, the Tudor Revival style house featured a steeply-pitched slate roof and prominent chimneys. The upper section was done in both the half-timber style and red brick, while the lower section was done in Lannon stone.

Harry S. Johnston

Johnston was involved in his family's confectionery business. The business began in 1848 when a Scottish immigrant, Alexander H. Johnston, established the A. H. Johnston Confectionery & Cracker Company at North 2nd Street and West Wells Street in Milwaukee. When Alexander died in 1866, his sons, including Robert, inherited the company. In 1890, the company joined American Biscuit & Manufacturing Company and moved its plant to East Erie Street. In 1894, American Biscuit joined with two other companies to form National Biscuit Company.

Robert left National Biscuit in 1899 to form the Robert A. Johnston Company. He built a factory at the corner of Florida Street and Clinton Street, now known as South 1st Street, in the Walker's Point area on Milwaukee's southeast side. Later, the factory moved to 4023 West National Avenue in West Milwaukee, and at that time, the company employed 1,000 people. Upon the death of Robert in 1907, his son, Harry S. Johnston, became the president and treasurer, and he headed the company for forty-five years until he retired in 1952. Harry died in November 1967 at the age of ninety. The Johnston house is still located on North Lake Drive.

Dr. Arthur Patek House
Shorewood, Wisconsin

This architectural drawing was done in 1922 for Dr. Arthur Patek. Patek planned to build this home on North Newton Street in Shorewood; however, the house was never built. Dr. Patek was a physician, and in the 1920s, his office was located in the Goldsmith Building at 141 Wisconsin Avenue, Suite 508.

A God-Given Talent: Peter Brust, Architect, His Work and Legacy 1906-2006

Harry M. Miller House
Shorewood, Wisconsin

The Shorewood home of Harry M. Miller was designed in 1922 by the architectural firm of Brust & Philipp. Located at 3938 North Stowell Avenue in Shorewood, the Tudor Revival style house cost a total of $12,300.

Edwin Wolff House
Shorewood, Wisconsin

The Edwin Wolff house, located at 2731 East Beverly Road in Shorewood, is done in the Tudor Revival style. The architectural firm of Brust & Philipp designed the home in 1921.

Edwin Wollaeger House
Shorewood, Wisconsin

The Edwin Wollaeger house, located at 2632 East Beverly Road in Shorewood, was built on the former site of the Milwaukee Country Club. In 1911, the country club moved to River Hills and the land in Shorewood was developed into a residential area. The architectural firm of Brust & Philipp was commissioned in 1914 to design the English Arts and Crafts style house. The exterior of the house was done in stucco and featured bay windows. The unique front entrance of the Wollaeger house is very much like the Mrs. Sanford Cohen house, also designed by Brust & Philipp. [See Page 37.]

The interior of the Wollaeger house featured English Arts & Crafts style elements such as the oak wainscot and oak doors in the entrance hall. Other rooms featured beamed ceilings and patterned rugs, and oak furniture. The decorative features of the Wollaeger house were similar to Tudor Revival style features, except that the wood finishes of the Arts & Crafts movement were much lighter in tone.

Wauwatosa Commissions

Allan E. Hall House
Wauwatosa, Wisconsin

The Tudor Revival home of Allan E. Hall was designed in 1921, by the architectural firm of Brust & Philipp. Located at 1940 Wauwatosa Avenue, this Tudor Revival style featured a hipped roof and hooded entrances. The exterior of the house was clad in stucco, except for the half-circles of red brick above the first-floor windows. This half-circle technique was also used by Brust & Philipp on the Kaumheimer house in Shorewood. [See Page 64.] On the Hall house, plaster masks were mounted on the brick half-circles, but these masks do not appear on the original architectural drawings.

Allis Chalmers hired Allan E. Hall in 1909 to work at the company's district office in Seattle, Washington. In 1911, Hall moved to the Milwaukee area to work in the West Allis district office. He was promoted to manager of the milling machine department in 1920.

Dr. Rock Sleyster House
Wauwatosa, Wisconsin

In 1939, Dr. Rock Sleyster became the first Wisconsin doctor to head the American Medical Association. Sleyster served as the medical director of Milwaukee Sanitarium from 1919 to 1942. During his tenure as medical director, Sleyster's techniques and practices became a national model for the diagnosis and treatment of mental and nervous conditions.

The architectural firm of Brust & Philipp was commissioned in 1925 to design a house for Sleyster. The house was located at 7711 Chestnut Street directly behind the Milwaukee Sanitarium in Wauwatosa. The French Eclectic style home, with a semi-octagonal entrance tower and a stucco exterior, cost a total of $57,475. Farmhouses of Normandy, France, were the inspiration for this house. The French Eclectic became popular in America between the two World Wars. The house is still located at the original site and was recently renovated.

Henry Heun House
Wauwatosa, Wisconsin

The Henry Heun house was designed by the architectural firm of Brust & Philipp in 1921. Located at 633 North 76th Street, formerly known as 507 Cottrell Avenue, the Wauwatosa home was designed in the Tudor Revival style with a steeply-pitched slate roof and a brown brick exterior.

Fox Point Commission

Hunter Goodrich House
Fox Point, Wisconsin

Timothy Watson Goodrich established the T. W. Goodrich & Son Company, a manufacturer of linseed oil, in 1890. When Timothy died in 1906, his son, William, took over the company as chairman of the board. He changed the company name to William O. Goodrich Company, and he proceeded to build a new plant at 13th Street and Hopkins Road in Milwaukee.

William married Marie Pabst, the daughter of Captain Frederick Pabst, and raised six children, including Hunter. At the time of Hunter's birth in 1901, William and Marie resided in a Gothic Revival style home designed by Otto Strack at 2234 North Terrace Avenue.

Hunter earned a degree in civil engineering from Princeton University in 1923. After returning to Milwaukee, he became a mill manager for his father's company. Hunter married Polly Hackney, and they raised two children, Hunter Jr. and Polly.

Later, the Archer-Daniels-Midland Company of Minnesota purchased the Goodrich Company. Hunter continued with the company as the manager of the New York plant.

The architectural firm of Brust & Philipp designed a home for Hunter and his wife in 1926. Located at 7748 North Club Circle in Fox Point, the house was done in the English Tudor Revival style. The upper exterior was done in stucco and the lower exterior in brick. The house is at the same location and remains faithful to the original design.

Wisconsin Architectural Archive

River Hills Commission

Mrs. Louis A. Sherman/ Frederick G. Riesen House
River Hills, Wisconsin

The architectural firm of Brust & Philipp designed a Colonial Revival style home for Mrs. Louis A. Sherman in 1924. According to Peter Brust's archival records, a remodel was done in 1931 when Georgia and Frederick G. Riesen owned the home. It is unclear if Mrs. Sherman was related to Frederick and Georgia Riesen. According to the 1910 Census, Rhoda M. Sherman lived with Georgia and Frederick G. Riesen. It is possible that Rhoda was Georgia's mother.

The address listed in archival records is 7790 North River Road in River Hills. The home remains on the same site surrounded by a grove of trees. However, it appears that the address was changed slightly since the 1930s. Frederick Riesen held the River Hills village office of supervisor in 1930. According to city directories, he was also the treasurer/secretary for the Paul Riesen's & Sons general contracting firm. This contracting firm provided masonry services on a number of Brust & Philipp projects.

A pencil drawing of the Riesen House

Residential Commissions Outside the Milwaukee Area

D. P. Lamoreux Mansion
Beaver Dam, Wisconsin

The Tudor Revival style mansion of D. P. Lamoreux is no more. After many years of delayed repairs and neglect, the mansion was in such a deteriorated state that the cost of restoration was astronomical. The home was razed in 1981.

Known by his middle name, Percy, Donald Percy Lamoreux was the youngest child of Silas Wright Lamoreux, a successful industrialist. Percy spent his youth in Mayville, Wisconsin, where his father's business successes allowed his family to be part of Mayville's high society. Their home on Buchanan Street was witness to many social events.

Percy graduated from Mayville High School and attended the University of Wisconsin-Madison, where he graduated in 1895. Shortly after, Silas moved his family to a home on Park Avenue in Beaver Dam, Wisconsin, and established a new industrial foundry, Beaver Dam Malleable Iron Works.

After college, Percy held a number of employment positions. He worked as a civil engineer and as a private secretary to the general commissioner in the United States Land Office in Washington, D.C. He also spent three months at the Exchange Bank in Mayville before moving to Seattle, Washington. In Seattle, Percy ran steamships from Seattle to Alaska. It was in Seattle that Percy met his future bride, Isabella Holmes, whom he married on November 19, 1898. They traveled back to Beaver Dam and settled at 310 Park Avenue. Percy took a position in the clerical department of this father's company. Percy and Isabelle raised two children, Fred, born in 1900, and Bertram, born in 1906. Percy was soon promoted to treasurer and manager of

The Tudor Revival style exterior of the Lamoreux Mansion home was comprised of a number of building materials. The lower section was done in Lannon stone with the upper section done in stucco. The bay section was done in dark-stained wood beams and stucco.

the company. When his father died in 1909, Percy was named president and general manager.

For a man of Percy's social status, building a mansion was fairly predictable. In 1908, Percy and his wife traveled to Europe to study the architectural styles of the homes there, and like many of the affluent, they were greatly impressed with the English Tudor style. In 1909, Percy hired the architectural firm of Brust & Philipp to design such a home for his family. At the time, the firm was the largest architectural firm in the state of Wisconsin. Since the house was to reflect the English Tudor Revival style, the exterior materials were of stone, stucco, and wood. Bays of multi-paned casements windows, with heavy stone frames, also reflected the style. The home's foundation was made of poured concrete, with first-floor walls twenty-one inches thick. Quality of workmanship and materials were a priority.

The interior also reflected this quality of workmanship and materials. The paneled walls, oak woodwork, and pine-ceiling beams epitomized the true English manor that the home attempted to mimic. The grand hallway boasted oak paneling with oak leaves carved into the stairway newel posts.

According to a recent Beaver Dam newspaper article (*Citizen Newspaper*, February 19, 2000), the mansion featured four full baths, a vacuum system, electric lights, and central heating. The article also described the mansion as having a main hall, dining room, living room, kitchen, playroom, service porch, servants' hall, and solarium on the first floor. The solarium was connected to the house by a glassed-in corridor. The second floor contained seven bedrooms, each with a walk-in closet. The attic, like the English manors, contained servant rooms.

The house was built on a three-acre lot at 208 La Crosse Street in Beaver Dam. The building site chosen for the home was not near the fashionable upper-class neighborhood. Instead, it was built on a site high above Beaver Dam Lake. Unlike future communities that found the lakeshore a refuge for the society's elite, Beaver Dam Lake was mainly used for industrial purposes. The factories not only found the lake a handy source for water, but they also found it as a handy place for depositing sewage. Not until after World War II did the Beaver Dam lakeshore become a popular site for the more affluent of the town's population.

Unfortunately, the Lamoreux family lived in the mansion for only six short years. Lamoreux's company failed in 1916, and both the company and the house were sold to Western Malleables, Inc. Lamoreux and his family left very quickly for Canada, settling in Brantford, Ontario. Some speculated that Lamoreux experienced financial problems, and he needed to flee the country to escape prosecution. No business records were found. However, Lamoreux was successful in his business ventures in Canada. He was appointed vice president of Canadian Car and Foundry Company, Ltd., in Montreal. In 1922, Lamoreux formed the company of Lamoreux-Kelly, Ltd. He died on July 12, 1955, at the age of eighty-one.

When Lamoreux left Beaver Dam in 1916, E.E. Symthe, the new president of Western Malleables, Inc., occupied the mansion on La Crosse Street. When Symthe died, the mansion was used as a dormitory to house

factory workers. In 1922, the Lutheran Deaconess Hospital purchased the mansion for $30,000. The architectural firm of Brust & Philipp was hired to remodel the mansion to reflect its new use as a hospital. [See Page 176 for Lutheran Deaconess Hospital.] The mansion was demolished in 1981, but a small porch of the house was attached to one of the hospital additions. The mansion was featured in an issue of *American Architect* on May 24, 1916.

The main hall featured rounded doorways, quartered sawed oak paneling, and a stone floor.

The living room of the Lamoreux mansion contained many elements of the Tudor Revival style. The beamed ceiling, the animal skin area rugs, and paneled walls reflected this style.

The dining room at the Lamoreux mansion

Dr. Edwin J. Albrecht House
Mayville, Wisconsin

Dr. Edwin J. Albrecht of Mayville was a first cousin of Richard Philipp. In 1914, Dr. Albrecht hired the architectural firm of Brust & Philipp to design him a home in Mayville at 19 North Walnut Street. The Dutch Colonial style home featured a side-gambrel roof. Dr. Albrecht's granddaughter, Jeanne Young, now owns the house. Richard Philipp spent part of his childhood in Mayville before his father moved the family to Milwaukee.

Dr. Albert James Hodgson House
Waukesha, Wisconsin

The city of Waukesha was well known during the late 1800s and early 1900s for its mineral spring water and health spas. One of the most well-known companies of spring water was the Bethesda Mineral Spring Company. Dr. Albert James Hodgson, a general medical practitioner, was the vice president of this company. He also established a spa in Waukesha to treat diabetes, kidney aliments, and Brights disease. Hodgson was a nationally recognized authority in the treatment of these diseases.

When Hodgson retired from his medical practice, he commissioned the architectural firm of Brust & Philipp in 1924 to design him a Pueblo style home at 1008 East Broadway in Waukesha. According to a newspaper article *(Waukesha Freeman,* November 11, 1996), the exterior walls were made of tile and covered in stucco. The article went on to say that the flat roof was built with a parapet that was crowned in blue, brown, and tan-colored tiles; the tiles were done in the mission style. Also, a small tiled roof covered the large oak front door. The interior, according the newspaper article, featured a beamed plaster ceiling with a tile floor and a fireplace that featured an ornamental inlay. The house is still located on East Broadway in the city of Waukesha.

Oscar A. Richter House
Manitowoc, Wisconsin

The home at 846 North 8th Street in Manitowoc was built as a wedding present for Oscar and Ruth Richter who were married in 1921. Ruth's father commissioned the architectural firm of Brust & Philipp in 1925 to design this Colonial Revival house for the couple. The exterior was done in red brick with pilasters at the front entrance.

At the time, Richter was the vice president and director of the Manitowoc Hotel Company, and in 1937, he was the president of the Richter Vinegar Corporation. The home on North 8th Street is now owned and occupied by the law firm of Kaminski and Pozarski.

Dr. W. Grant Hatch House
Santa Cruz, California

Sometime in the early 1920s, the architectural firm of Brust & Philipp designed a home for Dr. W. Grant Hatch in Santa Cruz, California. The home was done in the Mission/Mediterranean Revival style. The drawing included here, depicting the Santa Cruz house, was published in the July 1925 issue of the *Western Architect*. The firm of Brust & Philipp also designed a home for Dr. Hatch in Rockford, Illinois. [See next page.]

Dr. W. Grant Hatch House
Rockford, Illinois

The architectural firm of Brust & Philipp designed the Dr. W. Grant Hatch residence in Rockford, Illinois. The home is a fine example of the English Tudor Revival style, with a steeply-pitched roof and bay windows. The upper story featured stucco and wood shingles, and the lower story featured red brick.

No records or drawings for this home could be found in the Brust & Philipp archival information. The home was featured in an issue of *American Architect* on September 6, 1916, and the periodical clearly attributes the house design to the architectural firm of Brust & Philipp. According to Rockford assessment records, the house was built in 1905. It could be speculated that either Peter Brust or Richard Philipp just completed designing the home when the firm of Brust & Philipp was founded in 1906; hence, the design was attributed to the firm of Brust & Philipp.

Little information could be found about Dr. Hatch. The federal census listed him as a physician. His wife's name was Amy, and the couple raised two daughters, Eleanor and Harriet. The census listed his address as 1419 National Avenue in Rockford.

The home is still located at the same site and is beautifully maintained.

A drawing from the *American Architect* shows the physical layout of the Hatch home.

Harry E. Dankoler, Sylvan Lodge Sturgeon Bay, Wisconsin

Harry E. Dankoler was born in Sturgeon Bay in 1863. He was orphaned at the age of seven and was placed in an orphanage in Madison, Wisconsin. At the age of eleven, Dankoler was displaced again when the Madison orphanage closed. He then returned to the place of his birth.

Once in Sturgeon Bay, he got a job with the newspaper office, *Door County Advocate*. He enjoyed the newspaper business, and at the age of twenty, he set a record for hand typesetting speed. In 1883, Dankoler, along with his brother, Ernest, published the *Calumet County News* in Chilton, Wisconsin; the paper shut down one year later. The brothers then moved to Milwaukee and published three newspapers, *Saturday Star, Milwaukee Daily Review,* and *South Milwaukee Star*. After Ernest retired, Dankoler published the *Milwaukee Daily Record*. He also worked for the *Milwaukee Sentinel* and the *Milwaukee Daily News*.

Dankoler and his wife had two sons; one died at birth, and the other son, Sylvester, died at the age of twelve. When his wife died in 1908, Dankoler left Milwaukee and moved back to Sturgeon Bay. Sadly, this was not the way that Dankoler wanted to return to his place of birth. His plans were to someday retire to Sturgeon Bay with his wife and son, Sylvester. In the 1890s, he had created a small sign for his retirement home that read Sylvan Lodge.

The land that Dankoler purchased in 1908 was comprised of twenty acres at 4304 Bay Shore Drive in Sturgeon Bay. Over a four-year period, Dankoler developed Sylvan Lodge, and in 1912, the architectural firm of Brust, Philipp & Heimerl was hired to design the main lodge. Later the firm designed alterations and additions. Dankoler lived at the lodge and devoted his life to his writing and collecting. In 1941, he wrote the book, *The Ice Age and the History of the Earth*.

The current owners of Sylvan Lodge, Jeff and Mary Campbell, retain the original blueprints for the lodge. They decided to retain the name of Sylvan Lodge in honor of Dankoler. Sylvan Lodge presently offers its facilities to organizations for retreats. The sign that Dankoler created so many decades before remains on the same pillar.

Dankoler was also known for creating the Door County Historical Society in 1939. The society began with a $1,000 donation, plus Dankoler's own personal collection of 1,500 items. Donations from other organizations and fundraising efforts totaled $18,000. The Door County Historical Society building was then constructed, and Dankoler became its curator. At the end of his life, Dankoler lived in an apartment at the museum. He died at the age of ninety-two while vacationing at his winter home in Alva, Florida, near Fort Myers.

Theسsign that Dankoler created in the 1890s

Arthur Hayssen House
Sheboygan, Wisconsin

The architectural firm of Brust & Philipp designed the Arthur Hayssen house in 1927. The house is located a block or so from Lake Michigan at 85 Lake Court in Sheboygan. The two-story house was designed in Colonial Revival style. Hayssen was the president and treasurer of the Hayssen Manufacturing Company, a company that made bread-wrapping machines.

Above, a recent photograph shows the Hayssen house. This house was built from the second design plan executed by Brust & Philipp.

Right, the first architectural plan done for Hayssen was in the Queen Ann style.

Jean C. Vollrath House
Sheboygan, Wisconsin

The English cottage of Jean C. Vollrath, located at 1925 North 4th Street in Sheboygan, was designed by the architectural firm of Brust & Philip in 1922. At the time, Vollrath was a department superintendent of the Vollrath Company, located in Sheboygan. In 1942, he became the president of the company. The Vollrath Company was established in 1874 and was incorporated in 1884 as the Jacob J. Vollrath Manufacturing Company. The company manufactured porcelain-enameled ware. [See Page 151 for the Vollrath Company commissions.]

Mrs. J.R. Riess House
Sheboygan, Wisconsin

The architectural firm of Brust & Philipp was commissioned by Mary Vollrath Riess in 1923 to design a house at 1024 North 7th Street in Sheboygan. The exterior of this English Tudor style home was done in stucco and featured a number of bay windows. The architectural firm was also commissioned in 1926 to design alterations to Riess' summer home on Elkhart Lake.

Mary Vollrath was the daughter of Jacob Vollrath and was married John Riess in 1880. The couple raised two children: Minnie, born in 1882, and Dewitt Frank, born in 1886.

John Riess was the son of Frank Riess. Frank Riess was born in Rhineland, Germany, and immigrated to America in 1848 where he was involved in the jewelry business in Wilkes Barre, Pennsylvania. Frank moved his family to Milwaukee in 1859. John attended the German and English Academy in Milwaukee and then studied law in the office of Carter, Pitkin & Davis. John was admitted to the bar and relocated to Chicago where he became a member of the law firm of Shepard, Riess & Shepard. In 1882, Riess sold his interest in the Chicago law firm and moved to Sheboygan to join his father-in-law's business, the Vollrath Company. In 1884, the Vollrath Company was incorporated, and Riess was named secretary/treasurer.

John Riess was a Republican in his political views, and in 1893, he was chosen to be a delegate to the National Convention of the Republican League of the United States. John died on October 20, 1906. It was after his death that Mary commissioned the firm of Brust & Philipp to design her new home on North 7th Street. The house was later razed. [See the next page for interior photographs of the Riess home.]

Mrs. J.R. Riess House, Continued

Top and bottom left, the library of the Riess home reflected the Tudor Revival style with mosaic tile decoration above the mantel.

Top right, the entrance hall of the Riess house featured dark ceiling beams and arched doorways with a leaded-glass entrance door.

Bottom right, tapestries decorated the hallway and stairway walls.

Jerry Donohue House
Sheboygan, Wisconsin

The Jerry Donohue II house was built in Sheboygan in 1897. It appears that sometime around 1920, the architectural firm of Brust & Philipp was hired by Jerry Donohue II to design an exterior and interior remodel of this home at 504 Ontario. The exterior was remodeled in the Tudor Revival style. Unfortunately, no architectural drawings were found for this remodel.

Donohue graduated from the University of Wisconsin with a Bachelor of Science degree in 1907. He traveled to Birmingham, Alabama, to work as an engineer for the Tennessee Coal, Iron & Railroad Company.

Donohue left the company in 1910 and moved to Sheboygan, where he practiced as a consulting engineer and surveyor. Donohue married Leila Marion Bishop in 1911. During the planning of Kohler Village, Donohue's engineering company, Jerry Donohue Engineering Company, was selected to direct all the engineering work for the village.

Jerry Donohue Engineering Company was incorporated in 1921, with Donohue appointed as chairman. In 1929, Donohue left the company when Governor Walter Jodok Kohler Sr. appointed him chairman of the Wisconsin Highway Commission.

Donohue returned to work as an engineering consultant at the Jerry Donohue Engineering Company in 1931. His company designed and supervised sewer construction, paving, sewage and water treatment plants, and drainage projects. The company still exists today. Donohue belonged to various national and local societies involving engineering and public works.

In 1941, he published an atlas, *Geographical and Historical Atlas of Sheboygan County, Wisconsin*, and dedicated it to the memory of his late friend, former Governor Walter Jodok Kohler Sr. When Donohue died suddenly in 1943, his wake took place in his home on Ontario Street. The Donohue house remains at the same site in Sheboygan.

Riverbend, the home of Walter J. Kohler Sr.

Riverbend House
Kohler, Wisconsin

Walter J. Kohler Sr., the owner of the Kohler Company, commissioned the architectural firm of Brust & Philipp in 1923 to design his Kohler home, known as Riverbend. The Kohler Company, a family owned business, manufactured plumbing fixtures and gasoline engines. Walter J. Kohler was involved in politics and served for one term as governor of Wisconsin in 1928.

Riverbend is located at 1161 Lower Falls Road in Kohler. It was designed in the Tudor Revival style, and the total cost of the mansion was $1 million. Typical of the Tudor Revival style, Riverbend was designed with the usual steep gables, dormers, and leaded-glass windows. This magnificent home overlooked the Sheboygan River on a forty-acre estate. Landscaped by the Olmstead Brothers of Brookline, New York, the landscape design included a polo field, a green house, a lily pond, small formal gardens, a picnic pavilion, and a covered walkway connecting the house to the carriage barn. Walter and his wife, Charlotte, traveled widely in Great Britain and Europe, and they were greatly influenced by the architecture they observed there. The interior space of Riverbend was designed with more than fifty rooms, which included a main hall, dining room, library, kitchen, breakfast room, pantry, solarium, and ten bedrooms. Also, each bedroom contained a bathroom and a dressing room.

Kohler died in 1940; his wife, Charlotte, died in 1947. At the time of Charlotte's death, her son, John Michael, and his wife, Julilly, acquired Riverbend and shared it with their four children. Decorating tastes in the 1920s ran towards darker interiors with

Front detail of the main entrance

heavy draperies, allowing little light to penetrate the interiors. Dark upholstery and the fumed oak and walnut furniture added to the dark interior. John and Julilly desired a lighter, brighter interior. To achieve this effect, the walls and ceilings were painted white to better reflect the sunlight coming through the windows. Actually, they found that the white walls contrasted very nicely with the beautiful dark furniture. Draperies were constructed of lighter and brighter fabrics. The bedrooms were given a lighter touch by paint and wallpaper in pastel shades.

Walter and Charlotte's children donated Riverbend to the National Trust for Historic Preservation in 1980. The house was then placed on the National Register of Historic Places. In 1986, the Kohler Company purchased back the mansion for $500,000 from the Trust. When restoration started in the year 2000, the property had sat vacant for fourteen years. With the help of a government tax credit of 25 percent, the restoration of Riverbend got underway. It was important to the Kohler Company that the restoration was done in a way that was faithful to the original design. Whenever possible, the same materials and colors were used.

To accommodate a new luxury resort, the original house of approximately 28,000 square feet was expanded by more than 10,000 square feet. The resort opened in 2001 and is for private members only. Because of the restoration efforts, Riverbend will be part of the Kohler tradition for many years to come. Riverbend was featured in the August 1924 issue of *Western Architecture*.

Top, the dining room and breakfast room were separated by portieres, and the floor was done in reddish-toned Moravian tiles.

Above, chauffeur's cottage at Riverbend

Kohler's Riverbend Home, Continued

The living room at Riverbend featured tapestries decorating the walls.

Above and bottom left, Riverbend's great entrance hall, with a floor of Vermont granite, was accented by Kurdistan rugs. The Tudor Revival style was also reflected in the dark-stained beamed ceiling.

William H. Killen House
Appleton, Wisconsin

The architectural firm of Brust & Philipp designed a house for William H. Killen and his wife, Margaret, in 1915. Located at 205 Prospect Avenue in Appleton, the house was later razed, and the Oneida Street Bridge is now in that location. It appears from city directories that the Killen family lived at the residence sometime between 1915 and 1918. In 1919, Albert Ellis occupied the house. No photographs of the house were found.

Dr. Charles Babcock House
Manitowoc Rapids, Wisconsin

Dr. Charles Babcock was born in Illinois and was educated in New York, earning a degree in dentistry at a New York college. Babcock came to Milwaukee in 1890 and practiced dentistry until his retirement in 1924.

Dr. Babcock commissioned the architectural firm of Brust & Philipp in 1923 to design him a retirement home in Manitowoc Rapids, which is now part of the city of Manitowoc. Babcock's house in Manitowoc Rapids Township was listed in a 1920s city directory as being located at "ns Rapid rd 1 w Soo Line." Babcock's second wife, Mary, the daughter of John Schuette, president of the Manitowoc State Bank, grew up in Manitowoc. A few years later, after the completion of the house, Richard Philipp, who was no longer with the firm of Brust & Philipp, designed a guest cottage for Babcock's Manitowoc Rapids property.

Babcock spent only a few years in the house, passing away in February 1927. The house was later razed. No photographs were found.

Mrs. Amelia. Puerner House
Jefferson, Wisconsin

After the death of her husband, Mrs. Amelia Heimerl Puerner commissioned the architectural firm of Brust & Philipp in 1917 to design her a new home at 304 North Main Street in Jefferson. The house was done in the Arts and Crafts style with a stucco exterior. Jefferson city records show that the house measured 2,600 square feet.

Amelia was the widow of William F. Puerner. William died in October 1912 from injuries he suffered from a fall at his store the month before. At the time of his death, he was secretary, treasurer, and general manager of A. Puerner & Sons Company, a mercantile business established many years before by his father, Andreas Puerner. William was survived by his widow, Amelia, and his seventeen-year-old son, Wilfred. It is interesting to note that Amelia was the sister of Julius Heimerl who was a partner in the firm of Brust, Philipp & Heimerl from 1911 to 1913.

Unfortunately, Amelia did not spend much time in her beautiful new home. Her son, Wilfred, served in World War I and sustained war injuries. Wilfred spent time recuperating at a military hospital. Worrying over Wilfred's injuries took a toll on Amelia's health, and she spent time recuperating at the home of her brother, Ferdinand, in Milwaukee. In January 1920, Amelia died suddenly at Milwaukee's St. Mary's Hospital just before undergoing surgery.

Amelia's son, Wilfred, lived to the age of sixty-one. He spent the last twenty years of his life at the Veterans Home in Woods, Wisconsin, where he was also employed. Amelia's beautiful house is still located on Main Street in Jefferson on a beautifully landscaped lot.

Isidore Heller House
Dunedin, Florida

Wisconsin Architectural Archive

Isidore Heller was a partner in the meat packing and butcher supply company, Wolf, Sayer & Heller, located in Chicago. In 1921, Heller commissioned the architectural firm of Brust & Philipp to design him a home in Dunedin, Florida. The firm previously designed a lake home for Heller on Big Cedar Lake, Wisconsin, around 1909. [See Page 89 for Isidore Heller's Cedar Lake house.] No photographs of the house in Dunedin, Florida, could be located.

Dr. Alexandre T. Nadeau
Marinette, Wisconsin

The architectural firm of Brust & Philipp was hired in 1922 to design a building for Dr. Alexandre T. Nadeau in Marinette at the corner of Newberry and Main Streets. This red brick Colonial Revival style building served as a residence and a doctor's office. The house address is 1424 Newberry Street and the office address is 1421 Main Street. The building is located across the street from St. James Lutheran Church designed by the firm of Brust & Philipp in 1921.

Dr. Alexandre Nadeau was born in Marinette sometime during the 1890s. He married Cecilia, and they raised a son, Alexandre Jr., who followed his father into the medical profession. Alexander Jr. and his wife, Heloise, also resided at the Newberry Street and Main Street residence.

Dr. Nadeau's father, John B. Nadeau, was a prominent figure in Marinette County history. John was born in 1850 in Concord, New Hampshire, and as an infant moved with his family to Quebec, Canada. As an adult, John arrived in Marinette in 1890 and engaged in the lumbering business, a career spanning thirty-one years. He served for many years as a superintendent for the Marinette Box Company. His brother, Napoleon Nadeau, was a millwright and owned Scofield, Arnold & Company, a mill in the city of Marinette. In 1920, John retired and died six years later, on December 28, 1926, while visiting family in Quebec.

Dr. Alexandre Nadeau's brother was also a doctor. Dr. E. (Eugene) G. Nadeau was a specialist in the treatment of eye, ear, nose, and throat diseases. He attended Marquette University in Milwaukee for medical school, graduating in 1914. After practicing medicine in Chicago, he settled in Green Bay, Wisconsin. In 1916, he set up what was to become a large, successful medical practice.

Not much personal information was gleaned about Dr. Alexandre Nadeau, the exception being a remembrance of a librarian at the Marinette Public Library. She recalled that the doctor was still practicing medicine well into his senior years.

Top, a photograph of the residential side of the Nadeau building

Middle, the office portion of the building

Bottom, this drawing shows screened porches at both ends of the house. The porches were later enclosed.

Summer Residence Commissions

Mrs. J. M. (Julilly) Kohler Chalet
Sheboygan, Wisconsin

In the early 1920s, the architectural firm of Brust & Philipp designed a Swiss chalet style summer home for Mrs. John Michael (Julilly) Kohler. It was built on lakeshore property she owned on Lake Michigan near Sheboygan. Architectural writer Rexford Newcomb found the design pleasing and said the following about the building:

The chalet is an American adaptation of the delightful folk-architecture of Switzerland, modified in such a manner as to remove its most insistent Alpine quality, a quality expressive of a geological formation, not to be found in the terrain of the Great Lakes area. Attention is called to the fact that in the structure a certain thrifty frugality is apparent without sacrificing anything of the comfort demanded in a modern American dwelling, and without the distortion of a quality that so often makes American adaptations of foreign spirit wholly ridiculous.[1]

Mrs. Kohler's husband, John Michael, was the son of Walter J. Kohler Sr. who owned the Kohler Company in Kohler, Wisconsin. The Chalet was featured in the August 1924 issue of *The Western Architect*.

[1] Rexford Newcomb, AIA, "Continuity of Personal Influence as Sensed in the Work of Brust and Philipp of Milwaukee," *The Western Architect* (July 1925), 88.

The dining room featured Jacobean furniture.

One of the Kohler children can be seen sitting on a bench in the gazebo on the Chalet's property.

Isidore Heller Summer House
Big Cedar Lake, Wisconsin

Isidore Heller was Hungarian by birth and immigrated to America, settling in Chicago. Heller became a partner in the meat packing and butcher supply company, Wolf, Sayer & Heller. This company was considered one of the most prosperous independent butcher supply companies in the American Midwest. According to the 1889 Milwaukee city directory, Heller also owned a butcher supply store in Milwaukee on Water Street.

Frank Lloyd Wright designed Heller a home in Hyde Park, Illinois, in 1897. This home is still located at 5132 North Woodlawn Avenue and was Wright's first in a series of homes using the Prairie style of architecture.

Isidore's wife, Ida, died in 1909 at the age of fifty-one. In that same year, Heller hired the architectural firm of Brust & Philipp to design him a Tudor Revival style summer home on a 4.8-acre site on Big Cedar Lake in Washington County, Wisconsin. This home on Boettcher Drive was probably used later as a year round home by Heller. He was listed in the 1920 federal census as living at the Cedar Lake home with three servants but no family members. Along with the butcher supply business, Heller may have been in the movie theater business. According to the Milwaukee city directory of 1919, Heller was listed as the president of the Standard Amusement Company.

The firm of Brust & Philipp also designed a monument for Heller in 1917, and a home in Dunedin, Florida, in 1921. [See Page 86 for the Florida commission.] The monument most likely was a grave monument for the Heller family cemetery that was located across the road from the main house at Big Cedar Lake.

One resident recalls the cemetery as having a large flat concrete platform from which rose a vertical headstone. The stone contained four bronze plaques, but only three were engraved. This was probably the monument referred to in the Brust & Philipp records. The resident went on to say that around 1974, the graves of the Heller family were moved from the Big Cedar Lake property to a Jewish cemetery in Chicago. At this time, it is not known which Jewish cemetery the graves and monument were moved to. The Heller home on Big Cedar Lake was featured in the October 1919 issue of *Architectural Record*.

Above and right, historical photographs of the Heller home

Left, this former carriage house was referred to as a stable in the records of Brust & Philipp. The carriage house contained an apartment on the second floor for servants, and it was designed around 1911. Presently, the renovated building is a residence.

Max E. Friedmann Summer House
Fish Creek, Wisconsin

Max E. Friedmann was the son of Albert T. Friedmann, an immigrant from Vienna, Austria. Albert began his employment with the Ed Schuster Department Store in 1884 as a bookkeeper and rose to the position of cashier and then to director of sales. Albert later married Ed Schuster's daughter and advanced further in the company, eventually becoming president of the Ed Schuster stores. [See Pages 153-155 for Ed Schuster commissions.] His two sons, Max and Ralph, joined the company, with Max taking over the presidency of Schuster's in 1933.

In 1926, the architectural firm of Brust & Philipp was commissioned to design a summer home for Max Friedmann at Fish Creek near Sturgeon Bay in Door County, Wisconsin. It is unclear whether Max Friedmann's estate was part of his father's estate or located on a property nearby. Albert Friedmann owned the entire area where Hidden Harbor Condominiums and Sunset Park are now located.

When the streets in Fish Creek were first laid out, some of the streets ran through Albert Friedmann's estate, dividing his property into sections. Albert Friedmann did not like that arrangement, so he negotiated a deal with the city. He offered to give the village a strip of land and in return, the streets running through his property would be closed and those strips of land turned over to him. The village was in favor of this exchange of property, and Sunset Park was created on the strip of the Friedmann property donated to the town.

No photographs of the Max Friedmann house, designed by the firm of Brust & Philipp, could be located; however, the drawings for the buildings are on file at the Wisconsin Architectural Archives and are included here.

The only building left from the Albert Friedmann estate is the coach house that now houses the Harbor Guest House. Renovations were done to the coach house, which included the addition of a second story.

"The Shack" designed by Brust & Philipp was part of the Max Friedmann estate at Fish Creek. The building is done in the chalet style very much like the Kohler Chalet designed for Mrs. John Kohler on her Lake Michigan property near Sheboygan. [See Page 88.]

Above and right, these drawings are of the Max Friedmann Lodge at Fish Creek. Because of the width of the drawing, the image is shown here in two sections. The drawing runs from left to right.

Walter and Toni Zinn Summer Home
Pewaukee Lake, Wisconsin

Fifteen years after designing the Toni Zinn house on North Hackett Street in Milwaukee, the architectural firm of Brust & Philipp was commissioned to design a summerhouse for Walter and Toni Zinn on Pewaukee Lake. Completed in 1922, the summerhouse was called Apple Green Lodge. According to a granddaughter of Walter Zinn, the house was razed in 1980, but the Zinn family still owns the property. The exterior and interior of the summerhouse gave one the sense of a hunting lodge. The exterior was of stucco and shutters decorated the windows. A screened porch extended across the full length of the lodge providing a mosquito-free environment.

The photographs on this page show an interior that reflected the English style. The mounted deer heads, antlers, and animal skin rugs fit the hunting motif.

Guido Hansen Summer Home
Pine Lake, Wisconsin

Guido Hansen hired the firm of Brust & Philipp sometime between 1906 and 1912 to design a Colonial Revival style lake cottage on Pine Lake. Guido, son of Theodore Hansen, was a partner in the Hansen Storage Company founded by his father in 1902.

The land purchased by Hansen on Pine Lake near Apple Lane has an interesting past. In 1910, S.C. Herbst purchased twenty acres of the Sands Farm on Pine Lake. The land was then divided up between Herbst, Hansen, Frank Mann, and Adolph Finkler. A newspaper account tells of a controversy surrounding the sale of the property. When Mrs. Sarah Sands, the owner of the property, sold the land, her daughter, Mrs. Mary Gunther, was very opposed to the sale. Mary, who lived on the property at the time, took her mother to court, attempting to have her mother judged incompetent. Mary lost the case and was appealing the decision when six armed men, accompanied by a private detective, tried to physically evict her from the summer cottage. The group successfully ejected Mary from the home, and the property was eventually taken over by the new owners.[1]

Guido's lake cottage was featured in the book *American Country Houses of Today*, published in 1912. The book provided the following description:

> From the pillared entrance, semi-circular in plan, and brave with canopy and tiled floor, the windows with their arched recesses overhead and oriel at the stair landing, the loggia and covered porch extending to the servants' quarters, from the stately fashion

Guido Hansen

Top, the exterior of the Hansen house featured pillars much in the keeping with the Colonial Revival style. A granddaughter of Guido Hansen said that the home is no longer in the Hansen family but stills exists at its original location.

Above left, the breakfast room was done in the Colonial Revival style with white woodwork and white furniture.

Left, the living room was a large open space with a doorway connecting it to the dining room. The arched staircase lead to the upstairs rooms. A large covered porch extended across the length of the living room.

in which the living room ceiling is treated, the scheming of the minor rooms, the unusual stairway, the detailing of the fireplace, and in many other ways do we note the attention which has been bestowed upon small things, things of great importance.

It is pleasing to see from the views that the owner realized that upon the furnishing and decoration much depends. He has kept it simple. He has also arranged to introduce into the kingdom a sense of brightness and good cheer. Possibly, the color has much to do with this, for we find no little care has been exercised in that regard.[2]

The rear of the Hansen house with its circular driveway

[1] William F. Stark. *Pine Lake* (Sheboygan, Wisconsin: Zimmerman Press 1984), 237.
[2] *American Country Houses of Today.* (New York: Architectural Book Publishing Co., 1912.), 147.

Emmanuel D. Adler Summer Home Oconomowoc Lake, Wisconsin

Sometime between 1906 and 1912, the architectural firm of Brust & Phillip was commissioned by Emmanuel D. Adler to design him a summer home on Oconomowoc Lake in Wisconsin. Adler was part of the David Adler & Sons company that specialized in ready-made men's clothing. [See Page 23 for the David Adler & Sons company commissions.] The following is a description of the house from the book *American Country Homes of Today* published in 1912:

The living-room is flooded with sunshine in the cheerful little cottage recently built by Mr. E. D. Adler on the broad shore of Lake Oconomowoc. It is so deep in the woods as to be practically out of sight to the casual visitor....The long gracefully pillared colonnading spells character, bringing once again a whisper from the days of the classics, when philosophies, ambitions and temples were intimately associated. It exercises a singular charm in so small a place, broadening it, and increasing the importance of its position immediately above the lawn-like meadow, which extends to the water's edge. The roof of the corridor becomes a series of balconies for the bedrooms overhead. The house is well schemed, having a square central hall from which the living and dining rooms open. It has also a double staircase and porches that extend in three directions, so that they may woo the breeze from every side as well as the sunshine. Is it not because of the perfume as well as the movement of these giant trees that people build so frequently in the wood?[1]

[1] *American Country Houses of Today.* (New York: Architectural Book Publishing Co., 1912.), 277.

H. M. Graham House
Brinson, Georgia

According to Brust & Philipp archival records, the firm was commissioned by H. M. Graham in 1907 to design a home in Brinson, Georgia. Unfortunately, no photographs are available and no information could be found for a H .M. Graham.

Carl Hansen Summer Home
North Lake, Wisconsin

The architectural firm of Brust, Philipp & Heimerl designed two cottages for Carl Hansen in 1911 on his lake property in North Lake. Hansen came from Denmark as a young man to help his uncle, Ramus Frederickson, who owned the North Lake Brewery. Ramus Frederickson immigrated to America from Lollard, Denmark, in 1866 with Christian Hanson. Together, they founded the North Lake Brewery. The brewery produced 100 barrels per year.

Carl purchased the brewery in 1913 from his uncle. It was said that during Prohibition the North Lake Brewery hid the brewery in the basement of the tavern and served the beer upstairs. Carl Hansen ran the brewery until 1920.

The cottages designed by Brust & Philipp are located on North Lake near Highway 83. The drawing pictured on this page is of the larger of two cottages built on the property. Both buildings, designed by Brust & Philipp, were greatly altered over the years, and they are unrecognizable from the drawings. It should also be noted that some of Hansen's descendants, living in North Lake, spell the name Hanson.

Chapter 3
Brust & Philipp-Ecclesiastical Commissions, 1906-1926

Churches, Rectories, Religious Schools in the Milwaukee Area

Holy Redeemer Catholic School
Milwaukee, Wisconsin

A small group of North Milwaukee residents gathered on May 12, 1897, with the intention of establishing a new mission church, Holy Redeemer Parish. At the time, the town of North Milwaukee was a fairly rural community with some manufacturing.

The wooden structure on the far right was probably part of the wood-frame school Brust & Philipp designed in 1922. The one-story building, on the far left may be the barracks added at a later date. The brick building, designed by Brust & Philipp, was built in 1930.

The Archbishop agreed to their church request and the first church building was erected at North 38th Street and West Courtland Avenue at a cost of $2,000. Twenty-six families attended the new mission church. Mass was celebrated by Father Joseph S. Fischer who came by bicycle from St. Boniface Church every other Sunday. The first permanent pastor was Father Theisen.

The church school was established on September 15, 1922, and was staffed by four Sisters from the School Sisters of St. Francis of Layton Boulevard in Milwaukee. In the same year, the architectural firm of Brust & Philipp designed a wood-frame school; the total cost of this building was $9,699. Classes were held in the church while the new school was under construction.

Enrollment in the school doubled and then tripled, necessitating the addition of a two-room barrack building in October 1927. Between 1922 and 1930, enrollment was around 500 students.

The firm of Brust & Philipp was hired in 1930 to design a new Romanesque Revival style brick structure; the total cost was $76,583. More additions were made to the school at 4717 North 38th Street in the 1940s and 1950s. The brick structure designed by Brust & Philipp is still in use.

Due to declining enrollment, Holy Redeemer School closed in 1987, and the building is now rented to a charter school. The Holy Redeemer Parish merged with St. Albert's Catholic Church and St. Nicholas' Catholic Church in 1991, and the new parish was named Blessed Trinity.

A view of the 1930 school building from the alley

St. Mary's Catholic Church Hall
South Milwaukee, Wisconsin

On May 26, 1893, the Archdiocese of Milwaukee established St. Mary's Catholic Church in South Milwaukee. The new church building, located at 800 Marquette Avenue, was dedicated on April 11, 1894.

Father John N. Schiltz persuaded the congregation in 1910 to build a new parish hall. The architectural firm of Brust & Philipp designed the brick Romanesque Revival style building, measuring 50 feet by 100 feet. It was completed on May 15, 1910. The parish hall was considered a social center for the parish. The basement contained a bowling alley, pool and billiard tables, and card and reading tables. A temperance bar served only soft drinks, and clubrooms were open to the public. The upper hall contained the auditorium that seated 700 people. In the rear of the upper hall was a reception area with a coat check, toilet facilities, and ticket rooms, and above the upper hall was an area containing a gallery used for kindergarten classes.

The parish hall was remodeled in 1974. Although greatly altered, the hall still occupies the same site and is still in use. St. Mary's recently merged with other South Milwaukee Catholic parishes and is now part of Divine Mercy Catholic Church.

St. Joan of Arc Catholic Church
Delafield, Wisconsin

St. Joan of Arc Catholic Church, located at 120 Nashotah Road in Delafield, was established to serve the needs of the summer residents who owned or rented lake cottages. The parish was incorporated on July 6, 1920, with Monsignor Traudt as pastor. Land for a church was purchased from Mr. Schruedenback for $1,450.

The architectural firm of Brust & Philipp was hired to design a Spanish Mission Stucco style church. Father Traudt's design choice came under opposition from some parish members who felt that the stucco would not hold up to the cold Wisconsin winters. Tile was used under the stucco rather than the concrete used today. The Spanish Mission style design choice won out; some parishioners actually left St. Joan over the disagreement. The stucco did fail and was redone in 1969. The cornerstone was laid on August 12, 1923, with Archbishop Messmer officiating.

The firm of Brust & Brust went on to design the new church school in 1953. In 1997, the St. Joan of Arc chapel, designed by Brust & Philipp, was razed when the new church was built. Some religious articles from the old chapel were incorporated into the new church. The old church was determined eligible for listing on the National Register of Historic Places in 1997, but it was not listed to due to the church's objection.

Layton Park English Lutheran Church
Milwaukee, Wisconsin

The Layton Park English Lutheran Church was established in 1891. An early settler, Victor Seerup, decided to start up a Sunday school in the Layton Park neighborhood located near South 27th Street and West Lapham Street on Milwaukee's south side. From 1891 to 1892, the Sunday school group met wherever it was convenient. In 1893, the Gethsemane Lutheran Church was established, and the Pastor of Gethsemane allowed Seerup's group to meet in his church. Seerup's group asked the pastor of Trinity Church, Harry Olsen, to oversee their Sunday school and to conduct English services at Gethsemane. On February 9, 1908, Reverend Olsen conducted the first service at Gethsemane church at South 24th Street and West Harrison Avenue.

In September 1908, Seerup's group decided to purchase two lots at the corner of West Grant Street and South 24th Street with the intention of having their own church building. Within the week, a vacant Methodist church was purchased and moved to the vacant lots. The first service was held in the church basement on March 14, 1909. In 1910, the congregation purchased a third lot.

It was on March 4, 1918, that the congregation became affiliated with the English District of the Missouri Synod. Over the next few years the parish was involved in constructing church buildings. A parsonage was built on the third lot in 1919. Shortly after, the old church was moved to the rear of the property to make room for the new church; the old church was to become a parish hall. The architectural firm of Brust & Philipp was commissioned to design the new Gothic Revival style church at 2820 West Grant Street. The Layton Park English Lutheran Church was dedicated on May 20, 1923.

Due to a drop in membership, the church building was sold in April 2005 to Lad Lake, a center for at-risk youth headquartered in Douseman, Wisconsin. Lad Lake intends to use the buildings as an alternative secondary school. The Layton Park English Lutheran Church was featured in the October 1924 issue of the *Architectural Record*.

The arched ceiling and wooden beams reflected the English Gothic style.

St. Anne's Catholic Church and Rectory
Milwaukee, Wisconsin

At the time of its founding in 1894, St. Anne's Catholic Church was a German-speaking parish. The cornerstone of the first church was laid on November 19, 1894, and the church was completed in 1895. Within a few short years the congregation outgrew the church building. The overcrowded conditions were not surprising, since the church building not only housed the church but also the school and convent. To alleviate the crowding, a new convent, designed by Herman Esser, was built in 1904. Peter Brust was working for Esser at the time that the convent was designed. In 1908, the architectural firm of Brust & Philipp was commissioned to design a Colonial Revival style rectory for St. Anne's parish at a total cost of $12,732.

A new church was built in 1921 on a site northwest of the old church at 2477 North 36th Street. The firm of Brust & Philipp designed the church in the Northern Italian Romanesque Revival style. St. Anne's closely resembled the St. Joseph's Chapel that the firm designed for the School Sisters of St. Francis on South Layton Boulevard.

The stained-glass windows for St. Anne's were created in Innsbruck, Austria, and were shipped in twenty cases, each crate weighing 180 pounds. It took three weeks to install the windows. T.C. Esser worked with Brust & Philipp on the interior. Among the many stained-glass windows are the images of St. Elizabeth, St. Agnes, St. Augustine, and the Holy Family. Also in the sanctuary is a window of Christ blessing children.

St. Anne's is no longer owned by the Milwaukee Archdiocese. The Mercy Memorial Missionary Baptist Church owns the church.

Top right, the interior of St. Anne's Catholic Church

Above, St. Anne's rectory designed by Brust & Philipp in 1908

St. Augustine of Hippo Catholic Church
Milwaukee, Wisconsin

The congregation of St. Augustine of Hippo, located at 2530 South Howell Avenue, outgrew their church building by 1907. The architectural firm of Brust & Philipp was hired to design the new church, and the Elias Stollenwerk Company was hired to construct it. The total cost was $35,000. The church, measuring 77 feet by 140 feet, was dedicated on November 26, 1908. The church, designed in the Romanesque Revival style, featured a tall pointed spire. The symmetrical facade was designed with rounded arched doorways and was accented with heavy corbelling. Tan brick was used for the exterior, with ornamental brickwork and cut limestone trim.

In a ceremony on June 6, 1914, three bronze bells were installed in the church tower and then blessed. In the Catholic tradition, the bells were named. The largest bell was named for St. Mary and St. Augustine, the medium bell named for St. Joseph, and the smallest bell for St. Peter. Later, Brust & Philipp designed an addition for the convent at 2523 South Graham Street, and in 1920, the firm designed a brick-veneer facade addition for the rectory. St. Augustine parish is still an active parish.

St. Anthony on the Lake Catholic Church
Pewaukee, Wisconsin

St. Anthony's on the Lake is located at W280 N2101 Prospect Avenue in Pewaukee. Like St. Joan of Arc Catholic Church in Delafield, St. Anthony's was established to serve the needs of the summer lake residents. When requested by the lake residents to establish a church, Archbishop Messmer agreed to assign a priest if there were at least thirty attendees. The first mass was celebrated on Sunday, June 30, 1918, at the home of Mrs. Siegfried in Auer Park; the mass drew forty-six residents.

In 1920, residents elected Peter Brust, who rented summer cottages on Pewaukee Lake, as the chairman of the building committee. He prepared a sketch for a proposed chapel, and Mrs. Siegfried donated a plot of land at Angela Road and Louis Avenue. The Gothic Revival style chapel was completed at a cost of $1,100.

However, the parish soon outgrew the chapel. The chapel was moved 150 feet in 1936 and enlarged. However, in 1963, the old chapel was no longer adequate for parish needs and was in need of extensive repairs. The school hall was used as a temporary church, and the 1920 chapel was sold to be used as a private residence. A new St. Anthony on the Lake Catholic Church was dedicated in 1999.

St. Michael's Catholic School and Rectory
Milwaukee, Wisconsin

St. Michael's Church, located at 1445 North 24th Street, was established in 1884 with the purpose of preserving the German culture, language, and identity. A significant number of churches in Milwaukee were built for specific ethnic groups.

The architectural firm of Brust & Philipp designed the Romanesque Revival style school building in 1923. The building contained sixteen classrooms, four bowling alleys, and a cafeteria, all at a cost of $150,000. The building remains at the original site.

The firm of Brust & Philipp also designed the rectory, which was completed in March 1926. The rectory is still in use and retains its original thick tile roof. The convent on the church grounds was purchased from the School Sisters of Notre Dame, and the firm of Brust & Philipp was hired in 1928 to design the alterations for the building at a total cost of $6,000. The firm also did some remodeling work on the church in 1928. St. Michael's is still an active parish.

Top, St. Michael's rectory

Above, St. Michael's School

St. Patrick's Catholic Church
Milwaukee, Wisconsin

Archbishop Henni established St. Patrick's Catholic Church on the south side of Milwaukee in 1876. The intention of establishing the parish was to serve a growing number of Irish and other English speakers. The first church was built at 7th Street and West Washington Street in the summer of 1876. The church school was established in the fall of the same year. In 1895, a new church was erected and a new rectory was later built.

The architectural firm of Brust & Philipp was hired in 1925 to remodel the rectory with the total cost of the remodel totaling $2,000. The firm most likely added the Colonial Revival entrance at the front of the rectory. The firm was also hired in 1926 to remodel the church at the cost of $5,892. St. Patrick's is still an active parish. [See Page 124 for the St. Patrick's Convent commission.]

St. Stephen's Catholic Church
Milwaukee, Wisconsin

In the 1840s, immigrants from Cologne, Germany, settled in the southeast section of Town of Lake. The neighborhood was known as New Coeln, the name based on the German city of Cologne, spelled Koeln in German. In 1847, Catholic members of the community built St. Stephen's Church at 5880 South Howell Avenue. By 1884, the church proved too small for the growing congregation; therefore, a second church was built. The architect was Mr. Druiding of Chicago. Five years later a rectory and school were constructed.

St. Stephen's congregation witnessed two fires during the early 1900s. In May 1908, a fire gutted the church and damaged the rectory, and all that remained were the original brick walls. The architectural firm of Brust & Philipp designed a restoration plan using the original walls of the old Gothic Revival style church.

Fire again destroyed the church in 1926, leaving only the original walls still standing. Again, Brust & Philipp were hired to design the restoration of the church. A new rectory was also built at this time. The total cost to rebuild the church and build a new rectory came to $52,000.

St. Stephen's is now part of the city of Milwaukee. It is still an active parish. However, the church is up for sale, and once it is sold, a new church will be built at the corner of 13th Street and Oakwood Road in Oak Creek, Wisconsin.

The rectory built in 1926

St. Peter Claver Catholic Church
Sheboygan, Wisconsin

On January 15, 1888, St. Peter Claver was canonized. Fifteen days later, a new parish in Sheboygan, Wisconsin, was named for him in celebration of his canonization. Father J. P. Van Treeck was appointed pastor of the new St. Peter Claver congregation. The church/school/convent combination was erected that same year, with the Sisters of St. Agnes of Fond du Lac, Wisconsin, staffing the school.

Within two decades, the church proved too small for the growing congregation. At a meeting on October 25, 1906, parishioners discussed the inadequacy of the combination building and decided that a new church was needed. The firm of Brust & Philipp was hired to design the church. The new church at 1444 South 11th Street was completed in 1908. The total cost of the church was $50,000. The church was done in the German Gothic style with the exterior done in Sturgeon Bay stone. The seating capacity was 800 parishioners. Bishop Fox of Green Bay dedicated the church on June 21, 1908. St. Peter Claver Catholic Church is still an active parish.

St. Rose of Lima Catholic Church
Fredonia, Wisconsin

A group of Catholics held a meeting at the Joseph Hiltgen's Hall in Fredonia on March 11, 1909, to discuss the possibility of establishing a Catholic church in their community. With no church of their own, Catholics in Fredonia attended mass in the nearby towns of Dacada, Little Kohler, and Waubeka. Donations were sought from residents to finance a church, and a petition was sent to Archbishop Messmer on March 26, 1909. The Archbishop approved the community's request. Reverend P. J. Delles was assigned as pastor, and the name of St. Rose of Lima was selected on May 5, 1909.

The firm of Brust & Philipp was hired to design the Romanesque Revival style church at 305 Fredonia Avenue. The church was built of concrete blocks made by Frank J. Meyer's block-making machine in a barn across the street from the church. Stucco covered the bricks on the church's exterior. At the time the cornerstone was laid in September 1909, there were sixty parishioners. A school was built at the same time as the church. This school would later house the rectory until the new rectory was built in 1917. St. Rosa of Lima is still an active parish.

Churches, Rectories, Schools Outside the Milwaukee Area

St. Paul's Catholic Church
Combined Locks, Wisconsin

As in many Wisconsin rural communities, Catholics in the village of Combined Locks lacked their own church. They were forced to attend mass in Kimberly, Little Chute, and Kaukauna. However, in 1923 hopes were realized, and a new parish was organized in Combined Locks. The new church was named St. Henry's, but the name was changed to St. Paul's in honor of Paul Smith, a very dedicated parish member.

The first church was housed in the old fire-damaged school, which was purchased by the Combined Locks Paper Company from the school board for $5,000. The old school was remodeled as a church, with the design work performed by the architectural firm of Brust & Philipp. Along with designing the remodel of the church, the firm of Brust & Philipp designed a new rectory.

The first mass in the remodeled school was on Christmas Eve 1923 and was officiated by Reverend Henry Halinde, the first pastor of St. Paul's. The Combined Locks Paper Company owned the church buildings from 1924 until 1946, at which time the company officially gave the buildings to the congregation. A new church was built in 1963 at 410 Wallace Street. St. Paul's is still an active parish. [See Pages 210-212 for the Combined Locks commissions.]

Combined Locks Golden Jubilee Kimberly Public Library

St. Alphonsus Catholic Church
New Munster, Wisconsin

Immigrants from Munster, Germany, settled in Kenosha County in the 1840s, establishing the community of New Munster. Up until 1849, Catholics from New Munster attended mass in Burlington or relied on the circuit-riding priests who visited the area infrequently. In 1851, the New Munster community established St. Alphonsus Catholic Church, constructing a stone church at a cost of $5,000. A larger brick and wooden Gothic style church was erected in 1882 for $12,000.

Sadly, a fire destroyed the ca. 1882 church on January 13, 1907. The firm of Brust & Philipp was responsible for designing the new red brick Romanesque Revival style church in 1908. Parish members pitched in to haul, by horse-drawn wagons, the building materials for the new church. The total cost of the church, according to Brust & Philipp records, was $17,000. St. Alphonsus at 6301 344th Avenue is still an active parish.

St. Matthew's Catholic School
Campbellsport, Wisconsin

St. Matthew's Catholic Church in Campbellsport was established at the request of a small group of Catholics who banded together in 1864 to ask for their own parish. At the time, the town was known as New Cassel. In 1874, the first resident pastor, Father Anton Michels, was appointed.

The new church school opened in September 1874, staffed by three teaching Sisters from the order of the School Sisters of St. Francis. The Sisters erected their Motherhouse in New Cassel, and Father Michels was their spiritual advisor.

The archival records for the architectural firm of Brust & Philipp state that design work was commissioned for St. Matthew's School around 1921. According to church records, it was during this year that the old school, built in the 1880s, was enlarged. The upper floor, formerly the parish hall, was converted into two classrooms. An addition was designed for the east side of the building that housed a stairway and cloak-

St. Matthew's school, built in the 1880s, was not designed by Brust & Philipp. They most likely designed the remodeling in 1921 that accommodated more classroom space.

rooms. The firm of Brust & Philipp probably did these alterations. The old school was razed after a new school building was completed in 1956. St. Matthew's Church, located at 406 East Main Street, is still an active parish.

Holy Trinity Catholic Church
Jericho, Wisconsin

Holy Trinity was established at Jericho on January 27, 1871, and remained a mission church until 1878. Reverend Hugo Praessner was appointed pastor in the early 1880s, and a new frame church was built. In 1914, sparks from a nearby barn fire burned the church to the ground. Therefore, the building committee decided that a brick church would be more substantial as well as more architecturally beautiful.

The architectural firm of Brust & Philipp was selected to design the new church. The cornerstone was laid on October 15, 1915, and the church was dedicated on August 15, 1916. The Gothic Revival style church seated 480 parishioners. The altars were a combination of quartered-sawed oak, onyx, and marble. Holy Trinity Church is still located at the intersection of County Highways C and H, but the parish recently merged with other parishes in the area.

St. James' Evangelical Lutheran Church
Marinette, Wisconsin

According to their fiftieth anniversary celebration booklet, the Congregation of St. James Evangelical Lutheran church wanted to break away from the old world languages and present services in the English language. The first service at St. James, conducted by Reverend W. C. Stump, was held in the Arcade Building on Stephenson Street and Hall Avenue in Marinette on May 12, 1918, with thirty people in attendance. The congregation was officially organized on June 2, 1918, and it was incorporated on September 17, 1918. The congregation later bought a building on Main Street for $4,000 and remodeled it into a chapel. However, as membership grew, it was decided in 1920 to build a new church.

The architectural firm of Brust & Philipp was hired to design an English Gothic Revival style church. The cornerstone was laid on July 24, 1921, and the church was dedicated on April 1, 1922. The cost of the new church was $63,192. St. James is still located at 1402 Main Street and is in handsome condition. Directly across the street from the church is the Dr. Alexandre Nadeau residence/office also designed by Brust & Philipp.

The periodical, *The Western Architect*, published plates of the church in their July 1925 issue. Architectural writer Rexford Newcomb said the following about the church:

> If the reader will survey the plates presented here with--sketches as well as photographs--he will note an extreme simplicity of line and mass, a quality always acceptable when accompanied by beauty of form, interesting texture and variety of color. In this way, a simple little brick church like that of Saint James, at Marinette, Wisconsin, commands an attention not granted many a more ambitious scheme.[1]

[1] Rexford Newcomb, AIA, "Craftsmanship in Architecture," *The Western Architect* (July 1925), 71-72.

St. Mary's Catholic Church
Kansasville (Dover), Wisconsin

The parish of St. Mary's was founded in 1867, and a church was built the following year. When the old church needed to be replaced, the architectural firm of Brust & Philipp was hired in 1907 to design a English Gothic Revival style church. The exterior was done in a red Montezuma Indiana brick, trimmed in Bedford stone, and topped with a Bangor slate roof. The church measured 88 feet long by 38 feet wide, with a seating capacity of 210 people. The tower rose 53 feet from the water table to the cross. The cost of the church was $14,000 and was paid for through fundraising events and subscriptions. To reflect the Irish heritage of the parish, stained-glass windows with Irish-influenced images were installed and Celtic crosses decorated the belfry and the church entrance. St. Mary's was dedicated on December 1, 1907. The church, located at 23211 Church Road, is still an active parish.

St. Mary's of the Visitation Catholic School
Marytown, Wisconsin

St. Mary's of the Visitation Catholic Church, located on Highway G in Marytown, was founded in 1849 by a group of European immigrants. A parishioner, Mathias Burg, donated sixty acres to the church. Some of the lots were sold, and the money was used for building a permanent log church in 1897. The first resident pastor was Reverend Fabian Bermadinger. When the log church was destroyed by fire in 1879, a new, bigger church was built of quarry rock. When another fire in 1897 partially destroyed the church, a new church was built. The interior of the new church featured rich woodwork, a carved altar, beautiful statues, and stained-glass windows.

A new red brick school, financed by contributions and fundraising activities, was built in 1923. The architectural firm of Brust & Philipp designed the school in the Tudor Gothic style with a front parapet and side parapet gables. The building contractor was George Hayes.

Above, an historical photograph of St. Mary's School

Left, a recent photograph of the school shows that the windows were changed for heat efficiency reasons.

Combination Buildings

For many newly established parishes, their first building served as both church, school, and parish hall. This church/school/parish hall combination building was an economical way for beginning parishes to attain a place of worship. As the parishes grew, a separate church building was erected, and the old combination building was taken over by the school. The architectural firm of Brust & Philipp designed a number of these combination buildings.

Holy Angels Catholic Church/School
Milwaukee, Wisconsin

The architectural firm of Brust & Philipp submitted the lowest bid and won the commission to design the Holy Angels Catholic Church at 3785 North 11th Street. Completed in 1917, the Gothic Revival style building was a combination of a church, school, and social center with the church on the first floor, the school on the second, and the basement housing the parish hall and stage. Stone salvaged from the demolition of the Plankinton House Hotel in Milwaukee was used in the construction of the combination building. Sisters of Charity of the Blessed Virgin Mary from Dubuque, Iowa, staffed the school.

A new church building was constructed in 1927, and the old combination building was used just as a school. The combination building is still being used as a school; however, Holy Angels Catholic Church no longer exists.

Zimmerman Design Group

St. Boniface Catholic Church
Milwaukee, Wisconsin

Established in 1888, St. Boniface Catholic Church was located at 2609 North 11th Street in Milwaukee. In 1907, Father Stemper was given discouraging news from the city inspectors of schools. It was reported to Father Stemper that the old church and school buildings were unsafe, so a new church and school were needed. In August 1907, a group of eighty parishioners voted to spend $35,000 to build a new building.

The architectural firm of Brust & Philipp provided the Romanesque Revival style design for the two-storied red brick building. This eight-room building would house both the church and the school. A new church was later built, and the old combination building was used just for the school. St. Boniface was well known during the 1960s when Father Groppi, a civil rights activist, was a priest there. The combination building, designed by Brust & Philipp, was later razed.

St. Leo's Catholic Church
Milwaukee, Wisconsin

St. Leo's Catholic Church was established in 1909 at 2458 West Locust Street on property that was part of the Mayhew subdivision. According to the building permits, the architectural firm of Brust & Philipp designed the Romanesque Revival combination church/school in March 1909. The permit lists an estimated cost of $32,000. The School Sisters of Notre Dame taught at the school. Later, a new church was built, and the old combination building was then used just as a school. This building is still in use as a school, housing the St. Leo's Catholic Urban Academy.

St. Florian's Catholic Church and School Milwaukee, Wisconsin

St. Florian's Catholic Church was established in 1911 to serve Catholics in the small industrial town of West Milwaukee. St. Florian's began as a mission church of the Holy Cross Catholic Church, located on the northwest side of Milwaukee.

Church services were first held in an old public building. Archbishop Messmer appointed Father Joseph Ritger as pastor, but Ritger stayed for only one year. The Capuchins from Holy Cross Catholic Church returned after Ritger left and the order financially supported St. Florian's. The Capuchins helped the parish find a permanent location on South 46th Street and West Scott Street. However, the Capuchins hoped to disconnect from the daily running of St. Florian's.

The Capuchins suggested to Archbishop Messmer in 1913 that he contact the Discalced Carmelites at Holy Hill. The order expressed interest in establishing a monastery in Milwaukee. The Discalced Carmelites agreed to take over St. Florian's, but Archbishop Messmer stipulated that the new church building needed to be a church/school combination building. In 1913, Father Irenaeus Berndl was established as the first Carmelite pastor of St. Florian's. [See Page 129 for the Discalced Carmelite Monastery commission at St. Florian's and the Discalced Carmelite Monastery commission at Holy Hill in Hubertus, Wisconsin.]

On September 15, 1913, Father Irenaeus, along with his parishioners, decided to build a Romanesque Revival style combi-

The 1913 church/school combination building, designed by the firm of Brust, Philipp & Heimerl for the St. Florian's Congregation, was razed when the new school was built.

The basement church served the St. Florian's Catholic Church congregation from 1923 to 1938, at which time, the upper church was completed. The firm of Brust & Philipp also designed the Carmelite Monastery pictured on the extreme left side of this photograph. [See Page 129 for the Carmelite Monastery at St. Florian's.]

nation building at the corner of South 45th Street and West Scott Street. The architectural firm of Brust, Philipp & Heimerl was hired to design the new building.

During construction in February 1914, someone tried to set fire to the uncompleted building by dumping gasoline on the church floor; fortunately, the fire mysteriously extinguished itself. Some believed that the fire was extinguished due to the intercession of St. Florian, the protector against fires and the patron saint of firefighters.

The new combination church/school building was dedicated on April 19, 1914. The church was on the first floor, with the four-room school on the second.

By 1923, with a growing parish and school, a new separate church was needed. Money was tight, so a long-term building plan was devised. The firm of Brust & Philipp was hired to design the new church.

The church basement, completed in 1923, housed the temporary church. This church basement accommodated the celebration of mass until enough money became available and the upper church was completed. The upper church, located at 1233 South 45th Street, was subsequently completed in 1938. [See Page 216 for the St. Florian's upper church commission.]

St. Rita's Catholic Church
West Allis, Wisconsin

St. Rita's Catholic Church of West Allis was established as a mission church in January 1922. The pastor of St. Mathias Catholic Church in Milwaukee was chosen by Archbishop Messmer to direct this mission church. The church was named for St. Rita of Cascia. The first mass was celebrated on Sunday, July 6, 1924, in a tent rented from the State Fair Park.

According to Brust & Philipp archival records, the architectural firm did sketches for a St. Rita's School. In all likelihood, the firm was commissioned to design the new St. Rita's combination church/school/parish hall building.

The Gothic Revival style combination building, located at 2318 South 61st Street, was completed in October 1924. As a combination building, the basement served as the church, the first floor was divided into four classrooms, and the second floor housed the parish hall. The exterior was done in a tan-colored face brick with Bedford stone trim. The cost of the new building was $60,000, not including furnishings. The church, measuring 108 feet by 60 feet, seated 460 people. A new church was later built; however, St. Rita's still utilizes the old building.

Top, exterior of 1924 St. Rita's church/school/parish hall combination

Above, the interior of the 1924 basement church

Chapels

Sacred Heart Mortuary Chapel
St. Francis, Wisconsin

The Sacred Heart of Jesus Cemetery adjoins the Sacred Heart of Jesus Catholic Church property at 3635 South Kinnickinnic Avenue. The first burial was in 1876. The graves of early settlers buried at St. Aemilian's Orphanage were moved to the Sacred Heart Cemetery in 1888. According to a 1918 souvenir church booklet, the cemetery's physical closeness to the church allowed many parishioners to visit the "Silent City" every Sunday. The cemetery expanded as time went on with additional land being purchased by Sacred Heart Church in 1923. Later, three acres were purchased from the St. Francis Seminary for $3,500.

A Romanesque Revival style mortuary chapel was built in the cemetery in 1914. The cost was $1,000, and Peter Brust designed the chapel at no cost to the parish. The chapel was torn down, but the imprint of its foundation can still be seen. Near the original site of the chapel is the above ground crypt of Father Peter Grobschmidt, who was the first Sacred Heart parishioner to be ordained a priest.

The 1918 souvenir church booklet also said, "May we never forget the beautiful Catholic custom of taking good care of the graves of our departed and frequently visit the City of the Dead to pray for them and learn to die well."[1]

[1] *Souvenir Golden Jubilee. Sacred Heart of Jesus Congregation, 1868-1918* (St. Francis, Wisconsin: Sacred Heart of Jesus Congregation, 1918), 19.

Interior of the Sacred Heart Mortuary Chapel

Luther Memorial Chapel
Shorewood, Wisconsin

Evangelical Lutheran Church of East Milwaukee was officially organized in March 1906. Edwin Wollaeger was the first to serve as president of the church. [See Page 67 for the Edwin Wollaeger house commission.] The lots for the new chapel were purchased in 1917. In that same year, East Milwaukee became Shorewood, and the name of the chapel was changed to Luther Memorial Chapel.

The architectural firm of Brust & Philipp was commissioned to design the new Gothic Revival style Luther Memorial Chapel in 1924. The cornerstone was laid on August 24, 1924, and the chapel was dedicated on Sunday, May 17, 1925.

A newspaper article (*Shorewood Radio*, 1923) states that the building committee expected the chapel to conform to the standards of Lutheran architecture. Working closely with the building committee, the architects made sure that certain specifications were met. The chancel was to be in proportion to the rest of the building. The altar was to be built high enough to command attention, and the pulpit was to be enclosed and elevated so that the entire congregation could see the speaker. The balcony needed to be designed in accordance to the Lutheran standard that stated that the choir be heard but not seen. The chapel was described as being honest throughout. It was important to the committee that the designers avoid anything theatrical or showy, but rather followed simple and subdued lines.

The final cost of the Gothic Revival style chapel, including furnishings, was $100,000. This Lutheran house of worship seated 500 people. The chapel, located at 3833 North Maryland Avenue, still exists at the same location with some additions having been made to the church.

Top, the chapel was dedicated on May 17, 1925, and the church pastor, Reverend O. F. Engelbrecht, officiated.

Left, an historical photograph of the chapel

Convent Commissions

There were a number of convents for which the architectural firm of Brust & Philipp did design work. Among them were School Sisters of Notre Dame, Sisters of St. Francis of Assisi, School Sisters of St. Francis, Sisters of Mercy, Dominican Sisters of Perpetual Rosary, Carmelite Sisters, Dominican Sisters of Racine, and Sisters of St. Agnes. Of all these convents, the School Sisters of St. Francis hired the firm for the most commissions.

In 1922, the firm of Brust & Philipp was hired by the School Sisters of St. Francis to design Alvernia, a Catholic high school in Chicago. Brust was required to apply for a license to practice architecture in the state of Illinois. The application for the Illinois license contains an informative narrative written by Peter Brust about design work commissioned by the School Sisters of St. Francis. [A facsimile of the application is included on Page 264.] Peter Brust wrote the following in his narrative:

Our practice has a normal growth. We began with small buildings and have had larger and larger commissions from our earlier clients. To illustrate, for St. Joseph's Convent [School Sisters of St. Francis] we first enlarged a small house, then built an addition to their powerhouse, then St. Mary's Hill hospital for mental cases. Then we enlarged Sacred Heart Sanitarium three times and built a Nurses' Home for St. Mary's Hill. We then built the Convent Chapel [St. Joseph's Chapel], after that a home for student Sisters [St. Francis House of Studies] at the Catholic University of Washington, D.C. We are now building a large addition to the convent costing $500,000 and are also preparing plans for a high school for girls [Alvernia] in Chicago. It is for this job we desire registration in the state of Illinois.[1]

[1] State of Illinois Architectural Registration, (November 25, 1922).

The School Sisters of St. Francis, Milwaukee, Wisconsin

The Convent's Early Years

In 1873, three Sisters, Alexia Hoell, Alfons Schmid, and Clara Seiter, left Schwarzach, Germany, in hopes of establishing a religious community in America. Chancellor Otto Von Bismarck of Germany, was closing religious communities such as those in Schwarzach. Bismarck believed that the German government, not the Catholic Church, should determine moral laws. The government stripped power from the bishops and expected them to obey the State or face prison. Religious groups left Germany voluntarily or were threatened with expulsion. It wasn't until 1888 that Bismarck realized that he had overstepped himself and thus permitted the Sisters to take their vows and wear religious garb.

When Alexia, Alfons, and Clara arrived in Milwaukee, the School Sisters of Notre Dame graciously took them in. While there, they met Father Anton Michels who offered them a teaching post at St. Matthew's School in New Cassel, Wisconsin, now known as Campbellsport. St. Matthew's did not have a school at this time, but parishioners, like many other rural parishes, were anxious for a school. New Cassel was settled in

Mother Alexia Hoell

Mother Alfons Schmid

1844, and by the 1880s, it boasted a flouring mill, a sawmill, three churches, and a district school.

Once at St. Matthew's, the three Sisters renewed their vows, and the new order of the School Sisters of St. Francis was established on April 18, 1874. The arrival of the teaching Sisters thrilled the parishioners. The parishioners quickly gathered necessary articles for the school/convent building. Mother Alexia, however, entertained in her mind a long-term building plan. Determined to obtain a separate convent building, she signed a contract with John Fellenz's construction company to build them a convent. With no money down, she signed a contract for a new convent building. The cost of the new convent was $10,950, with a building completion date just five months away. This was the beginning of Mother Alexia's building plans. Even though money was scarce, the Sisters possessed much faith in St. Joseph that he would provide for them.

Once the Sisters were settled in their new, comfortable convent, Mother Alexia turned her attention to finding a suitable location for another school. In 1884, Mother Alexia purchased land in Winona, Minnesota, with plans to build a boarding school. St. Mary's Academy in Winona was dedicated in December 1885. However, problems existed between Mother Alexia and John Ireland, Archbishop of St. Paul, Minnesota. Archbishop Ireland wanted the order to be a diocesan community, whereas the Sisters wanted to remain as an independent order. Also, Archbishop Ireland, of Irish heritage, did not want the German language spoken in the Catholic schools; English he felt should predominate. He feared that if these schools were allowed to speak German that "ghetto Catholics" would be created. These disagreements lead Mother Alexia to sell St. Mary's to the St. Paul Diocese and look elsewhere for a new convent.

The Motherhouse

Archbishop Heiss of the Milwaukee Diocese suggested that Mother Alexia view Greenfield Park, outside of the Milwaukee city limits, as a possible site for a new convent. Mother Alexia came to Milwaukee in 1886 to view this property at what was then South 22nd and West Greenfield Avenue. There were two buildings on the property, a dance hall and a bowling alley.

The convent farmhouse was located on forty acres of land at the corner of South 92nd and West Howard Avenue in Milwaukee, about four miles from the Motherhouse. The School Sisters of St. Francis convent purchased the land in 1901 from the Walter family. The farm furnished milk, eggs, and vegetables to the Motherhouse and the Sacred Heart Sanitarium. The architectural firm of Brust, Philipp & Heimerl made alterations to the farmhouse in 1913. The farmhouse remodeling was one of the first commissions Brust & Philipp completed for the School Sisters of St. Francis. The farmhouse was later razed, and the location is now the site of Clement Manor, a senior residence.

Mr. Knurr owned the property, and Mother Alexia purchased the land with a down payment of $100. She received the $100 in a letter from an unknown donor on the very day she was leaving for her trip to Milwaukee. Mother Alexia then obtained a loan for $2,000 from benefactors in Milwaukee and $2,000 from relatives in Chicago. Mr. Druiding from Chicago was hired as the architect, and the building was completed in January 1888. (Druiding was also the architect for the 1884 St. Stephen's Church in New Colen/Town of Lake.) The convent building was named for St. Joseph and opened as a boarding and day school. Unfortunately, there was a fire on March 3, 1890, that destroyed the convent and took the life of Sister Blanche. After the debris was cleared away, a new convent was built at a cost of $80,000 and was dedicated on May 2, 1891. The architect of the new convent was Herman Paul Schnetzky of Milwaukee.

The Sisters were known as the Franciscans from Greenfield Park. When Greenfield Township was annexed into Milwaukee some streets were renamed, and the convent's address became 1501 South Layton Boulevard. The Sisters then became known as the Layton Boulevard Franciscans.

Two years after the Motherhouse was completed, Mother Alexia was ready to tackle a new building project. This project was the Sacred Heart Sanitarium. Impressed by the resort she visited in Woerishofen, Germany, Mother Alexia decided in 1895 to open a hospital that would use the Kneipp Program. The Kneipp Program used water baths and massage therapy for those seeking cures for various illnesses. Monsignor Sebastian Kneipp wrote a well-received book, *My Water Cure*. While she was still in Europe, Mother Alexia directed Sister Alfons to make plans to build such a hospital in Milwaukee. The new Sacred Heart Sanitarium would offer patients therapeutic bathing facilities, water cures, and massage therapy. [See Pages 182-188 for the Sacred Heart Sanitarium commission.]

Motherhouse Addition

As the School Sisters of St. Francis order grew in Milwaukee, it was decided by Mother Alfons to expand the Motherhouse. An addition, designed by the architectural firm of Brust & Philipp, was placed on the

The addition designed by Brust & Philipp for St. Joseph's Convent is at the extreme right. St. Joseph's Chapel, also designed by Brust & Philipp, is at the extreme left. The 1891 convent building featured the pointed tower and was designed by architect Herman Paul Schnetzky of Milwaukee.

north end of the building, at the corner of South Layton Boulevard and West Greenfield Avenue. The L-shaped addition, completed in 1922, housed the music department, dining rooms, classrooms, bedrooms, an infirmary, priests' apartments, and a novitiates' wing. The new addition also housed the Seraphic Press, which was formerly known as the St. Joseph Press. The Seraphic Press produced needed income for the order. Begun in 1917, the Seraphic Press provided bookbinding services and the printing of holy cards and stationary. It also published school newspapers and missionary magazines. This new Romanesque Revival style addition provided the Seraphic Press a pressroom, photography rooms, and a room in which to compose.

St. Joseph's Convent Chapel

Mother Alexia wasn't the only one who liked to build. Mother General Alfons, the co-founder of the religious order shared that interest. She dreamed of building a chapel that would be named for St. Joseph, the foster father of Jesus Christ. The chapel would be dedicated to the Lord, and the chapel would be built in such a way to do justice to what Mother Alfons felt the Lord deserved. She also wanted to provide a magnificent environment in which to pray and experience sacred music. Mother Alfons felt the present chapel was much too small. In her mind, no expense would be spared in order to emulate the best cathedrals of Europe. A number of Sisters traveled to Europe with Father Theisen from March to July of 1912. The trip allowed them to absorb the beauty of the many cathedrals of Europe. The chapel of Mother Alfons' dreams began to take shape in her mind. Upon her return to Milwaukee, this vision of St. Joseph's Chapel was to become a reality through the efforts of the architectural firm of Brust & Philipp. This project for the School Sisters of St. Francis would be the most glorious of all the projects done by this architectural firm.

Shortly after Mother Alfons' return from Europe, World War I began. It was a hazardous time to sail, and many merchant and passenger ships were attacked as they sailed to and from the continent. Since the building materials for the new chapel were being imported from Europe, the attacks on merchant ships was of great concern for the Sisters. Many prayers were said as the vessel was loaded in Rotterdam, Holland, with building materials from Italy, Austria, and Switzerland. Approval for departure was obtained from Washington, D.C. Perhaps the round-the-clock prayers said by the Sisters were rewarded, because the shipment arrived in perfect condition.

The construction of this Italian Romanesque Revival style chapel at 1501 South Layton Boulevard got underway in 1913, and it was to take four years to complete at a cost of $600,000. The roof alone cost $200,000. The chapel measured 200 feet by 90 feet and sat 500 people. The dome rose 70 feet above the sanctuary. Seven kinds of marble from all over the world were used in the interior of the chapel, including

St. Joseph's Convent Chapel

the white Italian Carrara marble used for the three altars in the main chapel. All three altars were exquisitely carved and inlaid with colored stones. Ten columns of Mexican marble, walls of Formosa marble from Germany, American marble from Colorado, and marble from Greece made for a very international flavor in the main chapel. In the Adoration Chapel, located directly behind the main chapel, marble from France was used.

The 115 stained-glass windows were imported from Innsbruck, Austria, designed and constructed by the Tyrolese Art Glass and Mosaic Company. These windows depict Jesus, Mary, the saints, and various Christian symbols. These windows make up the largest collection of Austrian stained glass in the United States.

The seven large mosaics in the main chapel, as well as the one large mosaic in the Adoration Chapel, were also done by the Tyrolese Art Glass and Mosaic Company. As with the stained-glass windows, the mosaics also depicted the saints and biblical scenes. Local craftsmen did the sanctuary floor, which was comprised of mosaics. The Stations of the Cross, carved from hard maple, lined the interior walls of the nave. A ninety-year-old man in St. Ulrich, Switzerland, carved the stations.

Archbishop Messmer consecrated the chapel on March 19, 1917. Since then, not much has changed in the chapel except for the lower level of the chapel. The original dormitory area was remodeled and now contains offices for the convent. Even with quality materials and workmanship, restoration over time is a reality. Much restoration was done, particularly to the stained-glass windows.

St. Joseph's Chapel was recognized in 1973 by the Milwaukee Historic Preservation Commission and was given landmark status. The chapel, with its excellent acoustics, is a perfect setting for choral and instrumental concerts. It is a truly magnificent chapel, one that truly reflects Mother Alfon's dream. The chapel was featured in an issue of *American Architect* on May 1, 1918.

A stained-glass window in the chapel

Interior of St. Joseph's Convent Chapel

Exterior of St. Joseph's Convent Chapel

St. Francis House of Studies
Washington, D.C.

The architectural firm of Brust & Philipp designed St. Francis House of Studies in Brookland, Washington, D.C., for the School Sisters of St. Francis in 1917. A number of Sisters attended the Catholic Sisters College, an extension of the Catholic University in Washington, D.C. The Sisters needed a permanent place to stay while they attended the college. The total cost of the Mediterranean Revival style building was nearly $28,000. In 1948, the building was sold to the Sisters of St. Joseph of Missouri.

Alvernia Catholic High School
Chicago, Illinois

It was during Mother Alfons' third term as Mother Superior that the religious order decided to build Alvernia High School on Chicago's northwest side. It was the first high school established by the School Sisters of St. Francis, and it was established at the request of Cardinal Mundelein of Chicago. When the architectural firm of Brust & Philipp was commissioned to design the school in 1922, the firm needed to file an application with the State of Illinois in order to practice architecture in that state. [See Page 264 for the Illinois Application.] Father John H. Theisen, chaplain of the School Sisters' convent, commuted weekly to Chicago from Milwaukee to observe the building of the Tudor Gothic Revival style school. Theisen also wanted to make sure that the completion deadline of September 1924 would be met.

The school did open in September, but it was far from completed. Since there were no doors, visitors were able to wander in and out. On the first day of school, there were 170 freshmen and sophomores. The building wasn't dedicated until May 3, 1925, some eight months after it opened. The total cost of the building was $818,000.

Low enrollment in the 1980s caused many Catholic high schools to close their doors. Unfortunately, Alvernia was no exception. The school at 3901 North Ridgeway Road was sold to the Chicago Public School system in 1989.

Sisters of St. Francis of Assisi, St. Francis, Wisconsin
St. Coletta's Institute Administration Building
Jefferson, Wisconsin

In the mid-1850s, Bishop Henni of Milwaukee encouraged German Catholics to come to America to serve as missionaries to the newly arrived Catholics in the Milwaukee area. In Ettenbeuren, Bavaria, Father Anton Keppeler recruited five men and six women in response to Henni's request. The group arrived in Milwaukee in May of 1849 and settled on the shore of Lake Michigan in an area known as Nojoshing Woods in Town of Lake. Nojoshing, pronounced No-Josh-Ing, is a Chippewa Indian word and means straight tongue. The land at this location protrudes out into Lake Michigan like a straight tongue. At one time, the land was home to a large Chippewa encampment.

These six women from Ettenbeuren, Bavaria, established the order of Sisters of St. Francis of Assisi. Their Motherhouse is still located at 3221 South Lake Drive in what is now the city of St. Francis.

The Sisters of St. Francis of Assisi founded the St. Coletta's Institute in Jefferson in 1904. The institute was established to support individuals with developmental problems and other disabilities. This mission still continues today.

The architectural firm of Brust & Philipp designed the administration building for the St. Coletta's Institute in 1915. The exterior of the Colonial Revival style building appears to be in its original condition, although the front entrance was modernized. It was at St. Coletta's that the late Rose Kennedy, sister of President John F. Kennedy, spent much of her adult life. [See Page 28 for St. Mary's Institute designed by Peter Brust in 1904 for the Sisters of St. Francis of Assisi.]

Above, this historical photograph shows the original front entrance of the administration building; note the Sister on the porch and children on the left.

Right, a recent photograph of St. Coletta's administration building shows a remodeled entrance.

Sisters of Our Lady of Mercy
Convent/Academy
(St. Clara's Home)
Milwaukee, Wisconsin

When the Sisters of Mercy closed their Motherhouse in Fond du Lac in 1885, St. Patrick's Convent in Milwaukee became their temporary home. The order intended to erect their Motherhouse in Milwaukee. In 1902, under Mother Evangelist's guidance, the Sisters of Mercy order built Our Lady of Mercy Convent on South 15th Street and West National Avenue in Milwaukee. This building served as the order's new Motherhouse and also housed the Our Lady of Mercy Academy, a day school for girls. The new building provided a dormitory for fifty boarding students. Newspaper advertisements (*Catholic Citizen,* January 1904) describe the Lady of Mercy Academy as having a "thorough course, including music, instrumental and vocal, drawing, painting, stenography and typewriting, bookkeeping, plain and fancy needlework."

The Motherhouse was moved in 1924 to the new Mercy High School building, and Our Lady of Mercy Academy became St. Clara's Home for Girls. [See Page 125 for the Mercy High School commission.] According to a newspaper advertisement (*Catholic Herald,* May 1928), the purpose of St. Clara's was to provide a home for "young women who came to Milwaukee in search of work and who might otherwise be exposed to the dangers that attend young women alone in a big city."

According to a letter from Peter Brust to the Sisters, dated March 6, 1926, the architectural firm of Brust & Philipp was hired to add another dormitory to St. Clara's. [See accompanying letter.] Later, in 1949, the architectural firm of Brust & Brust was commissioned to design the installation of an elevator at a total cost of $7,568. The building at 1527 West National Avenue is now used for senior housing.

Brust & Philipp did not design the Our Lady of Mercy Convent, later known as St. Clara's; however, the firm was hired to make alterations to the building in 1926.

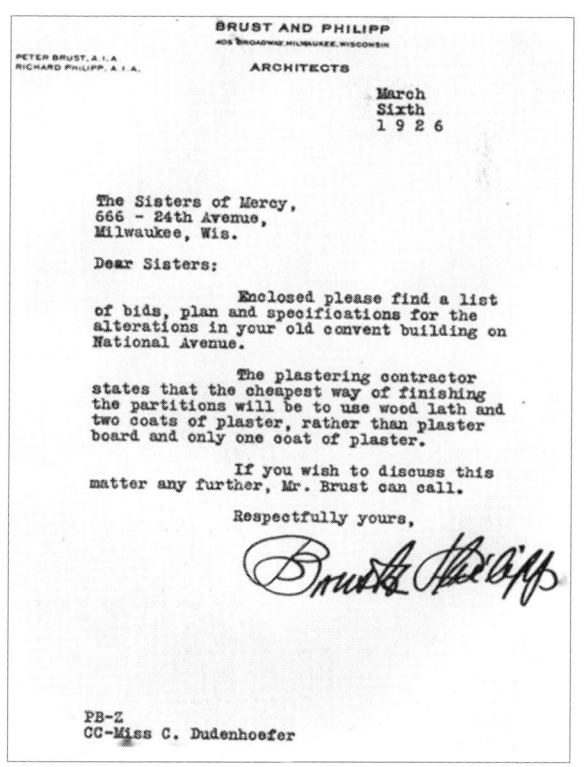

The firm of Brust & Philipp sent this letter to the Sisters of Mercy in regards to a remodeling project done in 1926 at St. Clara's, located at South 15th Street and West National Avenue. This letter is courtesy of the archives of the Sisters of Mercy, Chicago.

St. Catherine's Home for Working Girls
Milwaukee, Wisconsin

The Sisters of Mercy established Mercy Home in 1895 at the request of Milwaukee Mayor John Koch. The home's mission was to provide a temporary residence for girls, mainly those from small towns, while they adjusted to independent city living. St. Catherine's first site was on West Michigan Street, and housed twenty-five women.

In 1913, Mercy Home changed its name to St. Catherine's Home for Working Girls, and in 1916, a Tudor Gothic Revival style building was erected at 1201 West Michigan Street. It is not known if the architectural firm of Brust & Philipp designed this building; however, archival records show that the firm did some work on the building in 1938. Many times, the architect who designed the original building was called in to design additions or to do remodeling work. Unfortunately, building permits are no longer available for the building.

Marquette University needed to expand, so they purchased St. Catherine's Home in 1965 and razed the building. St. Catherine's relocated to 1032 East Knapp Street on Milwaukee's northeast side in June 1966. The apartment building, built in 1951, accommodated 240 women.

Over its history, St. Catherine's served over 20,000 young women and is still located at its East Knapp Street location. The facility is now known as St. Catherine's Residence and houses 125 women.

St. Catherine's Residence

St. Patrick's Catholic Church Convent
Milwaukee, Wisconsin

St. Patrick's Catholic Church, located at 723 West Washington Street, was established in 1876; the church school was opened in fall of that year. In 1885, Bishop Heiss of Milwaukee asked the Sisters of Mercy in Fond du Lac, Wisconsin, to staff the school. The Sisters of Mercy closed their Motherhouse in Fond du Lac, and the convent at St. Patrick's became their temporary Motherhouse.

When the new rectory was built in 1895, the old rectory was moved to the rear of the school to serve as the convent. In 1920, when it was time to build a new convent, the architectural firm of Brust & Philipp was commissioned to design a red brick Romanesque Revival style building. The building is still located on the same site.

Chapter 3 – Brust & Philipp–Ecclesiastical Commissions 1906-1926

Mercy Catholic High School
Milwaukee, Wisconsin

In an attempt to promote Catholic high school education, the Sisters of Mercy decided to build Mercy High School. Mother Superior Bernadine Clancy bought the Comstock farm at West Mitchell Street and South 29th Street for the new school. Designed by the architectural firm of Brust & Philipp, the four-story Romanesque Revival style school was built at a cost of $412,264. The building was highly praised by architectural writer Rexford Newcomb who said, "Rarely has the writer encountered a finer use of simple brick work than that employed in the Convent of Our Lady of Mercy, Milwaukee."[1]

The school opened in the fall of 1925 and accommodated 400 students. It also provided a new Motherhouse for the Sisters. The enrollment for the first year was 250. The school was closed in 1973 due to low enrollment, a situation that plagued many of the Catholic high schools in the city. The school building at 1720 South 29th Street was sold to the City of Milwaukee, and it was converted into senior housing.

[1] Rexford Newcomb, AIA, "Craftsmanship in Architecture" *The Western Architect* (July 1925) 71-72.

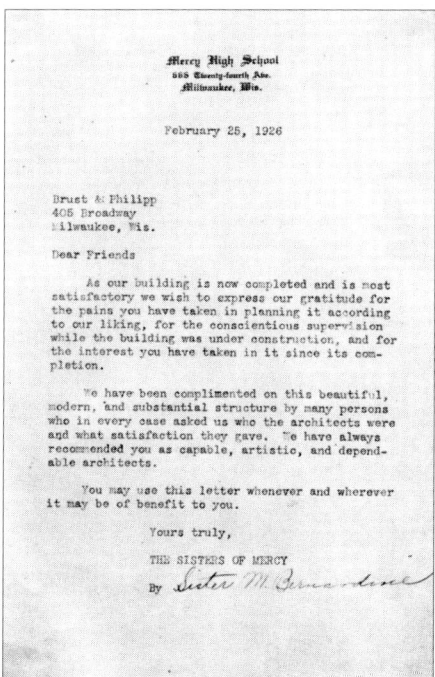

An interior photograph shows a vault-like Gothic ceiling.

Left, this letter was written by the Mother Superior of the Sisters of Mercy Convent to the firm of Brust & Philipp in 1926. Peter Brust probably used this letter as a reference for future commissions. The letter is from the archives of Zimmerman Design Group.

Sisters of St. Agnes
St. Florian's Church Convent
West Milwaukee, Wisconsin

Parishioners of St. Florian's Catholic Church at 1233 South 45th Street in West Milwaukee desired a parish school, and on September 15, 1913, their wish was realized. Archbishop Messmer asked the Sisters of St. Agnes to teach at the new St. Florian's School. [See Pages 231-232 for more about the Sisters of St. Agnes of Fond du Lac, Wisconsin.] The first Sisters arrived at St. Florian's in 1913. The Sisters of St. Agnes commissioned the architectural firm of Brust & Philipp to design a Romanesque Revival style convent at St. Florian's in 1916. The total cost of the building was $19,000. The building was later razed. The thank-you letter below is from the Sisters of St. Agnes to Peter Brust after the completion of St. Florian's Convent. The letter is from the archives of the Zimmerman Design Group.

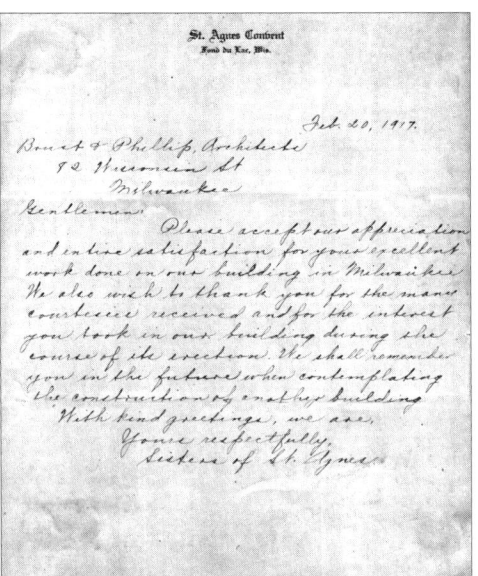

The Carmelite Sisters of the Divine Heart of Jesus Convent Chapel
Wauwatosa, Wisconsin

The Carmelite Sisters of the Divine Heart of Jesus order was founded in Milwaukee in 1912. Sister Anna Maria Tauscher, along with several other Sisters, arrived from Germany to establish an order in America. With the approval of Archbishop Messmer, the order established an orphanage for girls on South Pierce Street in Milwaukee. In 1916, the religious order purchased a home at 1230 Kavanaugh Place in Wauwatosa, and then proceeded to purchase the house next door. A chapel that connected the two buildings was built in 1919. This may be the commission that the architectural firm of Brust & Philipp mentions in their records in regards to the Carmelite Sisters. The Wauwatosa building permits for this property do not contain historical information before 1920. Along with establishing a new Motherhouse, the Carmelite Sisters established the Home for Boys.

Dominican Sisters of Perpetual Rosary Monastery Milwaukee, Wisconsin

The Dominican Sisters of Perpetual Rosary Monastery is located at 217 North 68th Street in Milwaukee. The order was founded in 1880 in Calais, France. In 1890, four French Sisters established an American community in the city of Hoboken (Union City), New Jersey. Six Sisters from the New Jersey monastery, led by Mother Mary of the Rosary Garnier, O. P., founded the Milwaukee community in 1897.

The Milwaukee order lived for about two years in a building near North 12th Street and West State Street. In the spring of 1899, the order moved to St. Martin's Parish in Hales Corners, Wisconsin. In 1926, in order to be closer to Milwaukee, the order built the monastery on North 68th Street. The Dominican Sisters order is cloistered, and it is known for its around-the-clock praying of the rosary. Also, each Sister spends at least one hour per day in private prayer.

The architectural firm of Brust & Philipp designed the Neo-Classical style monastery on North 68th Street in 1926. Peter Brust's sons, Paul and John, went on to design additions to the convent in 1957, 1959, 1960, 1961, 1968, and 1969. The total cost of the 1957 convent addition came to $330,782.

Interior photographs of the convent chapel

Dominican Sisters of Racine
Holy Rosary Academy
Sturtevant, Wisconsin

Sister Maria Benedicta Bauer and Sister Maria Thomasina Ginker from Bavaria, Germany, founded the religious order of the Dominican Sisters of Racine, Wisconsin, in 1862. The two Sisters were joined later by ten other religious women. They purchased property in Corliss, now known as Sturtevant, to build their Motherhouse. The school they established was aimed toward children of German immigrants.

The architectural firm of Brust & Philipp was hired in 1908 to build a school for the Dominican Sisters. The Colonial Revival style building featured an imposing colonial entrance. The architectural firm was also hired by the Sisters to design the St. Ann's Home for Elderly Ladies. This home housed elderly laywomen from the Racine community. The firm of Brust & Philipp also designed a power plant for the academy. Brust & Philipp records show that the total cost of the academy buildings designed by the firm was $129,350.

The order sold the Holy Rosary Academy complex in 1921 to a Franciscan order located in Pulaski, Wisconsin. By moving their seminary to Sturtevant, the Franciscans hoped to attract students from the large Polish populations of Milwaukee and Chicago. The purchase of Holy Rosary Academy included a large four-story, three-wing building that accommodated 189 students. It also provided offices and room for the administration, large dormitories, classrooms, a study hall, dining hall and kitchen, library, small gymnasium, infirmary, and utility rooms. The property consisted of 160 acres of land affording ample space for a beautiful campus, a park in front of the school and friary, and greatly needed farmland and buildings. A fire in January 1956 destroyed the administration building designed by Brust & Philipp. Fortunately, no one was hurt in the fire.

Due to financial difficulty, St. Bonaventure closed in 1983. In 1991, the Racine Correctional Institution opened on the site. Father Melvin, the order's archivist, jokingly remarked, "The students always felt the place was like a prison, and now it really is one." Some of the St. Bonaventure buildings remain; however, it appears that the none of the buildings designed by Brust & Philipp remain. Venture Architects, a joint venture of Zimmerman Design Group and Kahler Slater, designed the new prison complex.

Below, Holy Rosary Academy

Bottom, St. Ann's Home for Elderly Ladies

Monastery and Seminary Commissions

Discalced Carmelite Friars
Carmelite Monastery at Holy Hill
Hubertus, Wisconsin

The monastery at Holy Hill in Hubertus was founded by the Discalced Carmelite Friars, a reform order of the Carmelites. The word discalced means the wearing of sandals or going barefoot as part of the rules of the religious order. The Discalced Carmelite Friars came from Bavaria, Germany, in 1906, at the invitation of Archbishop Messmer who hoped that the order would consider joining the Holy Hill community in Hubertus.

In 1919, the order commissioned the architectural firm of Brust & Philipp to design their monastery/friary at Holy Hill. The Romanesque Revival style monastery was dedicated in 1920, and it served as a novitiate from 1921 to 1943, and then again in 1982. From 1934 to 1953, the monastery served also as a minor seminary. The second floor oratory and choir served as a cafeteria in the 1940s, and beginning in 1955 the building also served as a retreat center. The building, located at 1525 Carmel Road, is now known as the Old Monastery Inn and Retreat Center.

Carmelite Monastery, St. Florian's
West Allis, Wisconsin

St. Florian's Catholic Church, located at 1233 South 45th Street, was established in 1911 in the Milwaukee industrial suburb of West Milwaukee. It began as a mission church of the Capuchin Holy Cross parish located on the northwest side of Milwaukee. Archbishop Messmer appointed Father Joseph Ritger as pastor, but he only remained for one year. The Capuchins returned and were instrumental in finding a permanent location for the parish at South 45th Street and West Scott Street. Wishing to disconnect themselves from the daily running of St. Florian's, the Capuchins suggested to Archbishop Messmer that he contact the Discalced Carmelites at Holy Hill who expressed interest in establishing a monastery in Milwaukee. The Discalced Carmelites agreed to run St. Florian's, and Father Irenaeus Berndl became the first Carmelite pastor of St. Florian's in 1913.

The architectural firm of Brust & Philipp was hired by the Carmelites to build them a monastery on the St. Florian's Church property. The Carmelite community selected an Italian Renaissance style building that accommodated the monastic requirements. The three-story building's exterior was done in red brick. The building was completed on November 6, 1917. When St. Florian's church was completed in 1923, a passageway connected the monastery and church. The monastery remains at the same site and is part of St. Florian's Catholic Parish.

Salvatorians, Society of the Divine Savior
Salvatorian Monastery at Mother of Good Counsel
Milwaukee, Wisconsin

Reverend Francis Jordan was the founder of the Society of the Divine Savior. Jordan, along with four other members of the Salvatorian order, arrived in Wisconsin in 1896. They were granted 240 acres of property that would become the first permanent Salvadorian community in America. In 1924, the order decided to build a headquarters near a large city, so land was purchased on West Burleigh Street in Milwaukee.

The architectural firm of Brust & Philipp designed the Salvatorian Monastery in the Romanesque Revival style. The monastery served as the American Provincial house for six years. It was called the Salvatorian House of Studies and was also known as The Monastery. The total cost of the building was $35,569.

The parish of Mother of Good Counsel later purchased the monastery to be used as a convent for the Sisters who taught at the school. Presently, the former monastery building is being used as a day care center. The address is 6825 West Burleigh Street.

St. Francis Seminary, St. Francis, Wisconsin
Esser Gymnasium, Pio Nono College
St. Francis, Wisconsin

The Esser Gymnasium was located on the grounds of Pio Nono College. In 1926, the T. C. Esser family made a contribution to the gymnasium building fund as a memorial to their son, Father Lawrence Esser, who was killed in an automobile accident shortly after his ordination. The architectural firm of Brust & Philipp designed the gymnasium in the Romanesque Revival style. The total cost of the building was $37,000. The building was later razed. The former location of Esser Gym is now part of Thomas More High School at 2601 East Morgan Avenue.

St. Aemilian's Orphan Asylum
St. Francis Seminary
St. Francis, Wisconsin

The cholera epidemic of 1849 left many children orphaned and homeless. To address the needs of these children, Bishop Henni of the Milwaukee Catholic diocese requested the help of the Sisters of Charity, who graciously took on the responsibility of the orphaned girls. In 1850, to serve the needs of the orphaned and homeless boys, Henni rented a small wood-framed house in Milwaukee. It was named for St. Jerome Aemilian, the patron saint of orphans and abandoned children.

After a fire destroyed the Aemilian orphanage in 1851, a new two-story brick building was erected. The School Sisters of Notre Dame were in charge of the children at that time. The orphanage was financially supported by the Aemilian's Society that solicited donations from their members at a rate of twenty-five cents per month.

After a serious outbreak of cholera, a larger building was erected in Nojoshing, which is now part of the city of St. Francis. There were forty-nine orphans, and the responsibility for their care was transferred to the Sisters of St. Francis of Assisi. The orphanage was located just south of the St. Francis Seminary at 3257 South Lake Drive.

A fire broke out in 1855 and destroyed the building. It was said that a carpenter started the fire accidentally. Milwaukee Catholics generously contributed money to replace the orphanage with a total of $2,500 being raised. The new building was built of brick, and a number of wings were added by 1894. In 1895, a kerosene lamp exploded setting off a fire that destroyed all but one wing of the orphanage. The school was again rebuilt.

The architectural firm of Brust & Philipp was commissioned in 1924 to design an addition for St. Aemilian's. No photographs or drawings are available for this commission. At the time of this addition, there were over 200 boys being housed at the asylum. Another fire, this time of an incendiary nature, broke out in the orphanage in 1930. The boys were temporarily housed in the seminary gymnasium.

The orphanage then moved to a former Lutheran seminary at North 60th Street and Lloyd Street in Milwaukee. It was expected that a new orphanage would be built on a thirty-seven-acre site at North 89th

This is a postcard image of St. Aemilian's Orphan Asylum taken around 1905. The firm of Brust & Philipp designed an addition to this building in 1924. No photographs or drawings were found for the 1924 addition.

Street and West Capital Drive, purchased by the archdiocese in 1937. It wasn't until almost twenty years later that the new St. Aemilian's was built on that site. The Milwaukee Archdiocese continued to operate St. Aemilian's until 1969, at which time the operation of the orphanage was turned over to St. Aemilian Child Care Center Inc. In 1989, the center merged with Lakeside Children's Center, which was formerly the Milwaukee Orphan Asylum, founded in 1850. The Center continues to provide residential treatment and outpatient services for children.

St. John's School for the Deaf Institute Chapel
St. Francis, Wisconsin

St. John's Institute for Deaf-Mutes opened on May 10, 1876. At that time, the school was a department of Pio Nono College and occupied the second floor of the gymnasium. In order to expand the teacher-training program at Pio Nono, Father Bruenner hoped to train teachers in the education of deaf children.

The quarters at Pio Nono soon proved inadequate for the deaf school, so a new building was erected south of Pio Nono at what is now 3680 South Kinnickinnic Avenue in St. Francis. The two-story brick building, measuring 40 feet by 70 feet, was completed by the end of 1879. Tuition was twelve dollars a month unless the families could prove that they were unable to pay the tuition.

St. John's severed its ties with the normal school in 1895, and Father Gerend became the head of the St. John's School for the Deaf. Machinery was installed at the school, and workshops were set up to manufacture church furniture and furnishings such as confessionals, altars, and statues. When the school was first erected, Sisters from Mount Alverno, Wisconsin, and Franciscans from St. Louis, Missouri, were in charge of the school. After 1885, the Sisters of St. Francis of Assisi taught at the school, performed household duties, and acted as housemothers.

In summer 1907, a fire broke out in the school attic and destroyed most of the school. All that was left was the west wing, and that area had to be used to house the thirty summer students and staff. The architectural firm of Brust & Philipp was commissioned to design a new Italianate structure resembling the red-tiled roofed monasteries of Europe that Father Gerend admired in his travels.

The firm of Brust & Philip went on to design a chapel addition to the school in 1922 at a total cost of $12,906. The chapel featured stained-glass windows depicting the life of Jesus. On the wall in the middle of the chapel was a large painting depicting Jesus healing a deaf mute.

Brust & Philipp went on to do other design work for St. John's, including a garage and a water tower in 1922. Peter Brust designed a north addition to the school in 1927, and a one-story addition in 1933. In 1930,

St. John's for the Deaf School built in 1907

A postcard image of the Italianate style school building designed by Brust & Philipp in 1907

Peter Brust designed St. Mary of the Angels Chapel on the grounds of the school. [See Page 215 for the St. Mary of the Angels Chapel commission.] In 1940, the firm of Brust & Brust designed alterations for the deaf school that cost a total of $12,155.

The ca. 1907 school building was razed in 1966, and Peter Brust's sons, John and Paul, partners in the architectural firm of Brust & Brust, designed a new school building. [See Page 241 for the St. John's for the Deaf commission.] The 1966 school building now houses Deer Creek Elementary, which is part of the St. Francis school district.

The entrance to the 1907 St. John's for the Deaf school

The chapel painting of Jesus healing a deaf mute

Above, the 1879 St. John's for the Deaf School

Below, the 1879 school after the 1907 fire that destroyed most of the building

Interior of the chapel

Salzmann Library
St. Francis Seminary
St. Francis, Wisconsin

The Salzmann Library, located in the St. Francis Seminary grounds at 3257 South Lake Drive, was named for Reverend Joseph Salzmann, one of the founders of the St. Francis Seminary.

An historical photograph of the Salzmann Library

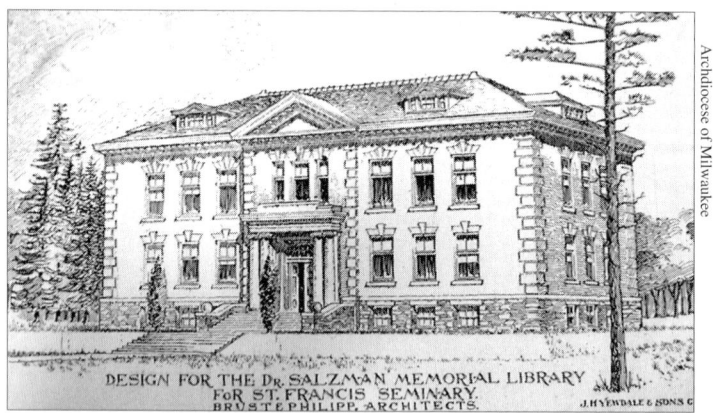

Above, Brust & Philipp did this drawing for the new library. These plans were probably for the library/gymnasium combination. However, these Colonial Revival style plans were discarded, and a new set of plans drawn up for a more Classical style building that housed only the library. It appears that the above drawing is very similar to the design of the Ernest Miller Gymnasium that Peter Brust designed for the seminary in 1927. Most likely, this discarded drawing was adapted for the gymnasium design.

Right, the 1960s addition, designed by Brust & Brust, is at the rear of the Salzmann library. The library remains at its original site.

Up until 1908, the seminary library was housed in the main seminary building. Discussions began in 1897 about building a separate library building. However, construction was delayed, because in 1902, the seminary found it necessary to construct a building that would serve as an infirmary and as a residence for the Sisters who worked at the seminary. [See Page 29 for the Sister's House and Infirmary commission.]

Early library plans sought to include a gymnasium, an assembly hall, and a dining room in the new library building. However, the directors of the seminary felt that those who contributed to the library fund expected a separate library building. Later in 1927, a new gymnasium, the Ernest Miller Memorial Gymnasium, was built and was designed by Peter Brust. [See Page 219 for the Ernest G. Miller Memorial Gym commission.]

The architectural firm of Brust & Philipp designed the Classical style library in 1908. The new library cost a total of $30,000 with a capacity of 40,000 volumes. The library debt was paid off in 2 □ years by alumni pledges.

As time went on, it was necessary to expand the library. In 1961, the architectural firm of Brust & Brust was hired to design an addition to be located on the back of the original library. This new addition added more reading areas, conference rooms, and a storage room in the basement. The original library was subsequently renovated. The second-floor museum area was turned into an area for bound periodicals, and the former living quarters in the old building became a space for audiovisual equipment, rare books, and workrooms.

Chapter 4
Brust & Philipp–Business Commissions, 1906-1926

Bank Commissions, 1906-1926

Banking in Wisconsin began as early as the 1830s when Wisconsin was a territory. As the territory grew, many people were accumulating wealth, and they needed a secure place to either store their money or to invest it. Unfortunately, the early banks were unsuccessful due to mismanagement; this, along with the Panic of 1837, contributed to their demise. Subsequently, territorial law outlawed banking from 1841 to 1848. After Wisconsin became a state, the state laws continued to outlaw banking until 1852.

The 1848 state constitution allowed voters to decide if banks should be allowed to exist. The banking referendum was placed on the ballot for the 1851 election. The Whig party favored banking, but the Democratic Party opposed it. The Whigs won out with the banking referendum being passed overwhelmingly. In 1852, the legislature passed a law that permitted free banking, and the minimum capital for each bank was set at $25,000.

Fond du Lac National Bank
(First Fond du Lac National Bank)
Fond du Lac, Wisconsin

Many of the banks currently serving the public in Wisconsin can trace their roots as far back as 150 years. The First Fond du Lac National Bank is one of them.

Firstar (Fond du Lac)

A.G. Ruggles, B.F. Moore, and Edward Pier founded the Bank of the Northwest in Fond du Lac in 1855 with money they brought with them from the East. The bank was so successful that it doubled its capital from $25,000 to $50,000 in a very short period of time. In 1864, the Bank of the Northwest took out a national charter in order to avoid the 10 percent tax that would soon be levied on state banks. The bank was now boasting capital assets of $100,000. Along with the new charter came a change of name to First National Bank.

On June 1, 1887, another Fond du Lac bank was founded--Fond du Lac National Bank. In 1902, the Fond du Lac National Bank moved to the Bischoff Building at 55 South Main Street. Around 1913, the architectural firm of Brust, Philipp & Heimerl was hired to design a remodel of this building giving the front a classical facade and a remodeled interior. The move to the Bischoff building doubled the size of the bank.

The First National Bank and the Fond du Lac National Bank merged in 1918 and changed the name to First Fond du Lac National Bank. The new bank existed under the charter of First National Bank.

The bank celebrated 100 years of banking history in Fond du Lac in 1955

and reverted back to the original national charter name of First National Bank of Fond du Lac. At the time, this bank was considered the eleventh largest bank in Wisconsin outside of Milwaukee.

From 1965 to 1967, the bank prepared for a new home. The old building at 55 South Main Street, the one Brust & Philipp remodeled, was demolished and the present structure was erected at the same site. In 1967, First National Bank of Fond du Lac changed its name to First Wisconsin National Bank of Fond du Lac. The bank is now U. S. Bank of Fond du Lac.

The lobby featured a leaded and stained-glass skylight framed in decorative plaster.

Security National Bank
Sheboygan, Wisconsin

John Ewing and his son-in-law, James Mead, traveled from Vermont to Wisconsin with the intention of starting a bank. Sheboygan was selected as a location because of its similarities to the countryside of Vermont. Mead and Ewing opened the German Bank in 1856 at the northwest corner of 8th Street and Pennsylvania Avenue in downtown Sheboygan. In 1866, George Cole was bank president, and he relocated the bank across the street. James Mead became president in 1873, but he was also involved with other business enterprises, such as the Phoenix Chair Company which he founded. Mead also co-founded the Crocker Chair Company. Mead was so influential in Sheboygan that the library was eventually named for him.

A new three-story bank was constructed at the corner of 8th Street and Commerce Street in 1882. Nine years later Mead died after serving for eighteen years as bank president.

By 1923, the bank needed to expand, and the architectural firm of Brust & Philipp was hired to design a seven-story structure including a roof garden. The total cost of the bank was $646,559. The bank was reorganized under a national charter and renamed Security National Bank. This seven-story building, located at 601 North 8th Street, was known at the time as Sheboygan's only skyscraper. De-

cades later, the building designed by Brust & Philipp was razed, and a new bank was built at the same site.

The Security First National Bank later merged with Security Financial Services Inc. and First Wisconsin Corporation in 1985. The bank became known as the First Wisconsin National Bank and is now a Firstar Bank.

*Above, note the vault-like ceiling in the dining room. This technique was based on the **Medieval Gothic** style and gave the impression of spanning space.*

Left, the flat ceiling was framed by a parged plaster decoration.

Bottom, a lounge area was furnished with English style furniture.

Marshall & Ilsley Bank
Milwaukee, Wisconsin

When Samuel Marshall established his first bank in 1847, it was located on North Water Street in Milwaukee. Marshall shared the space with a cobbler shop for two years. In 1848, Marshall moved across the street to the United States Block Building, located on the east side of North Water Street at East Clybourn Street. The following year, Charles Ilsley joined with Marshall creating Marshall & Ilsley Bank. In 1854, Marshall & Ilsley Bank rented space in the Furlong Building at North Water and East Clybourn. It was owned by Irishman John Furlong, a wholesale grocer and politician.

The Marshall & Ilsley Bank purchased their first building in 1871 from J. R. Treat, a real estate developer. This four-story brick building, located on the southeast corner of North Water and East Clybourn, exhibited the flavor of New Orleans architecture with its wrap around balconies. The bank remained in this build-

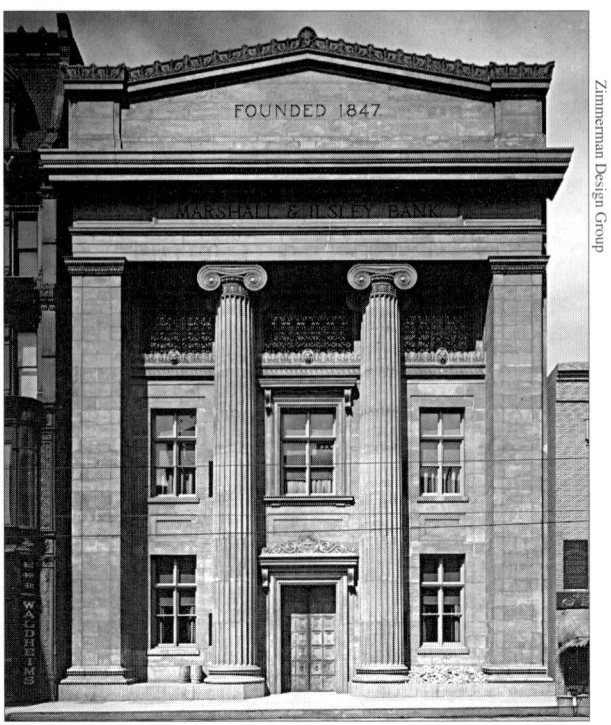

Front view of the 1913 bank

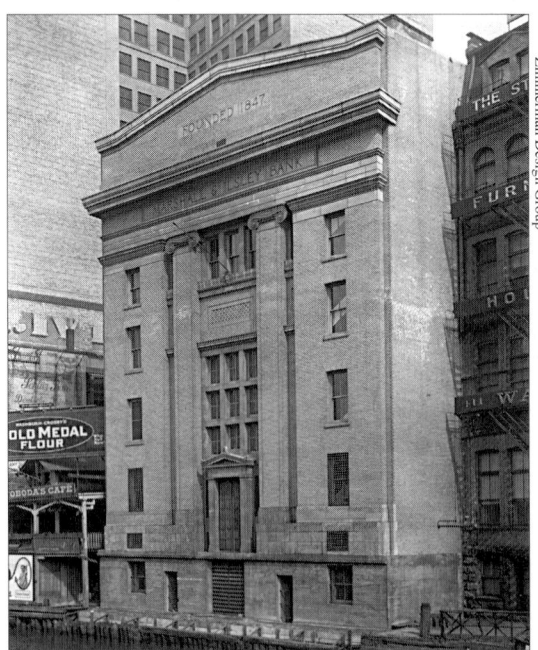

Rear view of the bank from the river

ing until 1884. With a growing business, the bank sold the Treat building and relocated to a three-story Italianate building. The building was purchased from a local tannery owner, Guido Pfister. The building, later known as the Marshall Block building, was located at the corner of East Wisconsin and North Broadway.

Marshall & Ilsley bank selected the architectural firm of Brust, Philipp & Heimerl in 1911 to design their first new bank building. The new bank location, located at 721 North Water Street, was less than two blocks from Marshall's first bank location of 1847. Staying near the original location was important to the company, as was staying near Milwaukee's downtown financial district. The 60-foot by 150-foot site on North Water Street ran along the Milwaukee River, and the site provided a rear terrace with a river view. The first decision to be made was the architectural style for the new bank building. Architect Richard Philipp accompanied the bank manager, John H. Puelicher, on a visit to the American Northeast. They visited banks that were known for their modern architectural style.

Chapter 4 – Brust & Philipp–Business Commissions 1906-1926

By the 1960s, a decision was made to build a new bank building. In 1966, a new bank building was completed across the street on North Water Street, replacing the 1913 structure. When the old 1913 structure was razed in the early 1970s, those who worked in the old structure expressed fond memories of working in the building. Fondest memories were those of the lunchroom's river view and the sounds of the tugboats.

Left, the Colonial Revival style was reflected in the pillars, the coffered ceiling, the arched doorway, and the chandelier.

Below, the lobby featured a leaded-glass skylight and coffered ceiling.

A classical style was chosen for the new bank building. The facade, with two Ionic columns, featured an architrave with ornately carved details. Inside the lobby, the column motif was repeated. A skylight provided additional light to the lobby during daylight hours. Tiffany shaded lamps illuminated the lobby during the evening. Potticino marble was used for the bank counters and for the floor. Wood panels lined the walls, and walnut furniture filled the space. On the east side of the building, flanking the lobby entrance on North Water Street, were two executive offices and boardrooms. These two offices contained marble fireplaces. Desks of the bank officers were on a raised platform in the lobby. A brass railing on the platform served as

a divider from the rest of the lobby. A loft was created on the second and third floor overlooking the lobby and contained small offices. On opening day, April 21, 1913, more than 20,000 people passed through the bank doors.

St. Francis State Bank
Milwaukee, Wisconsin

Frederick N. Lochemes founded St. Francis State Bank in 1923 with a capital of $50,000. Lochemes served as the bank president, Leo J. Stein as vice president, and Roman Czechorski as cashier. Along with his duties as bank president, Lochemes also served as the St. Francis postmaster beginning in 1911. The post office was located on the northwest corner of South Kinnickinnic and St. Francis Avenues, and the bank was

Above, the first St. Francis Bank building was built in 1923 at 878 South Pennsylvania Avenue, now known as 3474 South Pennsylvania Avenue.

Below right, a recent photograph of the 1923 bank building shows that much remodeling was done over the years.

founded in the back room of this building. The former post office building is still located at that corner. Lochemes also organized the St. Francis Building & Loan, serving as secretary. Other officers of the St. Francis Building & Loan were Anthony Helminiak as president and William Gardner, as vice president. During the first year of operation, with assets of $13,300,

Frederick Lochemes

the Building & Loan issued $12,000 in loans for home building. As of 1930, the Building & Loan, with a capital stock of $5 million dollars and accounts close to $1 million, financed over 1,000 homes.

The architectural firm of Brust & Philipp was hired in 1923 to design a building at 3474 South Pennsylvania Avenue. The building was to house both the St. Francis State Bank and the St. Francis Building & Loan. The total cost of the red brick building, located at the corner of South Pennsylvania and East Morgan Avenue, was $13,300. At the time, East Morgan Avenue was known as Ludlow Avenue.

Due to the Great Depression, St. Francis Building & Loan sold the building on South Pennsylvania Avenue in 1931 to a printing company, and the bank was moved to the old post office building at the corner of South Kinnickinnic and St. Francis Avenues. In 1934, the bank relocated to 3521 South Kinnickinnic Avenue.

In 1946, a new bank building was built at 3555 South Kinnickinnic Avenue. Again, the bank outgrew its space, so it built a new building next door at 3545 South Kinnickinnic Avenue in 1958. The year 1977 brought a new addition that cost $450,000. Sometime after 1958, the bank changed its name to St. Francis Savings & Loan and then to St. Francis Bank in 1992.

The little red brick building designed by Brust & Philipp is still at the original location. The print shop sold the building in 1943 to Knights of Pythias of Bay View to be used as a recreation hall, and in 1985 the Ace Pigeon Club purchased it and held their meetings there. At the present time, Cream City Realty owns the building.

State Bank of Manitowoc
Manitowoc, Wisconsin

According to Brust & Philipp archival records, the architectural firm was hired to create drawings for the remodeling of the State Bank of Manitowoc, located at 806 Washington in Manitowoc. The 1920 drawings appear to be a remodeling project, and the drawings depict a classical style building with two-story columns. It is unclear if this remodeling was ever done. The sketches were marked as tentative sketches. The building, on which the remodel was to be done, is still located on the original Washington Street site.

According to the 1920 Manitowoc city directory, the bank officers for the State Bank of Manitowoc were Reinhard Rahr, bank president; Daniel C. Bleser, vice president; and W. Moore, cashier. The 1928 directory goes on to list Charles O. Drumm as assistant cashier and E. J. Zankle as teller.

By 1934, the Bank of Manitowoc was no longer listed in the Manitowoc city directories. However, it appears that the bank merged with the Manitowoc Savings Bank, which was located around the corner at 8th Street and Jay Street. The Manitowoc city directory for 1934 states the bank officers for the Manitowoc Savings Bank as Daniel C. Bleser, president; Reinhard Rahr, vice president; and E. J. Zankle, cashier. The fact that these men were also past officers of the State Bank of Manitowoc makes the speculation of a merger likely. Also, a drawing from the tax assessor's office shows that both bank buildings, the one at 806 Washington Street and the one at 8th Street and Jay Street, were physically connected by additions located to the rear of the buildings.

This tentative sketch was done for the State Bank of Manitowoc but most likely never used.

A contemporary photograph shows the site of what was once the Manitowoc Savings Bank. This is the building for which the drawings were produced.

North Avenue Bank
Milwaukee, Wisconsin

North Avenue Bank was established in Milwaukee in 1922. The architectural firm of Brust & Philipp designed a new bank building in 1925 at 3506 North Avenue, later known as 3508 West North Avenue. The total cost of the bank was $145,000. By the 1930s, the bank was a branch of the First Wisconsin National Bank. The former bank building is still at its original site and is owned by the New Covenant Missionary Baptist Church Inc.

The lobby of the bank featured a vaulted ceiling that reflected the Gothic style.

First National Bank of Stevens Point
Stevens Point, Wisconsin

On August 1, 1883, the First National Bank of Stevens Point opened, with a capital stock of $50,000. The bank was located at 403 Main Street in a former post office. The following is from a newspaper article (*Stevens Point Journal*, July 1883) that humorously describes the bank's new burglar-proof vault:

> When the First National Bank opens for business on August 1st, funds will be kept in a safe, which was purchased by Mr. Morse a few days ago. Those who entrust their funds to its keeping can therefore feel assured that they will be safe from destruction by fire as well as from the raids of nocturnal gentry, whose capital consists of drills, chisels, crowbars, gunpowder or dynamite.

The bank later moved to a building at 1059 Main Street and proceeded to remodel the building. A newspaper article (*Gazette*, April 30, 1902) described the interior of the bank as being decorated in the Art-Nouveau style with a beautiful skylight that threw a soft, mellow glow. Supposedly, it was the first and only bank in the country with such an interior.

The First National Bank purchased a site for a new bank in 1917. According to a newspaper article (*Gazette*, October 31, 1917), the bank purchased land and a building at 449-451 Main Street. The article stated that the new bank would be completed in 1918. Brust & Philipp archival records make reference to a commission for the First National Bank of Stevens Point. Included in archival materials is a drawing done in 1918. In all probability, these were the architectural plans that the bank expected to use for the new building. However, according to the bank's history, no new bank building was built at the 449-451 Main Street location. The plans for this new bank were probably scrapped. It wasn't until the 1950s that a new bank building was constructed.

However, some remodeling was done at the second bank location at 1059 Main Street. According to a newspaper article (*Stevens Point Journal*, 1921), a new brick addition was constructed in 1921 to house a new burglarproof vault. This addition was 25 feet wide by 35 feet deep. The main lobby was also enlarged and more customer windows were added. The firm of Brust & Philipp most likely designed these additions and alterations. Brust & Philipp records show that the firm did design work in 1920 and 1925 for the bank.

In 1953, the bank obtained the vacant property east of the Masonic Temple on Main Street; the property extended south to Clark Street. A new bank building at 1245 Main Street, previously known as 519 Main Street, opened in February of 1955. The bank was expanded in 1974 on the site of the old Masonic Temple. The bank is now an M&I Bank.

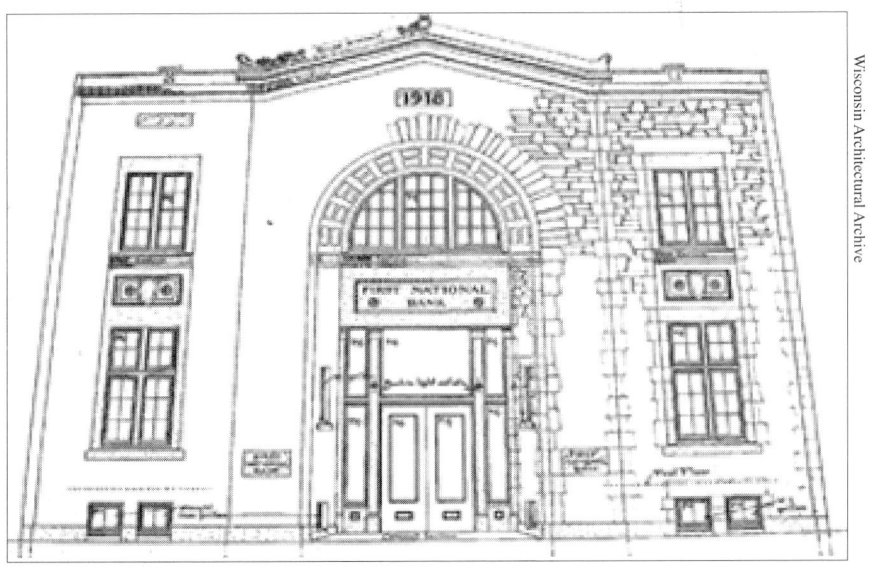

This drawing was done by the firm of Brust & Philipp in 1918 for the First National Bank of Stevens Point. It appears that this bank was never built. The blueprints, located at the Wisconsin Architectural Archive, are extensive and show the interior design in great detail.

Citizens Bank of Juneau
Juneau, Wisconsin

The Citizens Bank of Juneau was established in July 1891 with a capital of $10,000. Five individuals started the bank: W. E. Hallock, John Nelson, Theodore Hemmy, James Malone, and W. R. Rambusch. In 1892, Malone and Nelson sold their interests to the other three owners. A new charter was signed on January 27, 1896, and the bank opened for business under the new charter on February 3, 1896. Also, in February 1896, the bank was incorporated as a state bank with a capital stock of $25,000.

The bank was located at 105 South Main Street for its first fifteen years of operation. In 1906, the architectural firm of Brust & Philipp was hired to design the new bank building, which was located only a few steps to the south of the old bank building. A Juneau newspaper article (*The Independent* December 7, 1906) gave the following description:

> The new building is a solid brick structure of most modern design, beautiful in architecture, and its apartments judicially apportioned. The banking room is very handsomely equipped and occupies the main portion of the first floor. The business lobby is large and well suited to the patrons. Adjoining are private offices for the bank officials, and the vault room is large and systematically arranged.

In the early 1950s, the Citizens Bank needed to expand. A new bank was built a block away at Oak Street and Miller Street, and it was completed in October 1951. In 1981, the Citizens Bank became part of the Valley Bancorporation and changed its name to Valley Bank of Juneau.

The ca. 1906 building now houses the Rural Mutual Insurance and Laatsch Abstract Company. The former bank building retains its original façade, but unfortunately the name of the bank, Citizens Bank, was rubbed out of the stonework above the door.

Above, an historical photograph shows the Citizens Bank of Juneau shortly after it was built in 1906.

Bottom right, the 1906 bank is on the left. The building on the right housed the bank from 1891 to 1906. This image is from a postcard; note the little girl in the white dress running across the street.

Office Commissions, 1906-1926

Flambeau Paper Company
Park Falls, Wisconsin

Hugh Sherry was the first of his family to engage in the milling business in America. In 1849, he began his business in Neenah, Wisconsin, but he later moved to Minnesota. His son, Henry, remained in Neenah and continued the milling business. By the 1870s, Henry owned a shingle mill and a sawmill, operating one of the largest lumber businesses in the state.

Henry acquired the Cornell University land in the Flambeau River area of northern Wisconsin in 1885. Another sawmill and a dam were purchased in Park Falls, and Henry went on to secure water rights and rail service in Park Falls. In August 1890, his company, the Park Falls Lumber and Pulp Company, was incorporated as the Flambeau Paper Company. Unfortunately, the depression of 1897 left both Henry and his son, Edward, bankrupt. Slowly they worked to rebuild the family's financial holdings.

The architectural firm of Brust & Philipp was hired in the 1920s to design buildings for the Flambeau Paper Company in Park Falls. In 1922, the powerhouse was designed, along with a pulp mill. An office building at 200 1st Avenue was designed in 1923.

Along with his milling business, Henry and his son, Edward, established the Winnebago Realty Company and the Wisconsin Realty Company. Later, Edward took responsibility for both companies. Years later, Edward's son, Avery, born in 1904, joined his father in the business after graduating from Harvard. When Edward Sherry died on August 6, 1941, Avery headed the family businesses.

The Flambeau Paper Company was sold in 1947 to the Kansas City Star Company. After selling the paper company, Avery Sherry continued to preside over the Wisconsin Realty Company. [See Page 150 for the Wisconsin Realty Company commission.] Another paper company, Smart Paper, now occupies the Flambeau Paper Company office building designed by Brust & Philipp. The office building was placed on the National Register of Historic Places in 1985.

The Flambeau Paper Company office designed by the firm of Brust & Philipp in Park Falls was placed on the National Register of Historic Places in 1985.

Holeproof Hosiery
Milwaukee, Wisconsin

In 1873, Carl Freschl began manufacturing hosiery in Kalamazoo, Michigan. Freschl moved the company, Kalamazoo Knitting Works, to Milwaukee in 1882. The company was incorporated under the name of Kalamazoo Knitting Company.

Freschl developed a combination of yarns in 1899 that he believed would make woolen hosiery holeproof for at least six

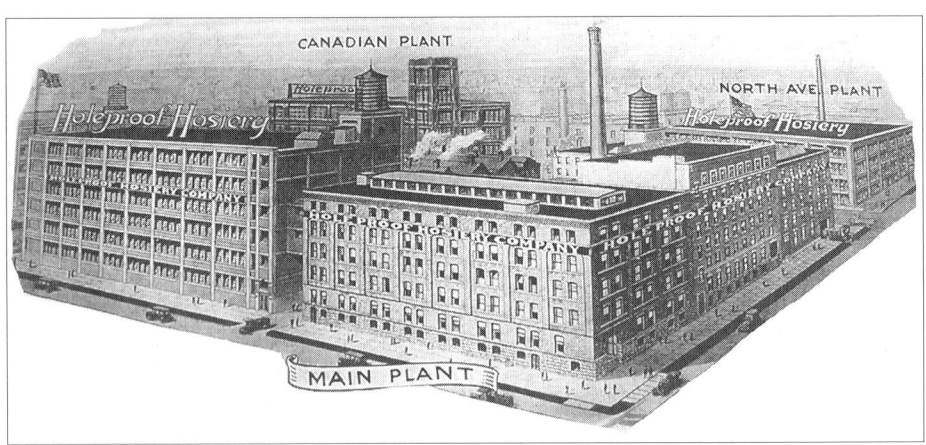

This drawing came from a company booklet produced in 1924. The drawing depicts the main hosiery plant in Milwaukee. It also depicts the Canadian plant and the North Avenue plant. The main building is the office building designed by Brust & Philipp.

Carl Freschl

months. The company then made up a quantity of socks using this newly developed yarn and distributed the socks to friends and business acquaintances. This practical test gave positive results, and the socks were offered to the general public with an absolute six-month guarantee.

As fashion changed and woolen socks went out of style, the cotton sock became fashionable, so the company developed the holeproof cotton sock. The company claimed that the cotton sock would be even more durable than the woolen socks. Also the cotton socks sold at twenty-five cents per pair compared to fifty cents for a pair of woolen socks.

The company's name was incorporated as the Holeproof Hosiery Company in 1904. Carl's sons, Max, William, and Edward, assumed management of the company in 1908. Within four years, production went from 40 dozen pairs a day to 1,500 dozen pairs. The company was then located in Milwaukee at 404 West Fowler Street, a block south of West Clybourn Street. Fowler Street no longer exists and is now the site of the downtown post office.

The architectural firm of Brust & Philipp designed an office building for Holeproof Hosiery Company in 1910 and a penthouse in 1913. The total cost of the both commissions was $64,900.

Holeproof was the first hosiery plant to be unionized. The company employed 500 employees. The 400 knitting machines produced over 1,500 dozen knitted items each day. Holeproof had offices in Chicago, New York, Canada, and England.

The company later moved most of its production to Georgia and Mississippi in order to stay competitive with other northern hosiery companies. The Holeproof buildings in Milwaukee, including the ones designed by Brust & Philipp, were later razed.

Holeproof Hosiery advertisement from *Saturday Evening Post* magazine of 1911 (Milwaukee Public Library)

Kempsmith Manufacturing Company
West Allis, Wisconsin

Frank Kempsmith was born in Philadelphia, Pennsylvania. He worked as a machinist apprentice in Philadelphia but eventually opened a machine tool shop in Springfield, Ohio. Kempsmith later moved to Milwaukee.

Once in Milwaukee, Kempsmith worked for the Whitehill Sewing Machine Company on Milwaukee's south side. In 1888, he opened the Kempsmith Machine & Tool Company on South Robinson Avenue in the Milwaukee neighborhood of Bay View. In a small, one-story frame building, with a workforce of fifteen men, the company developed the Number Three Universal Milling Machine, which was so successful that in 1892, the company received a single order of 300 machines. The company expanded at the corner of South Woodward Street and East Linus Street in Bay View doubling the company's workspace. Unfortunately, the Panic of 1892 caused the company to close its doors for eight months, and when it reopened, it produced small milling machines for the growing bicycle industry. During this time, two employees, E. J. Kearney and Theodore Trecker, left Kempsmith and opened a machine tool business, Kearney & Trecker, in the Milwaukee suburb of West Allis.

The Kempsmith Company doubled in size by 1899, but because of failing health, Frank Kempsmith sold the company in 1901 to Frank Wollaeger and Howard Browning. The company was reincorporated as Kempsmith Manufacturing. On July 9, 1910, ground was broken for a new factory on a ten-acre site at South 53rd Street and West Rogers Street in West Allis. Four new buildings were completed, including a three-story office building with 106,000 square feet. The architectural firm of Brust & Philipp designed the office building. The firm also designed some of the factory buildings. Brust & Philipp archival records list a total cost of $88,531. Brust & Philipp also were commissioned to design a garage for the plant in 1918. The total cost of the garage was $5,719.

The factory site was sold to Beta Realty Corporation for $100,000 in 1936. In the same year, Arkco Engineering, owned by Thomas Kattnig, a former employee of Kempsmith, purchased the Kempsmith Company and changed the name to Kempsmith Machine Company. The company is now located at 1820 South 73rd Street in West Allis. The office building that Brust & Philipp designed remains at South 53rd Street and West Rogers Street in West Allis.

Above, a recent photograph of the office building that was designed by Brust & Philipp

Below, this drawing shows the Kempsmith Company at South 53rd and West Rogers Street. The office building designed by the firm Brust & Philipp in 1910 is at the bottom left corner.

Frank Kempsmith

Wisconsin Realty Company
Milwaukee, Wisconsin

Wisconsin Realty Company, owned by Edward Sherry, commissioned the architectural firm of Brust & Philipp in 1923 to convert a single-family house at 785 North Jefferson Street in downtown Milwaukee into office space for his realty company. This Greek Revival style house, with an exterior of Cream City brick, was built as a family residence in 1858 for William A. Weber, a billiard table manufacturer.

After the remodeling, the Wisconsin Realty Company offices were located in two rooms on the second-floor of the renovated building. Sherry also used these second floor rooms for his other businesses, including Flambeau Paper Company, Winnebago Realty, and Flambeau Power Company.

From 1906 to 1935, Edward Sherry served as president of the Wisconsin Realty Company established in 1899 by his father, Henry Sherry. The largest real estate holding of the realty company was the Flambeau Paper Company in Park Falls, Wisconsin. [See Page 147 for the Flambeau Paper Company commission.]

Edward Sherry died on August 6, 1941. His son, Avery, subsequently took over the realty business. The upper floor of the Weber building now houses a beauty shop, while the lower floor houses a restaurant.

Top, a recent photograph of the former Weber house

Right, a drawing from the Brust & Philipp archival files at the Wisconsin Architectural Archives.

Vollrath Company
Sheboygan, Wisconsin

Jacob J. Vollrath established a business in Sheboygan making farm implements, cast iron stoves, steam engines, and cooking utensils. In 1873, Vollrath sold his business, Union Iron and Steel Foundry, to John Michael Kohler. Vollrath's new business focused on producing enameled cast iron and stamped sheet steel. Porcelain enamelware, a durable and inexpensive product, was very popular in Germany, but in America these products were not so widely available. In order to learn the process of enameling cast iron, Vollrath sent his son, Andrew, to Germany in 1873.

When Vollrath started his enameling business in the mid-1870s, he employed just six men; by 1881, he employed forty men and was grossing $50,000 in sales. Vollrath's company eventually became recognized nationwide. His new factory, Sheboygan Cast Steel Company, was built at 5th Street and Huron Street. In 1886, the company was renamed the Jacob J. Vollrath Manufacturing Company.

Jacob Vollrath died on May 15, 1898. His son, Andrew, then became president of the Vollrath Manufacturing Company. Jacob's widow, Elizabeth, died on November 6, 1906, at the age of eighty-four. Due to family disagreements, some of the heirs of Elizabeth's estate exercised their rights and bought out Andrew's shares of the company. When Andrew left the company, his brother, Carl, became president. In 1910, a new plant was built at 1236 North 18th Street, and the name was changed to the Vollrath Company.

The architectural firm of Brust & Philipp was commissioned to design a gatehouse in 1917 and an office building in 1920. The total cost of the structures was $120,000. It appears from the photograph below, that the brick office building was done in a Mediterranean Revival style. The facade featured inset tile decoration and the roof was done in tile. The office building and the gatehouse were later razed.

Jacob J. Vollrath

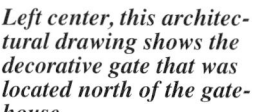

Top left and above, front entrance of the Vollrath office building that was designed by Brust & Philipp for the 18th Street factory.

Left center, this architectural drawing shows the decorative gate that was located north of the gatehouse.

Bottom left, the gatehouse designed by Brust & Philipp is visible on the bottom right area of the photograph. The decorative gate was already gone when this photograph was taken.

F. M. Prescott Steam Pump Company
West Allis, Wisconsin

F.M. Prescott

The F. M. Prescott Steam Pump Company, a manufacturer of mine pumps, was founded in Menominee, Michigan, in 1899 by Frederick M. Prescott. Soon after, the company moved to Milwaukee. Mine pumps were installed in the bottom of mineshafts to pump water from the bottom of the shaft to the surface of the excavation. The lives of the miners depended upon the successful operation of these powerful machines. The Prescott pumps were used widely in the mining operations across America, Canada, and South America. The high duty Corliss Pumping Engine was used in the copper mines of upper Michigan, operating at a depth of over 2,000 feet. Some of the mines using the Corliss Pump went as deep as 5,000 feet.

In 1903, the Prescott manufacturing plant was located at South 67th Street and West Greenfield, in West Allis. The plant employed about 500 men by 1910. In order to test the pumps, an enormous tank was built beneath floor level, and each pump was checked for both suction and proper discharge.

The architectural firm of Brust & Philipp designed a number of buildings for the F. M. Prescott Steam Pump Company. The office building was designed in 1910, and the total cost of the building was $47,000. The pattern shop was done at a total cost of $6,556, and the foundry was designed later at a total cost of $22,014.

It is unclear when Prescott Pump closed its doors, but by 1929, Milwaukee Electric Crane Manufacturing Company was located at the South 67th Street site. In 1936, the Harnischfeger Company took over the buildings. The buildings were sold in 1964, and from that date until 1968, the buildings were known as the West Allis Warehouse Buildings. The buildings were razed around 1985, and a bank is now at that location.

Above, is a photograph of one of the Prescott factory buildings designed by the firm of Brust & Philipp. The building was razed shortly after this photograph was taken in 1985. The building is depicted in the drawing at the left.

Left, this drawing of the Prescott factory complex was done some time before 1915. The firm of Brust & Philipp probably designed all of these buildings.

Store Commissions, 1906-1926

Ed Schuster Stores
Milwaukee, Wisconsin

When Edward Schuster came to Milwaukee at age fifty from Hamburg, Germany, in 1883, the population of Milwaukee was around 120,000. With some mercantile experience under his belt, Schuster found Milwaukee to be fertile ground for his aspirations in the dry goods business.

Upon his arrival in Milwaukee, Schuster joined with Jacob Poss and formed Poss & Schuster and Company. The small dry goods store was located at North 12th Street and West Walnut Street. A year later, Schuster went into business by himself and opened a store at 2107 North 3rd Street in Milwaukee. He purchased the building from Edward Housman and established the Ed Schuster and Company. Nineteen-year-old Albert Friedmann, who worked at Poss & Schuster as a bookkeeper, cashier, and director of sales, was hired by Schuster to work at his new store. Friedmann was born and educated in Vienna, Austria. He married Ed Schuster's daughter, and they raised two children, Max and Ralph, both of whom later worked for the Schuster Company. Max became president of the company in 1933. [See Page 90 for the Max Friedmann summer home commission.]

In an attempt to expand the business, the Schuster Company leased a new, larger building at North 3rd Street and West Brown Street. A fire broke out in 1893 and destroyed the West Harmon Street store, along with all the new fall stock. A new store was built shortly after. Two additions and a warehouse were added to the building by 1901.

The company opened a store in 1894 at North 12th Street and West Walnut Street in order to keep the Schuster name alive in the minds of the customers during the rebuilding of the West Harmon Street store. Charles Schuster, brother of Edward, became store manager of the rented storeroom that measured 25 feet by 90 feet. When the store outgrew the space, the store moved in 1900 to a building owned by Jacob Kutz at North 11th Street and West Winnebago Street. This building was 1,500 square feet. By 1910, a larger building was needed and the company purchased a site at North 12th Street and

The Schuster building at North 3rd Street and West Garfield Avenue still exists; however, the building is now completely wrapped in stucco and metal siding.

West Vliet Street. The architectural firm of Brust & Philipp was hired to design a building at this location. In 1923, the firm went on to design an addition to the building that ran west on West Vliet Street to North 13th Street. This facility was 235,558 square feet.

The Schuster building, located at 11th Street and Mitchell Street, is known as the Mitchell Street Mall. Retail stores are at ground floor level. The Milwaukee County Department of Health and Human Services offices and SER-Jobs For Progress are on the upper floors. A Pewaukee developer purchased the 160,000 square-foot building and will be designing apartments for the upper floors and new retail on ground floor level. It will be renamed the Schuster Historic Building.

In 1907, a few years before the West Vliet store was built, Schuster found a location for a store at North 3rd Street and West Garfield Avenue. It is unclear if the firm of Brust & Philipp designed this store, however, the firm of Brust & Philipp did design additions to the store in 1914 and 1918. In 1924, the firm of Brust & Philipp designed a garage at North 4th Street and West Garfield Avenue to house the delivery trucks. This store also accommodated the executive and sales offices.

Milwaukee's south side residents needed to travel a distance to get to the two Schuster stores on the north side. Ed Schuster saw this south side population as potential Schuster customers, so he decided to build a store at South 11th Street and West Mitchell Street. Schuster purchased the site from Philip Saxe and proceeded to hire the firm of Brust & Philipp to design a new building. The new Schuster store opened in October 1914, and Henry Heller, who worked for rival T.A. Chapman Company, became the store manager. In 1921, additions designed by the firm of Brust & Philipp were built east of the store along West Mitchell Street. In 1935, Peter Brust was commissioned to design another addition. In 1947, the firm of Brust & Brust was commissioned to install escalators in the West Garfield Street store.

When Capital Court Shopping Center opened in Milwaukee in 1956, the shopping center included a Schuster store. The firm of Brust & Brust was hired to collaborate in the designing of this new shopping center. [See Page 251 for the Capital Court commission.] In December 1960, all of the Schuster stores were sold to Gimbels and became Gimbels-Schusters.

Ed Schuster Stores, Continued

Above, the Schuster building at 12th Street and Vliet Street Store is now owned by Milwaukee County Department of Human Resources.

Left, Max E. Friedmann, president of the Ed Schuster Stores, wrote this letter in 1931 as a letter of recommendation. At the time, Peter Brust was applying for a commission to design a building for the U.S. Post Office in Wisconsin. No records were found to show that Brust was awarded the commission. This letter is from the archives of the Zimmerman Design Group.

Walter A. Zinn Store & Apartments
Milwaukee, Wisconsin

Walter A. Zinn's grandfather, Adolph C. Zinn, established Zinn Malting Company in 1874. The business was located in the old Schlitz Brewery building at 5th Street and Chestnut Street, later known as North 5th Street and West Juneau Avenue. American Malting Company absorbed Zinn Malt Company in 1893. Walter's father, Albert Zinn, organized the Milwaukee-Western Malt Company in 1903. Albert was president of the company, and Walter later took the position as president. In 1909, Walter hired the architectural firm of Brust & Philipp to design him a store with second-floor apartments located at 426-430 West Juneau Avenue. The building was later razed. No photographs of the building were found.

Frank J. Mann Store and Flat
Milwaukee, Wisconsin

Frank J. Mann was seventeen years old when he worked as a clerk for the T.A. Chapman Company in 1878. From 1880 to 1894, Mann was employed as a clerk, traveling salesman, and manager for Singer & Benedict, a wholesale clothing company. In 1894, Mann founded Mann & Gruber Company with Fred C. Gruber, dealing in the wholesale woolen business. The business was located at 545-547 North Water Street.

The architectural firm of Brust & Philipp was hired sometime around 1909 to do some design work for Frank Mann on a building at 933-935 North Jackson Street. The building was later razed; unfortunately, there are no building permit records available. Most likely this commission was a remodel of the store front and possibly the interior, since the total cost of the project was only $7,251. Apparently, the store was rented to the Moulten & Ricketts Company, which according to a 1911 city directory was a purveyor of paintings and antiques. The Mann building was featured in an issue of *American Architect* on March 1, 1916.

Herman L. Emmerich Drug Store
Milwaukee, Wisconsin

The architectural firm of Brust & Philipp designed the Herman L. Emmerich Drug Store in 1909. It is still located at 3116-3118 North Downer Avenue, across the street from the University of Wisconsin-Milwaukee campus. It is now a Quizno's submarine sandwich restaurant, and the upper units are still apartment rentals.

F. M. Theisen Office and Flat
Milwaukee, Wisconsin

F. M. Theisen was a Milwaukee dentist. He commissioned the architectural firm of Brust & Philipp in 1910 to design him a building. The building contained a storefront for Theisen's dental practice and a flat above to be used as his home. The architecture of the building has been identified as the German Renaissance style. The building is still located at 3731-3733 West North Avenue in Milwaukee. As can be seen in this recent photograph, the building was remodeled.

F. H. Bresler Galleries Showroom
Milwaukee, Wisconsin

Frank Durbin and Phillip Poposkey opened an art gallery in 1882 at 729 North Milwaukee Street that featured paintings and rare prints from the personal collection of Frederick Layton. In 1889, when Durbin and Poposkey retired, the business was sold to Frank H. Bresler of Manitowoc, Wisconsin. The gallery was renamed F. H. Bresler Gallery. Bresler traveled often to Europe to buy art to feature in his gallery.

The architectural firm of Brust & Philipp was hired in 1919 to make alterations to the gallery on North Milwaukee Street. According to building permits, partitions were built on the second floor, an elevator was installed, and a stairway was built that lead from the first floor to the second. Gothic vault-like arches were installed in the ceiling areas.

When Frank Bresler died in 1931, his daughter, Gertrude, continued the business until 1955, at which time, it was then sold to

Interior photographs of the Bresler Showroom show the richness of the art and furnishings offered by the gallery. The right center photograph shows the stairway designed by Brust & Philipp. The bottom photograph depicts the intersecting, barrel-vaulted ceiling.

John Seidel. Seidel continued to sell high museum quality art. Seidel later moved into the art appraisal business, which later became the focus of the business. The gallery business was sold in 1968 to a local paint company, T. C. Esser Company, located at North 31st Street and West Galena Street. The Esser Company also acquired the Eitel Brothers Framing Gallery on North 3rd Street with the intention of merging it with the F. H. Bresler Galleries. When this merger was completed, the result was the Bresler Eitel Framing Gallery.

Looking for a new business venture, Clive Buckley, the owner of the Buckley Cleaner and Launderers, bought the Bresler Eitel Framing Gallery in 1971. The year following the sale, Buckley decided to focus

Chapter 4 – Brust & Philipp–Business Commissions 1906-1926

only on the framing end of the business, and he proceeded to sell off the art inventory that included works by Picasso, Warhol, and Dali. To expand the business, the Bresler Eitel Framing Gallery was moved to 777 North Water Street.

The business continued to grow, and a decision was made in 1986 to build a new 12,000 square-foot facility at North 5th Street and West Walnut Street. Buckley retired in 1996, and the business was sold to William Gray. The framing business now offers over 1,000 wood moldings and 300 metal moldings. The business also offers art pieces done primarily by regional artists.

The Queen Anne style building at 729 North Milwaukee Street that housed the former F. H. Bresler Gallery is known as the James Conroy Building. The building, built in 1881, still exists with its classical styling. Some of the Brust & Philipp remodeling design work is still present, such as the Gothic ceiling arches on the second floor. The lower floor now houses a restaurant, and the second floor is used as office space. The Bresler Galleries Showroom was featured in the August 1924 issue of *The Western Architect*.

Photographs on this page depict how each showroom was furnished in the English Revival style giving the impression that one just entered a residential space. Some of the furniture displayed was of the Jacobean style and rich tapestries decorated the walls.

Left, the ceilings were designed in the Gothic medieval style with intersecting barrel vaults which gave the effect of greater spanning space.

Stein Studios
Milwaukee, Wisconsin

Simon L. Stein was one of the most prominent photographers in the history of Milwaukee. He was born in Rosshaupt, Austria, in 1854. He came to America, initially settling in Chicago to study photography with A. J. Lawson. Later, he came to Milwaukee and worked for Hugo von Broich. In 1879, Stein purchased the studios of Broich & Cramer and established his own studio at North 3rd Street and West State Street. He did business at that site until 1897, at which time he moved Stein Studio to 402 East Wisconsin Avenue in order to be more accessible to his cultured clientele.

Stein was known internationally. In 1900, Stein was asked to photograph Queen Victoria. Also, the Smithsonian Institute at Washington, D.C., asked Stein to contribute works to their exhibits.

Later, Stein's son, Julian, joined the business. Simon Stein died in March 1922, two months before his new studio opened at 733 North Milwaukee Street. The architectural firm of Brust & Philipp was hired to design the remodeling of the building on North Milwaukee Street. The Stein Studio was next door to the Bresler Galleries, which was also remodeled by the firm of Brust & Philipp. The Stein Studio building on North Milwaukee Street was later razed. The Stein Studio was featured in the July 1925 issue of *The Western Architect*.

These interior photographs show the intersecting, barrel-vaulted ceiling that gave a sense of spanned space. The furnishings are of the English Jacobean style.

Industrial Commissions, 1906-1926

A. F. Gallun & Sons
Milwaukee, Wisconsin

August F. Gallun was born in Osterweick, Germany, and was the fourth generation of the Gallun family to go into the tannery business; however, August's business would be located in America, not Germany.

At the age of twenty, August landed in New York City, eventually taking on work in the Yonkers' tanning industry. In the spring of 1855, he set out for the American Midwest, working his way through Chicago, and finally arriving in Milwaukee in 1858.

He quickly established a partnership, forming the Trostel & Gallun Tannery. The firm dissolved in 1885 with each partner establishing his own business. The Gallun Tannery prospered, becoming one of the leading leather manufacturers in the country, selling their goods all over the world. The company manufactured all kinds of leather, mostly for the shoe industry, using vegetable and chrome tanning in a number of colors, depending upon the fashions of the day.

August Gallun married Julia Kraus and raised four children: Albert, Ella, Edwin, and Arthur. As a youth, Albert attended the German-English Academy. When he left school, he entered his father's tannery business. In the late 1890s, Albert, took over A.F. Gallun & Sons, located at 1818 North Water Street. His brother, Arthur, became vice president.

In 1912, Albert commissioned the architectural firm of Brust, Philipp & Heimerl to design the Gallun hide house at the north end of the 1800 block of North Water Street. The firm was also hired in 1918 to design additions and alterations to the rear of the Gallun office building at 1818 North Water Street. The architectural firm of Brust & Brust went on to do alterations for A.F. Gallun & Sons in 1942.

Albert married Hedwig Mann in 1896 and raised two sons, Edwin and Albert Jr., and two daughters, Elinor and Gladys. Elinor married into the Prizlaff Hardware family, and Gladys married into the Brumdner family. The firm of Brust & Philipp designed a new home for Albert Gallun in 1914 on East Newberry Boulevard on Milwaukee's northeast side. [See Pages 46-47 for the Albert Gallun House.]

Albert's two sons eventually entered the business: Edwin in 1920 as vice president and Albert Jr. in 1921 as secretary and general manager. Albert Sr. retired from the presidency of Gallun & Sons in 1928.

August F. Gallun

In 1996, the Gallun office building at 1818 North Water Street was converted into the Gallun Tannery Apartments. In 2004, these thirty-one apartments were converted into condominiums. Some of the main tannery buildings across the street from the Gallun Tannery Apartments are also being developed into condominiums. It appears that the building designed by Brust & Philipp at the north end of the 1800 block of North Water Street will be part of this condominium project. The Gallun family still owns the former tannery property. The Gallun Tannery buildings on North Water Street were placed on the National Register of Historic Places in 1984.

Albert F. Gallun

A. F. Gallun & Sons, Continued

This ca. 1900 drawing is of the Gallun Tannery. The building in the background with the wide chimney is the Gallun Building at 1818 North Water Street built in 1894. The architectural firm of Brust & Philipp did not design this building; however, they designed additions and alterations to the rear of the building. (See photograph below.)

Above, the firm of Brust, Philipp & Heimerl designed the Gallun hide warehouse in 1912 on the north end of the 1800 block of North Water Street. The decorative cornice and the top floor of the building were later removed.

Additions and alterations were made to the rear of the 1894 Gallun building. (See drawing at top.) The design work by the firm of Brust & Philipp began in 1918 and extended to 1942 when the firm was known as Brust & Brust. The 1894 building was developed into the Gallun Tannery Row Apartments in 1996. The twenty-six rental units were converted into condominiums in 2004.

Lakeside Distillery
Carrollville, Wisconsin

In 1893, Mrs. Frank Brice and Q. A. Matthews bought 1,000 acres of farmland in the town of Carrollville, which was located on the shore of Lake Michigan in the southeast section of Milwaukee County. The city of South Milwaukee was located to the north, and the city of Oak Creek was located to the south and to the west. Brice and Matthews proceeded to sell 280 acres to the South Milwaukee Springs Distillery, later renamed Lakeside Distillery. Established in 1893, the owners of the distillery were two brothers, P.R. Carroll and John Francis Carroll. The distillery made high quality, near one hundred proof sour mash, whisky, bonded whiskey, bourbon whisky, and gin. The company employed between thirty and fifty workers from 1893 to 1919.

The village of Carrollville was originally named Carroll for the two brothers who founded the distillery, but another town on the train route was already named Carroll, so the town name was changed to Carrollville. Another theory about the town name was that it was named for a Mr. Carroll, a frequent train rider. His name was called out when the train approached his stop in the area.

A perk for the distillery workers was a daily ration of a quart of whiskey as a token of management's appreciation for the laborers' hard work. Workers of the distillery weren't the only ones to receive a perk. The following passage is from the book, *History of the Oak Creek Township*, by Mrs. Alfred J. Meyer:

> Farmers came from far and wide with great large barrels on horse drawn wagons to haul from there feed for their cattle. This feed was a by-product from the whiskey made at this distillery. Every morning there would be a long caravan of the huge barrel wagons coming down the often muddy roads. The cattle ate with great relish this hot, fragrant, and juicy food, fresh from the distillery.[1]

According to archival information, the architectural firm of Brust & Philipp was commissioned to design buildings for the Lakeside Distillery sometime between 1905 and 1919. Photographs are not available, but the buildings they designed are probably pictured in the drawing below. The drawing depicts the main distillery buildings, a refining building, a cattle barn, a warehouse, a pump house, a cooper shop, and an office building.

When the Eighteenth Amendment to the U.S. Constitution outlawed the sale of alcohol beverages in 1919, the Lakeside Distillery closed. The property was sold to Hynite Corporation, a company that made fertilizer from tannery scraps.

Carrollville is now part of the city of Oak Creek, and there is interest by city officials to redevelop the area; Bender Park, a Milwaukee County Park, is located on the south end of Carrollville. Still present in Carrollville are many of the homes that were

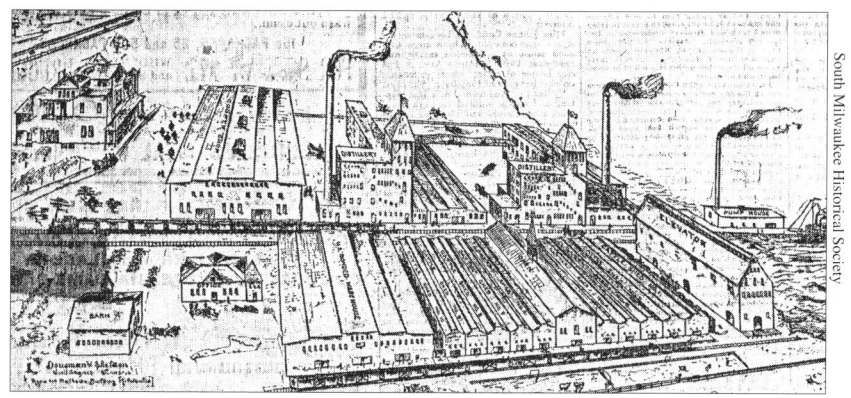

owned by Carrollville industries and were rented to their workers. Milwaukee County designated the former company town of Carrollville a Milwaukee County landmark.

This drawing is from a 1919 news article, and it probably depicts the buildings that the firm of Brust & Philipp designed.

[1] Mrs. Alfred J. Meyer, *History of the Oak Creek Townships* [197?], 7.

Luick Ice Cream Factory and Garage
Milwaukee, Wisconsin

John Luick spent most of his working years in the confectionery business. At the age of eleven, John was apprenticed to

The Luick Ice Cream Garage is now the Van Buren Loft Condominiums. [See Page 260 for the Van Buren Lofts.]

confectioner Henry Miller. At the age of seventeen he left the apprenticeship and enlisted in the Union Army, spending time at Harper's Ferry during the American Civil War. After his return from the war, John Luick began his confectionery business in Milwaukee on North Water Street in 1867. Six years later, he moved his store to North Milwaukee Street.

At that time, ice cream's popularity was just beginning in this country. At their confectionery store, John's wife, Elizabeth, cooked and churned the ice cream. It was said that Grover Cleveland was served ice cream for dessert when he attended a dinner at the Luick home. John Luick retired from the confectionery business in 1903.

John's son, William Ferdinand, followed him into the ice cream business. William began his apprenticeship in the family business at the age of sixteen. However, to gain more experience, William traveled to New York City to work for a confectioner there. After two years he returned to Milwaukee and re-entered the family business. However, after only six months, William took a position with the largest confectionery company in Chicago.

William returned to Milwaukee in 1897 and founded Luick Ice Cream Company. William hoped to develop a new process for making ice cream. Unable to convince his father to enter the wholesale ice cream trade, William set off on his own. Using his own savings and some loans, William purchased the necessary equipment and rented workspace. The ice cream was manufactured in a basement work area with the freezer cranked by hand. The daily output was only ten gallons per day, but William was not deterred. He was striving for a superior quality ice cream.

As the business grew, William purchased his first property in 1901 on North Jackson and East Ogden Street on Milwaukee's northeast side. Hand power for the cranking of the freezers was eventually replaced by gasoline motors and finally by electricity.

The architectural firm of Brust & Philipp was commissioned to design the Luick Ice Cream Garage in 1921. This five-story building cost a total of $96,000. Archival records show that in 1929, the firm designed an additional project at a cost of $11,000. [See Pages 44-45 and Page 51 for the William Ferdinand Luick House commissions.]

By 1945, Luick Ice Cream Company employed 650 people and his company was worth $2.5 million. Wisconsin dairy farmers were paid $1.5 million annually for their milk. The Sealtest Company eventually purchased Luick Ice Cream Company.

Maynard Steel Casting Company
Milwaukee, Wisconsin

Charles Maynard founded the Maynard Electric Steel Casting Company in 1907. Sylvester Wabiszewski purchased the company in 1913 and moved it to its present location at 2856 North 27th Street in Milwaukee. The first building erected on the South 27th Street site measured 120 feet by 300 feet. This is probably the building designed by Brust & Philipp in 1918. The total cost of the building was $33,950. In 1925, an addition was built measuring 200 feet long.

Before purchasing the Maynard Company, Wabiszewski was a prominent builder and mason contractor. In 1885, Wabiszewski immigrated to America from Poland, and upon arrival, he took an apprenticeship with a bricklayer. In 1888, he began his own general contracting business. He worked on projects designed by Brust & Philipp such as the Holy Rosary Academy in Sturtevant (Corliss). Other prominent buildings that Wabiszewski constructed were St. Vincent's Catholic Church, St. Lawrence Catholic Church, and Holy Ghost Catholic Church, all located in Milwaukee. In addition to the contracting business, Wabiszewski also became the vice president of the Mitchell Street Bank in 1907.

When Wabiszewski died in 1962 at the age of ninety-six, his sons, Ralph and Edmund, continued to manage Maynard Steel. Their sons, Ralph and Edmund Jr., in turn succeeded them.

Battery Light Company
Milwaukee, Wisconsin

Louis Allis owned the Battery Light Company, which was located at 427 East Stewart Street in Milwaukee on the Allis' original homestead farm. The Mechanical Appliance Company, also owned by Louis Allis, shared the same location. [See Page 22 for the Mechanical Appliance commission.] Allis hired the firm of Brust, Philipp & Heimerl around 1912 to design a factory building for the company at the East Stewart Street location. The total cost of this building was $28,000. The Battery Light and Power Company was incorporated in 1909 and manufactured storage batteries. It is unclear from building permits if the Battery Light building designed by Brust & Philipp was razed or was just greatly altered. No photographs of the building were found.

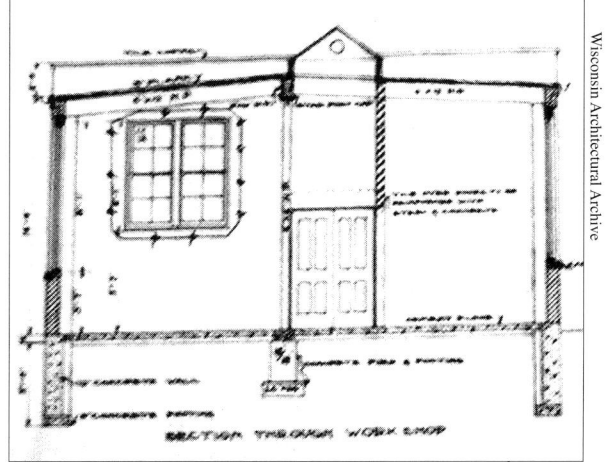

A drawing of the Battery Light Company

George Ziegler Candy Company
Milwaukee, Wisconsin

George Ziegler's family left Halsheim, Bavaria, Germany, in 1845 and bought farmland in Bristol, Wisconsin, which is located in Dane County. From the age of fifteen to eighteen, George Ziegler was apprenticed as a leather worker at the company of L. Pieron in Milwaukee. After a three-year apprenticeship, he worked for the firm of Bradley & Metcalf Shoe Company.

A contemporary photograph of the factory on Florida Street

On May 4, 1851, George married Barbara Boll. In the 1860s, George went into the confectionery business with his two brother-in-laws, John and Andrew Boll. Due to the loss of business during the American Civil War, both brothers were laid off from a candy company in Chicago. Ziegler's new confectionery factory was created in a home owned by the Boll family at North 13th Street and West Vliet Street in Milwaukee.

The Boll brothers made the candy, and Ziegler took care of the financial end while keeping his day job as a shoemaker. The Boll brothers' father, a tailor by profession, peddled the candy. The company prospered, and the brothers suggested that George quit his shoemaking job and work full time as the business manager. George finally quit his day job, and the firm of Boll Brothers & Company was founded.

Larger quarters were needed by 1865, and the company moved to the Lutz building on North 3rd Street, on what would later be the site of the Steinmeyer building.

The factory moved again to the Plankinton Building on West Wisconsin Avenue, then called Spring Street, near the future site of the Gimbel's Department Store. In 1867, Andrew dropped out of the firm, and the name was changed to Boll & Ziegler. After John died in 1873, George ran the business alone.

A fire destroyed the factory in 1882, and the company relocated to North Water Street. The business was incorporated in 1887 under the name of George Ziegler Company. The factory moved again in April 1908 to 402-424 West Florida Street. Herman Schnetzky was hired to design the new seven-story building. It may be the first building in the United States to be constructed with a concrete skeleton.

The George Ziegler Company was well known nationally for its American and French confections. The company was innovative in making improvements in the candy-making processes and inventing new ones. The company was the first to offer a peanut-chocolate bar called the Milk Chocolate Peanut Block. In 1911, they marketed the first wrapped candy bar called the Ziegler Giant Bar, containing peanuts and milk chocolate, that sold for five cents. This candy bar was also known as the Fox Trot bar in 1912.

Chapter 4 – Brust & Philipp–Business Commissions 1906-1926

When George died in 1904, all of his sons were working for the company. Charles was the financial manager, Frank was the superintendent of the factory, and Theodore and Andrew were assistants. Two other sons, George and H. T., also worked for the company in some capacity. [See Page 55 for the Charles I. Ziegler house commission.]

The architectural firm of Brust & Philipp was commissioned by the Ziegler Company in 1919 to build a one-story garage, measuring 26 feet by 100 feet, at a cost of $10,000. In February 1920, Brust & Philipp was commissioned to build an addition to the factory at the West Florida Street location. The seven-story addition measured 80 feet by 112 feet, and the total cost was $238,790. This building is still at its original site.

The George Ziegler Company endeared themselves to Milwaukee school children, when after World War II, the company gave each Milwaukee school child, both public and private, two Giant candy bars at Halloween time. The author of this book remembers receiving the two candy bars every year.

Unfortunately, the George Ziegler Company went out of business in 1972. Fifth generation descendants of the company, William and Mary Ziegler, opened their own company, Half Nuts, in 1990. The West Allis retail store sells assorted candies, including the Ziegler Giant Bars that are still poured in patented molds. The chocolate bar now costs $1.19. Many customers who were recipients of the two free Giant Bars in the 1950s and 1960s still find the taste heavenly.

A photograph on the cover of an old Ziegler candy box shows the George Ziegler Company building, including the Brust & Philipp addition, located on West Florida Street.

George Ziegler

Slocum Straw Works
Milwaukee, Wisconsin

The Slocum Straw Works manufactured ladies' straw and felt hats. Albert Slocum, a native of Massachusetts, founded the company in 1873 and located his factory on Mason Street in Milwaukee. Albert's brothers were pioneers in the millinery business in Milwaukee as early as 1867. Their factory was located on what is now the site of the Milwaukee Athletic Club. Slocum Straw Works was the first manufacturer west of New York to manufacturer ladies' hats. The company's main markets were in the Northwest and in the South. By 1881, the company employed 300 people.

In 1909, the company, then known as the Slocum Hat Corporation, moved to 1426 West National Avenue into a new two-story building. The company was also known as Northwestern Straw Works. Albert's son, Everett A. Slocum, became manager and executive head of the company five years before his father retired. When Albert died in 1925, Everett was the president and general manager.

The architectural firm of Brust & Philipp designed buildings for the Slocum Hat Corporation at 1412-1426 West National Avenue in 1919, 1925, and 1926. The Slocum Hat Corporation dissolved in 1956. The buildings now house the Astronautics Corporation.

Argola Investment Company Garage and Auditorium
Milwaukee, Wisconsin

The architectural firm of Brust & Philipp designed the Argola Investment Company Garage and Auditorium in 1916. The building at 922 North 5th Street was later razed. No photographs were found of the building.

Wisconsin Architectural Archive

Milwaukee-Waukesha Brewery
Waukesha, Wisconsin

In 1900, Charles Manegold Jr. and his son-in-law, August Lindemann, headed the Waukesha Imperial Spring Brewing Company. The company name was changed to the Milwaukee-Waukesha Brewery Company in 1903. The company brewed ale, stout, beer, malt tonic, mineral waters, and ginger ale; all were produced with pure Waukesha spring water. The company also owned manufacturing buildings near the 400 block of South Water Street in Milwaukee. Those buildings have been razed.

When the Eighteenth Amendment to the U.S. Constitution outlawed the sale of alcohol beverages in 1919, the company changed its name to the Fox Head Spring Beverage Company.

Brust & Philipp designed a new shipping room in 1920 at 227 Maple Avenue in Waukesha. The Brust & Philipp archival records list the name of the company as the Milwaukee-Waukesha Brewery.

When Charles Manegold died in 1928, and his daughter, Mrs. Emilie Lindemann, took over as president during Prohibition and the Great Depression eras. The name was later changed to the Fox Head Waukesha Corporation. The company resumed beer making in 1933 when Prohibition was lifted. Most of the Milwaukee-Waukesha Brewery buildings at the Maple Avenue location were razed, including the shipping room that the firm of Brust & Philipp designed.

Wisconsin Architectural Archive

E. A. Schroeter Warehouse
Milwaukee, Wisconsin

*N*othing could be found in the Milwaukee city directories for the E. A. Schroeter Company. According to the Brust & Philipp records, the warehouse designed by Brust & Philipp was located on North 5th Street near Juneau Avenue. The accompanying drawing is dated 1916.

Wisconsin Architectural Archive

Automotive Commissions, 1906-1926

Buick Motor Company Showroom
Milwaukee, Wisconsin

David Dunbar Buick was born in Scotland. As a young child, he immigrated to America with his family in 1856. As an adult, Buick was a successful plumbing inventor and manufacturer in Detroit, Michigan. By 1899, Buick's company, Buick-Auto-Vim, was producing gasoline engines. Buick was interested in developing a vehicle powered by such an engine.

In 1903, Buick's financial backer, Benjamin Briscoe Jr., sold out his interest in the Buick company to a group of wagon makers in Flint, Michigan. James H. Whiting, owner of the Flint Wagon Works, along with the other wagon works directors, decided to move the business to Flint. David Buick moved with the business to Flint. In January 1904, the Buick Motor Company was dissolved and reincorporated as the Buick Motor Company of Flint.

In the summer of 1904, the company built the first Flint Buick automobile, the Model B Buick. William "Billy" Durant, who owned the Durant-Dort Carriage Company, took control of the Buick Company in November 1904. Durant was the largest producer of horse-drawn vehicles in the country, and he was considered Flint's carriage king. Durant successfully marketed the new Buick, getting an order for 1,000 vehicles in 1905 at a time when the company built only thirty-seven vehicles that year. In 1905, Durant moved the Buick assembly plant to Jackson, Michigan, and manufactured 700 of the Model C Buick. The four-cylinder Model D was produced in 1907. After gathering money from Flint banks and businessmen, Durant was able to build the country's largest assembly plant in the city of Flint.

Durant created a holding company, General Motors, in 1908, and eventually gathered together Buick, Oldsmobile, Cadillac, Oakland (later called Pontiac), and AC Spark Plug. By 1910, there were more than thirty companies in the General Motor holding company. Buick was the number one producer of cars in 1908, producing more cars than Ford and Cadillac combined.

The architectural firm of Brust & Philipp designed the Buick Motor Company Showroom in 1910 located at 510 East Wisconsin Avenue. The exterior of the building was done in a light-colored brick and the top of the building sported a decorative copper cornice. This three-story brick building is still at the same location but with a remodeled facade.

Milwaukee Public Library

Packard Motor Car Company Garage
Milwaukee, Wisconsin

The Packard Motor Car Company Garage was located at North 35th Street and West Wisconsin Avenue. In 1915, this area was part of Wauwatosa but was later annexed by Milwaukee. The architectural firm of Brust & Philipp designed additions to the garage in 1915 and 1926. The Packard Motor Car Company of Wisconsin was a division of the Packard Motor Car Company of Chicago. The Packard building was later razed, and no photographs were found. The drawing below appears to be of a automobile showroom rather than a garage; however, the term garage may have been used somewhat differently than it is today.

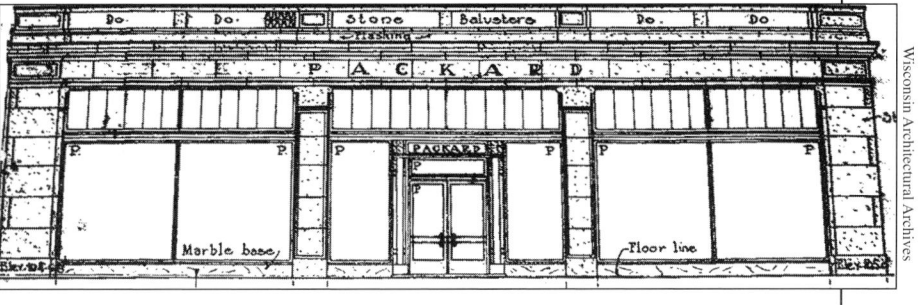

Filling Stations, 1906-1926

With the popularity of the automobile in the early part of the twentieth century, drivers needed refueling facilities. These roadside facilities popped up across the country to provide not only gasoline but also other related products, such as tires, lubricants, and batteries for automobiles.

Most of these filling stations were owned by large corporations. When the Standard Oil Trust was divided into separate companies in 1911, the Trust owned 90 percent of the nation's refineries. The Trust also owned most of the filling stations. By 1915, because of the popularity of the automobile, the large oil companies found it difficult to keep up with patrons' gasoline needs. Therefore, independent jobbers opened filling stations to provide gasoline for automobile owners.

O'Neil Oil and Paint Company was one of these independent jobbers. The company was incorporated in 1893 as O'Neil Oil and Paint Company and then was reincorporated in 1926 as O'Neil Oil Company. George O'Neil was a manufacturer and jobber of oils, paints, soap,

This unidentified photograph came from the Zimmerman Design Group archives. The station was designed by the firm of Brust & Philipp in the Mediterranean style.

and chemicals. In 1923, the architectural firm of Brust & Philipp designed an English Tudor style filling station for O'Neil at 2243 North Prospect Avenue in Milwaukee. The station was later razed. Unfortunately, no photographs were found, but the Wisconsin Architectural Archives has the drawings of the filling station.

These independent jobbers needed to create brand loyalty, so they stressed customer satisfaction. They presented themselves as local producers and also as neighbors with a more personable attitude than the larger, impersonal oil corporations. It was this desire for individuality that drove the independent jobber to design filling stations that were different from the larger oil companies.

The large oil companies came up with a standard design for all of their filling stations. One of the large corporations, Pure Oil, used the English cottage style designed by C. Petersen. The Pure Oil station featured white stucco walls and a steep, high-ended gabled roof with deep blue tiles. Ventura Refining Company of Los Angeles adopted the mission type building, and in 1931, Seaboard stations were done in the Spanish Mission style with stucco walls and tiled roofs.

The independent jobbers, however, wanted a one-of-a-kind design and therefore turned to local architects such the firm of Brust & Philipp to design their filling stations. The station owners hoped to convey the sense of a private home, bringing a sense of class and status to the station. Station owners sought to blend stations into the architectural style of the neighborhood. These stations reflected the popular house styles of the 1920s and 1930s, such as the English Tudor revival and the Mediterranean style. Each station looked like a small house that contained an office, one or two small storage rooms, and public restrooms.

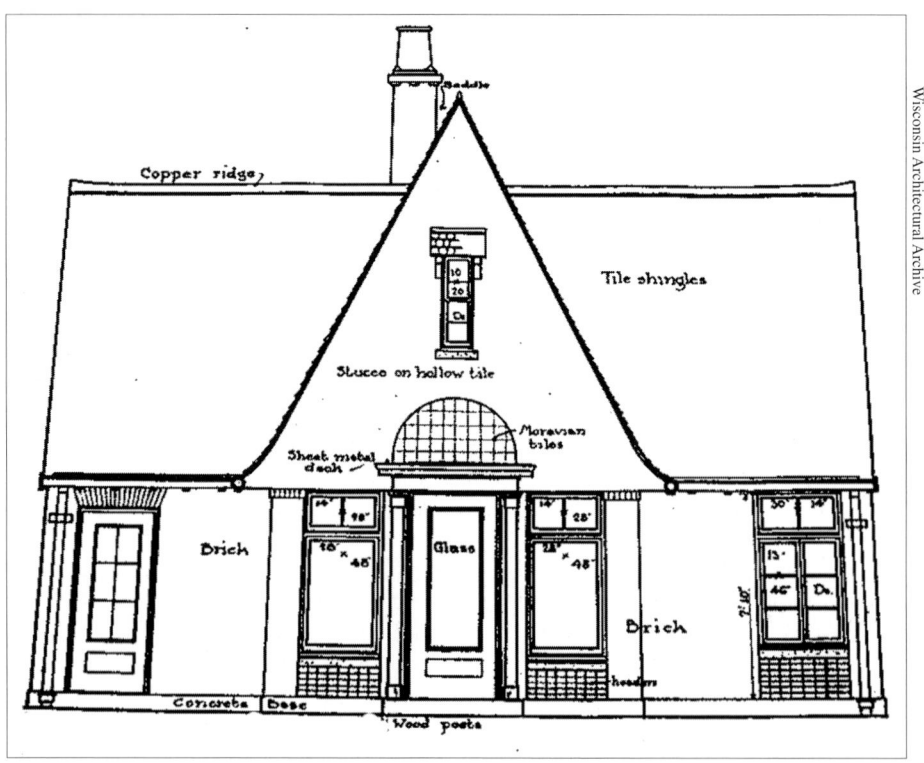

The O'Neil Oil and Paint Company filling station on Prospect Avenue was designed by Brust & Philipp in the English style.

Chapter 5
Brust & Philipp-Medical, Public, Memorial, Recreation, and Theater Commissions, 1906-1926

Medical Commissions, 1906-1926

Milwaukee Sanitarium
Wauwatosa, Wisconsin

Dr. James McBride, a former superintendent of the Milwaukee County Hospital for the Insane, established the Milwaukee Sanitarium in 1884 at what is now 1220 Dewey Avenue in Wauwatosa. McBride's mission was to treat people with nervous disorders, and he felt the best place to do this was in a peaceful, wooded environment, away from the city distractions. The hospital's location was known as the Harwood Estate, which overlooked the Menomonee River Valley. In 1894, Dr. McBride retired and moved to California. The hospital was then reorganized and renamed the New Milwaukee Sanitarium Association.

Dr. Richard Dewey took over as director of the sanitarium in 1895, and he developed the cottage system. Previously, Dr. Dewey practiced in Chicago, serving as head of the Illinois State Hospital at Kankakee. A number of buildings were constructed on the Milwaukee Sanitarium grounds between 1896 and 1897, including a nurses' dormitory, an office building, and a bathhouse that was equipped with hydro-therapeutic apparatuses.

The West House was constructed in 1906 with rooms, private baths, and a gymnasium with a hall, measuring 40

feet by 60 feet, for physical exercise and recreation. By this time, fifty patients could be accommodated at the hospital. Additional land was purchased that year bringing the total to twenty-eight acres. During his twenty-four years as director, Dr. Dewey developed a program that trained staff in the care of the mentally ill. Dr. Dewey was held in such high esteem that the street on which the sanitarium stands was named for him.

Dr. Rock Sleyster became medical director in 1919, and he served in that capacity until 1942. Under his leadership, the sanitarium emphasized the importance of psychiatric treatment. Dr. Sleyster was one of America's best-known doctors to specialize in psychiatry. Gerhard H. Schroeder, the executive director from 1919 to 1942, worked closely with Dr. Sleyster. Schroeder was responsible during his thirty-three years at the sanitarium for creating the beautiful hospital grounds. The thirty acres of hospital grounds included tennis courts, which were used as a form of rehabilitation. Along with outdoor rehabilitation, indoor therapy consisted of Zander equipment that provided passive exercise, such as the vibration treatment.

The architectural firm of Brust & Philipp was hired in 1919 to design the new main building, now known as Sleyster Hall. The Classical Revival style building housed a central dining room, lounges, patients' library, and a double-deck sun porch that was used year round. Architectural writer Rexford Newcomb said the following about the new building:

> The new Main Building of the Milwaukee Sanitarium, frankly American Colonial in inspiration, has in addition to a cleanly and sanitary hospital air, a certain residential charm, thus adding a note of hominess so often totally lacking in structures of this class.[1]

The firm of Brust & Philipp was also hired to design additions in 1921, 1924, and 1927, including a new gymnasium. The total cost of the main building was $131,500. [See Page 68 for the Dr. Sleyster house commission.]

Due to the efforts of Dr. William T. Kradwell who served the hospital for fifty years, the Milwaukee Sanitarium became a non-profit institution in 1954. The sanitarium would later become the Milwaukee Psychiatric Hospital. In 1993, the sanitarium joined Aurora Health Care, and the hospital became part of Aurora Behavior Health Services.

[1] Rexford Newcomb, AIA, "Continuity of Personal Influence as Sensed in the Work of Brust and Philipp, of Milwaukee," *The Western Architect* (July 1925), 88.

Above, the dining room featured rounded arched windows and a simple Colonial Style fireplace mantel.

Right, the sweeping staircase reflected the Colonial Revival style.

Below, the sitting room featured a tiled fireplace and overmantle.

Lutheran Deaconess Hospital
Beaver Dam, Wisconsin

Lutheran Deaconess Hospital began its operation in the old Percy Lamoreux mansion in Beaver Dam. The architectural firm of Brust & Philipp designed the mansion in 1909 for the Lamoreux family. [See Pages 71-73 for Donald Percy Lamoreux mansion commission.] In 1916, the Lamoreux mansion passed to E. E. Symthe when Symthe purchased Percy Lamoreux's failing business, Western Malleables, Inc. In 1922, the Lutheran Deaconess Association of Indiana purchased the mansion for $30,000.

The firm of Brust & Philipp was commissioned to remodel the mansion to fit the needs of a new hospital. The Lutheran Deaconess Hospital was dedicated on Sunday, January 29, 1922, with twenty-five patient beds. Later, an addition designed by Peter Brust was built to the west of the mansion. The architectural firm of Brust & Brust designed more additions in the 1950s.

The old Lamoreux mansion served as part of the hospital until 1952, after which the old mansion was used for offices and storage space. By this time, the mansion section of the Lutheran Deaconess Hospital was badly deteriorated. With a leaky roof and sagging floors, it would have cost $400,000 to restore the mansion. It was suggested that the mansion be used as senior housing or a community center. It was even suggested that the mansion be moved across the lake, but since the later hospital additions were sandwiched between the lake and the mansion, such a move was impossible. After much discussion, the mansion was razed in 1981. However, a little part of the mansion remains. A former enclosed porch of the mansion is attached to the hospital near the parking lot.

In 1972, Lutheran Deaconess consolidated with St. Joseph's Hospital of Beaver Dam and resulted in Beaver Dam Community Hospital, which is still in operation. The firm of Brust & Brust designed the St. Joseph's Hospital building in 1938. [See Page 233 for St. Joseph's Hospital commission.]

Above, the Lamoreux mansion can be seen in the foreground. At the left in the background are the additions made in later years. The small enclosed porch on the left side of the mansion is the only remaining portion of the mansion.

Below, a recent photograph shows the hospital additions made to the Lamoreux mansion. The mansion is gone, but the small porch remains.

The main hospital was designed by the firm of Brust & Philipp in 1919.

Columbia Hospital
Milwaukee, Wisconsin

Columbia Hospital of Milwaukee was established out of a need for a hospital medical center with extensive laboratory facilities. It was hoped that such a facility would encourage medical research. A group of laymen and one physician gathered to organize such a hospital; they were Bernhard Leidersdorf, Jacob Friend, John W. Mariner, Gustav Pabst, and Dr. Otto H. Forester. Gustav Pabst suggested the name, Columbia Hospital, and the name was agreeable to all present.

The group leased the Knowlton Hospital building near North 9th Street and West Michigan Street for their new hospital. The Knowlton Hospital and Training School for Nurses had been established in 1901 in a private home and served as a private and general hospital.

In July 1909, Articles of Incorporation were filed for the new Columbia Hospital. W. L. Lecron was appointed director and house physician. In 1914, sixteen acres was purchased near North Frederick Street and East Cramer Street on Milwaukee's northeast side. The hospital attempted to raise $500,000 to build the new hospital, but it wasn't until after World War I that construction started. The hospital opened on January 20, 1919, with eight patients transferring from the Knowlton building. This was the year of the great polio epidemic in Milwaukee. Through a community effort, $25,000 was raised for the research of polio. Columbia Hospital was selected to research this dreaded disease to discover the cause and a cure.

The new hospital contained sixty beds, with major medical departments and a School of Nursing. The architectural firm of Brust & Philipp was commissioned to design the new main hospital building and the new nursing school and dormitory. Both buildings are still located on the 3000 block of North Maryland Avenue. The cost of the project was $76,000 according to Brust & Philipp archival information. The Columbia Hospital School of Nursing, under the leadership of Miss Pouty, enrolled fifty-seven students and was affiliated with Milwaukee Children's Hospital and Milwaukee Downer College. Both buildings remain on North Maryland Avenue.

Above and inset, the inscription above the doorway says Columbia Hospital School for Nurses.

The Columbia Hospital School of Nursing designed by Brust & Philipp in 1919

Wisconsin Home for the Feeble-Minded
Chippewa Falls, Wisconsin

The Wisconsin Home for the Feeble-Minded in Chippewa Falls was established in April 1895 when the state legislature appropriated $100,000 for land and buildings. A Menomonee architect, John Charles, was hired to design twenty buildings. This institution at 2820 East Park Avenue was founded as a home for feeble-minded and epileptic males under the age of thirty and females under the age of forty. No cases of dementia or insanity were accepted if the conditions were developed after childhood. These residents received care and treatment for their conditions, and they also received education, especially industrial training. The center was designed to be a self-sufficient farm with labor furnished by inmates. Also, inmates were trained in cooking, sewing, and shoemaking. However, even with such training, few residents were released or placed in jobs outside the center. The number of residents at the center numbered 291 in 1898 and grew to 1,226 by 1920.

A new fifty-bed hospital was constructed in 1914. This was most likely designed by the architectural firm of Brust & Philipp. Archival records show that blueprints were drafted during that period for a project at the Wisconsin Home for the Feeble Minded in Chippewa Falls. Unfortunately, these blueprints are not available.

The superintendent of the center, A. L. Beier, requested in 1922 that the name of the home be changed to The Northern Wisconsin Colony and Training School. Beier felt that the term, feeble-minded, was an objectionable term. In 1976, the state legislature changed the name to Northern Wisconsin Center for the Developmentally Disabled. The center still exists and as of 1997, the center's population was 302.

Mendota Hospital for the Insane Madison, Wisconsin

Mendota Hospital for the Insane opened at 301 Troy Drive in Madison on July 14, 1860. When families or communities could no longer take care of their mentally ill members, the asylum became the place of last resort.

As the medical community began to treat mental illness as a disease, the name of the hospital was changed to the Mendota State Hospital. As time went on, with the advent of new treatments for mental illness, many patients could be treated at community hospitals and clinics. For those who required more specialized treatment, Mendota State Hospital was the place for them.

Mendota Hospital underwent dramatic improvements in 1906. That year, electricity was installed in the hospital, replacing gas and kerosene lighting. The result was better ventilation and less danger of fire. The newest treatment at the time was hydrotherapy, and such treatment was successful at Mendota.

Trained nurses were placed on all the infirmary wards in 1906. An industrial teacher who taught arts and crafts and needlework was hired in 1908. The nursing school started in 1910. That same year a ten-year building plan was unveiled.

Around the year 1911, the architectural firm of Brust, Philipp & Heimerl was hired to design a new nurses' dormitory in the Colonial Revival style. The nurses' dormitory, designed to house fifty nurses, was completed in 1914 at a total cost of $30,000. The basement was used for industrial rooms, one side for the men and the other for the women. Another new building was erected around that time to house patients with contagious diseases. The cost of that building was $40,000 and housed fifty-six patients and sixteen nurses.

The dormitory was razed in the early 1960s. No photograph was found of the nurses' dormitory; fortunately, the architectural drawings survived. The hospital's name was later changed to Mendota Mental Health Institute.

Above, a side view of the nurses' dormitory at the Mendota Hospital for the Insane

Right, a front view of the nurses' dormitory

Northern Hospital for the Insane Nurse's Dormitory
Winnebago, Wisconsin

Construction of the Northern State Hospital for the Insane began in 1871; the hospital opened in November 1875 with a capacity of 500 patients. The state appropriated $125,000 for the purchase of the site at 2100 Main Street and for the construction of the buildings. An additional 338 acres were purchased on the shore of Lake Winnebago, north of Oshkosh, for $26,000. The hospital was almost self-sufficient with patients participating in farming and lumbering. It was thought that fresh air and work, along with good nutrition, was an important treatment for the mentally ill.

By 1911, there were 1,831 residents at the hospital. The architectural firm of Brust, Philipp & Heimerl was hired to design a nurses' dormitory in 1912, and it was completed in the fall of that year. The new dormitory was designed to accommodate forty nurses and female attendants, and it provided all of the modern conveniences. Up until that time, nurses and attendants lived on the wards, working twelve-to fifteen-hour days. The nurses and attendants were allowed only one day off each month, with the hospital preferring that they take half-days off. The new dormitory building was long needed. It was felt that having rooms for staff away from the wards would lighten the burden of the women who were caring for the patients. The building designed by Brust, Philipp & Heimerl was later razed. The hospital, however, still remains and is now known as the Winnebago Mental Health Institute.

Top and bottom, both photographs are of the nurses' dormitory at the Northern Hospital for the Insane in Winnebago. The date of the top photograph is unknown. Note the lady with the parasol. The bottom photograph is identified as being taken in 1916. It appears that the Northern Hospital was very similiar in design to the Mendota Hospital on the previous page.

Sacred Heart Sanitarium
Milwaukee, Wisconsin

Mother Superior Alexia of the School Sisters of St. Francis felt that someday the Sisters would be called upon to care for the sick of the community. She favored the more natural ways of healing promoted by Monsignor Sebastian Kneipp in his book, *My Water-Cure*.

Mother Alexia decided in 1892 to set up a sanitarium in Milwaukee. She sent Sister Hyacinth to Baden-Baden, Germany, to take a course on the methods of massaging and water cures. When Mother Alexia was ready to build her hospital, she encountered opposition from Archbishop Katzer who wasn't too keen on the Kneipp Method of naturalness. While Archbishop Katzer was making up his mind, Dr. I. H. Hirschfield was setting up a training program for the Sisters who would staff the new sanitarium. The Sisters set up shop on the first floor of the Motherhouse. The sanitarium would be the first establishment in the United States to use the Kneipp Water Cure. Finally, Archbishop Katzer agreed to the founding of a sanitarium.

Above, a postcard image of Sacred Heart Sanitarium

Archbishop Katzer

The original Sacred Heart Sanitarium building, designed by Herman P. Schnetzky of Milwaukee, opened for business on December 23, 1893. Brust & Philipp designed additions for the hospital from 1912 to approximately 1927.

On April 29, 1893, land was purchased along Lapham Street and South Layton Avenue for the new sanitarium. Aton Czyak was paid $8,000 for the property. Once the $130,000 for the cost of construction was gathered, the construction of the three-story building commenced. Architect Herman P. Schnetzky, who had designed the St. Joseph Convent building in 1891, was commissioned to design the new sanitarium. The Sacred Heart Sanitarium, facing South Layton Boulevard, opened for business on December 23, 1893, with thirteen patients. After a rough start, the Sanitarium was functioning by the fall of 1894 with eighty patients.

Unfortunately, a smallpox epidemic forced the Sanitarium to close its doors until March 1895. Once it reopened, patients came for various reasons; some came to be treated for chronic illnesses and some just came to recuperate from such illnesses. Others came for treatment of nervous conditions. The hospital did not treat contagious or infectious diseases.

Various types of baths were used to treat the illnesses, such as the mud bath, using mud imported from Italy at a high cost of forty dollars a barrel. Carbonic acid baths, brine baths, hay flower baths, Turkish baths, Russian baths, and sulfur baths were also used for the treatment of rheumatism. A 1904 newspaper article published in the *Catholic Citizen* said that a patient could "steam himself in the fragrance of a delicious herb bath." The electric bath made use of the recently invented electric light bulb. The 1904 *Catholic Citizen* newspaper article goes on to describe the electric bath as permeating the whole body with the "genial warmth of innumerable incandescent lights giving the affect of a sunbath."

Along with therapeutic baths, patients could use the Zander Gymnasium that occupied a great portion of the main floor. In the gymnasium, patients were treated to message treatments by means of vibratory machinery that was imported from Sweden at a cost of $20,000. The sanitarium featured a state board certified pharmacist. Medical staff used X-rays for diagnostic purposes.

The 1904 *Catholic Citizen* article went on to boast of elegant reception rooms, lounging rooms, broad verandas, and spacious billiard rooms. Every effort was made to give the patients a feeling of a homelike and pleasant environment.

In 1912, the architectural firm of Brust, Philipp & Heimerl designed an addition that added eighty rooms, a sun parlor, a gymnasium, billiard room, bowling alleys, and a swimming pool. There was a new athletic field connected to the sanitarium by a

Above, the hospital chapel in the Sacred Heart Sanitarium designed by Brust & Philipp

Below, an interior photograph of the sanitarium lobby designed by Brust & Philipp

tunnel. It contained a suspended running track and tanbark floor for horseback riding. For people of financial means, this was the place to go for treatment or for a rest cure.

By 1914, the hospital occupied seventeen acres of land. Surrounded by a spacious, park-like area, with rustic seats from which patients could enjoy nature, the sanitarium developed a national reputation. However, due to this popularity, the sanitarium soon needed to expand.

The firm of Brust & Philipp was hired in 1917 to design a north-wing for the rapidly expanding sanitarium; the total cost for the north wing was $103,626. The following year the firm was hired to do some remodeling on the old building. In 1919, the firm designed the south wing and center wing, and the total cost of the two buildings was $264,725. The center-wing lobby was designed in 1919, and the total cost was $48,934. By 1928, additions were need for the center and south wings that were added in 1917 and 1919. Brust & Philipp designed additions to these wings at a total cost of $604,212. In 1919, a pavilion was also designed, and records show that design work was commissioned for this structure periodically until 1927. Other commissions were a root cellar designed in 1921 and a clinic in 1926 at a total cost of $48,964.

The main sanitarium buildings were razed in 1976; however, two building wings remain. The former center-wing addition, located at 1546 South 29th Street, now houses Clare Tower, which is owned by the U. S. Department of Housing and Urban Development (HUD). Clare Tower contains apartments for physically handicapped adults. The former south-wing addition, located at 1545 South Layton, is now used for convent offices. Both the south- and center-wing additions are pictured on the following page.

Above, an interior photograph shows the lobby at Sacred Heart Sanitarium that was designed by Brust & Philipp.

Right, the pavilion was located south of the sanitarium and was designed by Brust & Philipp.

Chapter 5 – Brust & Philipp–Medical, Public, Memorial, Recreation, and Theater Commissions 1906-1926

Sacred Heart Sanitarium, Continued

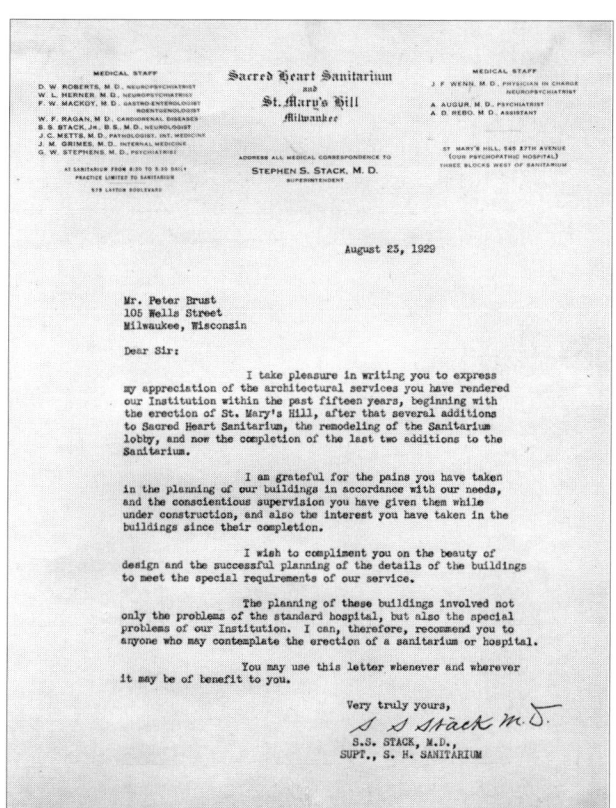

Dr. Stephen S. Stack of the Sacred Heart Sanitarium wrote this letter to Peter Brust in 1929. Brust probably used a copy of the letter as a reference for future employment applications. This letter came from the archives of the Zimmerman Design Group.

Above, the center wing lobby of the sanitarium, designed in 1919 by Brust & Philipp, featured a coffered ceiling. Mosaic tiles decorated the fireplace and multi-colored tile were used as a floor covering. The Continental Faience and Tile Company of South Milwaukee probably created the tiles. Note the Sister sitting on the far left reading.

Below, a photograph of the main dining room shows Colonial Revival style furnishings.

Sacred Heart Sanitarium, Continued

Right and below left, are two photographs of a small dining room that still exists in a two-story building that is attached to the south wing addition. Originally, this dining was attached to the larger, more formal dining room that was later razed. The leaded-glass windows of this small dining room are still intact along with the chandeliers. See the bottom of this page for an exterior photograph of this two-story building.

Above, a recent exterior photograph of the small dining room pictured at the top of this page

Inset right, a close-up shot of one of the leaded-glass dining room windows

Above, the former solarium is located on the sixth floor of the sanitarium's south wing addition. It is no longer used as a solarium but rather as a conference room. The solarium originally featured a glass ceiling, which was removed, but the Arts & Crafts tile on the walls and floor remain.

The wall and floor tiles were made by the Continental Faience and Tile Company of South Milwaukee, located at 909 Menomonee Avenue. Carl Bergmans was the company president and at one time worked with Frank Lloyd Wright and Russell Barr Williamson. The company made unglazed floor and wall tiles along with glazed faience tiles that were made from wet clay rather than clay powders. The company made tile from 1925 to 1943.

Chapter 5 – Brust & Philipp–Medical, Public, Memorial, Recreation, and Theater Commissions 1906-1926

Sacred Heart Sanitarium, Continued

Above and right, historical photographs of the center wing addition designed by Brust & Philipp in 1928

Above, is a recent photograph of the center wing addition. The building was sold in 1978 to the Department of Housing and Urban Development (HUD) and is now the St. Clare Tower and contains apartments for handicapped adults.

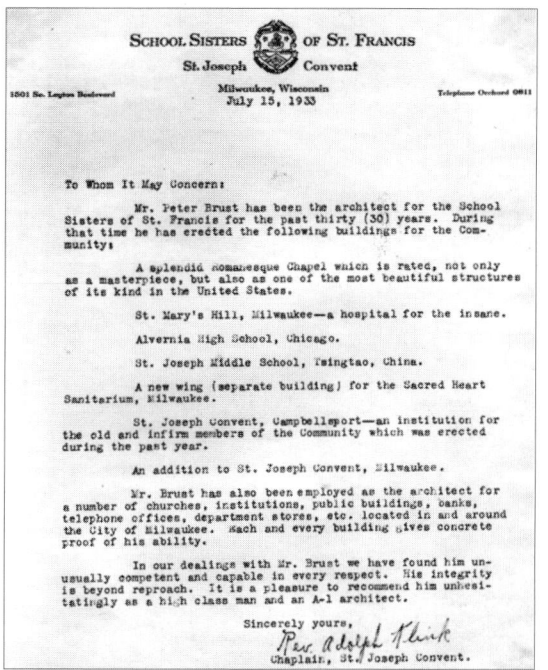

Reverend Adolph Klink, the chaplain for St. Joseph's Convent of the Sacred Heart Sanitarium, wrote this letter of recommendation in 1933. The letter was probably used by Peter Brust as a reference for employment applications. This letter is from the archives of Zimmerman Design Group.

Sacred Heart Sanitarium, Continued

Above, an historical photograph of the south wing addition

Above, a contemporary view of the south wing addition

Left, an aerial view of the former Sacred Heart Sanitarium shows the various additions that were done to the original 1893 building. The original building is located at the front of the building and contains the tower.

All of these buildings were razed except for the center wing addition and the south wing addition. Those two buildings are pictured in the top left section of the photograph.

St. Mary's Hill Hospital & St. Mary's Hill Nurses' Home
Milwaukee, Wisconsin

In the early 1900s, very little was known or understood about the disease of mental illness. When Sacred Heart Sanitarium began to attract patients suffering from mental disease, Mother Alexia saw a need for a separate mental health facility to treat the mentally ill and those with alcoholic and drug addictions. Mother Alexia purchased five acres of land two blocks west of the sanitarium at 1445 South 32nd Street. The site was on a hill, and the mental health hospital was appropriately named St. Mary's Hill Hospital.

The architectural firm of Brust, Philipp & Heimerl was hired in 1911 to design the new Colonial Revival style hospital building. It was completed in May 1912 with ten patients being admitted when the doors opened. There were six Sisters who cared for the patients, along with seven physicians including Dr. S. S. Stack and Dr. WenGlesky. At that time, hydrotherapy was the usual method of treatment in the care of the mentally ill. Wet sheet packs, tub baths, and salt glows made from sea salt and natural oils were used. However, the chief source of treatment at St. Mary's Hill was the Sisters themselves who tirelessly treated the patients with tender-loving care. Over the first fifty years of the hospital's existence, 16,000 patients were cared for at the facility.

In 1920, the architectural firm of Brust & Philipp designed the Colonial Revival style Nurses' Home, pictured at right, located at 1512 North 32nd Street, across the street from St. Mary's Hill Hospital. This home's location made it convenient for the nursing staff who worked at the hospital. The total cost of the residence was almost $28,000.

The hospital program of education and services was moved in 1974 to the St. Mary's Hospital building on North Lake Drive on Milwaukee's northeast side. The St. Mary's Hill building on South 32nd Street was renamed Maryhill in 1975, and it was used as a residence for retired Sisters who needed health care. In 1994, the property was sold to the Milwaukee Public Schools to house Grandview School, a charter school. Grandview serves students from ninth through twelfth grade.

St. Mary's Hill Hospital

St. Mary's Hill Nurses' Home

Public Commissions

South Side Library
Milwaukee, Wisconsin

The first attempt to establish a circulating English-language library on Milwaukee's south side was in 1858. Interested parties met in the basement of Hanover Street Congregation, at Hanover Street and Park Street, and the group formed the South Side Literacy Society. Hanover Street is now known as South 3rd Street and Park Street is now West Bruce Street. Books were purchased as well as a piano, and meetings were held in the Hanover church basement. Unfortunately, the society disbanded a few years later. The piano was donated to the church, and the books were given to C.A. Sontag Bookstore at South Reed Street and West Florida Street. Reed Street is now known as South 2nd Street. Sontag loaned the books to patrons for a user fee until all of the books disappeared.

On April 17, 1901, a legislative bill was passed allowing schools to present free lectures. This law encouraged the formation of literary societies, such as the South Side Association, which was formed on December 15, 1894, at a meeting held at South Division High School. After viewing a number of sites, the association decided to rent a space measuring 17 feet by 39 feet in the lower corridor of the high school. After purchasing a glass partition for seventy-five dollars, tables for eight dollars each, and wall cases for thirty dollars each, the library was open for business in March 1895.

Two years later, the association moved their library to South 2nd Street and West Greenfield Avenue. This library was considered a branch of the Milwaukee Central Public Library. However, south side citizens constantly called on the City Library Board to build them a new library building. According to George C. Nuesse in his book *Founding of the South Side Library*, the city promised that such a building would be built when the city treasury could afford it.

In 1903, the association moved their library back to South Division High School.

After fourteen years of promises from the City Library Board, the City of Milwaukee finally built a south side library at 931 West Madison Street. The beautiful, Classical Revival style library was designed by the architectural firm of Brust & Philipp and was completed in 1917. The total cost of the building was $47,000. The building's rusticated stone foundation was half exposed, and the upper exterior wall was comprised of brick. Four sets of Ionic columns were evenly spaced across the front entrance with a long flight of steps. This style was highly popular with libraries at the time. This classical style represented a number of things to the American public, including freedom, democracy, education, and opportunity. The purpose of the South Side Library, according to George C. Nuesse, was to encourage the studious and books lovers.

The library closed in 1966 when the Forest Home Library opened. In 1984, the building was turned over to the Milwaukee County, and the building now houses the Southside Neighborhood Service Center. The building was placed on the National Register of Historic Homes in 1988.

Top, the Gothic style vaulted ceiling gave the impression of spanning space.

Above, the main entrance of the library featured a Gothic style vaulted ceiling.

Right, the interior of the South Side Library featured arched doorways and leaded-glass skylights.

Milwaukee Detention House & Juvenile Court
Milwaukee, Wisconsin

The Milwaukee County Detention House and Juvenile Court Building, located at North 11th Street and West Galena Street, was erected in 1909 and was designed by the architectural firm of Brust & Philipp. The three-story brick building was done in the Classical Revival style and was erected at a total cost of $100,000. The first floor housed the Juvenile Court and Probation Departments, and the two upper floors were used for the detention of children. The kitchen was located on the top floor and contained three dining rooms that separated boys, girls, and staff. The upper floors also contained two classrooms, one for boys and one for girls. Segregation of the sexes was rigidly maintained. For recreation, there was an outdoor playground area, and for rainy days, there was a recreation room in the basement.

For sleeping quarters, the children slept in individual rooms, although there were a few small dormitories. For the boys, there were fifteen sleeping rooms on the second floor and eight on the third floor. There were nine sleeping rooms on the second floor and six on the third floor for the girls. There was no living or recreation areas on the second and third floors, so much of the children's free time was spent in their sleeping rooms. The building was erected with a planned capacity of sixty-five children, providing forty-three beds for boys and twenty-two for girls.

However, by 1946 the facility housed 110 children. Overcrowding was relieved by the removal of the dependent and neglected children to a county facility in the city of Wauwatosa. The removal of these children allowed for living rooms to be made available to the children on both the second and third floors.

Along with the growing numbers of children in need of detention, the building was also found to be inadequate for the court and probation department office needs. In 1946, suggestions were made to move the facility to county-owned land in Wauwatosa. The Detention Home and Juvenile Court were eventually moved to the Wauwatosa site, which provided room for a larger building and outdoor recreation space. The building designed by Brust & Philipp was later razed.

Washington Park Zoo
Milwaukee, Wisconsin

In 1892, the Washington Park Zoo was established in Washington Park, located at 1859 North 40th Street. At that time, Washington Park was governed by the City of Milwaukee. The zoo began with a small mammal and bird display, but by 1902, the zoo covered twenty-three acres and housed 800 animals.

The creation of zoological societies began in the 1890s, and these societies supported zoos by purchasing animals and conducting fundraisers. The mission of a zoo, according to the zoological societies, was to both educate and entertain the public.

The architectural firm of Brust & Philipp was commissioned in 1907 to design the first of three small animal buildings included in Washington Park's long-range plan. The Romanesque Revival style building measured 75 feet by 150 feet and was constructed of re-enforced concrete. The building was considered fireproof. Inside the small animal house, a sixteen-foot wide center space provided an area for zoo visitors, and it also contained a four-foot passage in front of the cages separating the visitors from the cages. This four-foot space also provided a space for zoo personnel. The cages were eight feet deep with a four-foot service passage behind the cages that allowed the animal handlers to service the animals. This service passage also allowed the animals to move from their cages to the outside summer cages. A description found in the 1907 *Annual Report of the Park Commission of the City of Milwaukee* reads as follows:

> Arrangement is made so the animal can stay in the inside or outside or pass in or out across the back passage by means of transfer cages that can be raised up out of the way when not in use. A small receiving cage runs along a track in the service passage, by which animals are received into the building and easily placed in any cage along the service passage.[1]

A mechanical ventilating apparatus run by electric motors forced warm fresh air into the building above the cages, moving the impure air to the bottom. The basement contained the heating and ventilating equipment, along with storage areas and feed rooms. The total cost of the building was $41,424.

The zoo commissioners, including Alfred C. Clas, the former employer of Peter Brust and Richard Philipp, inspected the building. According to the 1907 *Annual Report of the Park Commission of the City of Milwaukee*, the firm of Brust & Philipp was paid the second and final payment of $578 for their

design. Most likely the total architectural fee came to over $1,000.

The zoo became part of the Milwaukee County Park Commission in 1937 and grew to thirty-eight acres. The arrangement with the County Park Commission gave the zoo the resources it needed to grow and prosper. In 1958, the zoo moved to its present location at 10001 West Blue Mound Road in Milwaukee. Currently, the 200 acres of beautiful parkland is home to over 350 species of animals.

[1] *Annual Report of the Park Commissions of the City of Milwaukee*. (Milwaukee, Wisconsin: City of Milwaukee, 1907), 21-22.

Lake Park Children's Pavilion
Milwaukee, Wisconsin

Lake Park is situated on Milwaukee's northeast side at 3233 East Kenwood Boulevard. The City of Milwaukee Park Commission decided in 1906 to erect a new children's play area. According to the 1906 *Annual Report of the Park Commissioners of the City of Milwaukee*, "The children received considerable attention here and a new building at the playground was erected and a full assortment of apparatus installed."[1]

The new play area measured 115 feet by 225 feet space and was situated in a meadow near the old concert grove. Sand was hauled from the Lake Michigan beach, and the entire ground was graded and shaped. An oval gravel wading pool, measuring 68 feet by 91 feet, was added along with swings, a teeter tooter, a merry-go-round, a slide, and sand boxes. A jet drinking fountain with a cement base rounded out the play area. The cost of the new play area was $1,340.

The architectural firm of Brust & Philipp was commissioned to design the pavilion for the children's area. The building, measuring 30 feet by 70 feet, featured porches and was fitted with sanitary conveniences. The total cost of the pavilion was $3,779. According to the 1906 *Annual Report*, the firm of Brust & Philipp was paid $117 for their design work.

The pavilion designed by Brust & Philipp was later razed. Lake Park is now part of the Milwaukee County Park System.

[1] *Annual Report of the Park Commissioners of the City of Milwaukee.* (1906), 10.

In the background of this postcard image, the Lake Park Children's Pavilion can be seen. The playground equipment can be seen in front of the pavilion.

Left and right, two postcard images show children enjoying the playground equipment installed near the new Children's Pavilion.

Mitchell Park Pavilion
Milwaukee, Wisconsin

Mitchell Park is located at 2200 West Pierce Street in Milwaukee. Originally, this location was the site of a Native American village and was later the site of Jacques Vieau's trading post.

A legislative bill was passed in 1889 that permitted the City of Milwaukee to purchase land for park purposes. Land for Mitchell Park was one of the first plots purchased by the City under this bill. John Landrum Mitchell sold twenty-five acres of land to the City of Milwaukee for Mitchell Park and then donated another five acres. The park was named for Mitchell who was a State Senator from 1872 to 1873 and 1875 to 1878. Mitchell was the son of railroad magnate and financier, Alexander Mitchell. General "Billy" Mitchell, for whom the Mitchell International Airport is named, was the son of John Landrum Mitchell and the grandson of Alexander Mitchell.

By 1905, Mitchell Park had gained a reputation for its beautiful flowerbeds and was called the flower park of Milwaukee. Mitchell Park boasted more flowers than all of the other parks combined. The sunken garden was created in 1905, and in 1906, five more acres were annexed for the park so that more propagating houses could be built. These propagating houses provided flowers for Mitchell Park and for all the other parks in Milwaukee.

The old lake in the Mitchell Park was drained in 1907 and replaced by a concert grove with a new bandstand. A new lake was excavated, and a new pavilion was built on the northwest side of the lake. The architectural firm of Brust & Philipp was commissioned to design this new pavilion. The firm received a fee of $343; the total cost of the building was $10,515.

The new two-story building served boaters in summer and skaters in winter. The new pavilion was not completed in time for the 1907 summer season, but it was ready for the ice skaters that winter.

The upper floor contained restrooms and refreshment facilities. The frame building featured roughcast cement walls. The installation of drinking bubblers on the playground was innovative for the time. The bubblers did away with the old buckets and dippers.

In 1948, the 1907 pavilion was razed to make room for a new pavilion. The 1948 pavilion remains at the same location. Mitchell Park is now part of the Milwaukee County Park System.

Top, a 1907 photograph of Mitchell Park Pavilion

Above and left, postcard images of the 1907 Mitchell Park Pavilion

Memorials, 1906-1926

Kilbourn Park
World War I Memorial
Milwaukee, Wisconsin

Kilbourn Park is located on a twenty-nine-acre site that was donated to the City of Milwaukee by one of Milwaukee's founding fathers, Byron Kilbourn. The park is located at East North Avenue and North Bremen Street on Milwaukee's northeast side. The park is presently owned by the City of Milwaukee and is part of the Milwaukee Water Works Department. In 1873, a reservoir was built on the site with a twenty-one-million gallon water storage tank buried within a steep hill.

Located on the south-facing slope of the hill, just off of East North Avenue and Bremen Street, is a obelisk monument dedicated to the soldiers who fought in World War I. Funds for the monument were raised by the Sixth and Thirteenth Ward Memorial Association headed by August A. Moths. The unveiling took place on Veteran's Day, November 11, 1920. The architectural firm of Brust & Philipp designed the memorial, and sculptor John R. Menge Jr. executed it. The monument is done in White River granite with emblems of each branch of military service engraved on it. The front of the memorial reads, "In commemoration of those who fought for the freedom of the world 1917-1919." The back reads, "Erected by the citizens of the 6th and 13th wards." Enclosed in the base of the monument is a small brass box that contains the names of the former servicemen.

The City of Milwaukee plans to reconstruct Kilbourn Park. According to the City's plans, the obelisk memorial designed by Brust & Philipp will not be disturbed by the reconstruction. Some clean-up and clearing of vegetation around the obelisk will make it more visible from the street.

Above, a close-up view of the top back portion of the monument shows an insignia for a branch of the military service. Each side of the monument depicts a different branch of military service.

Left, a full front view of the Kilbourn Memorial

Social and Recreation, 1906-1926

Knights of Columbus
Milwaukee, Wisconsin

The Milwaukee branch of the Knights of Columbus, a Catholic social organization, was founded on June 24, 1900, when fifty-one men met at the Alhambra Hotel at North 4th Street and West Wisconsin Avenue, to establish such an organization. A second council, the Pere Marquette Council, was formed in 1904. Peter Brust was a member of this second council. Between 1900 and 1910, both councils held their meetings at various locations in the city; however, both councils sought a permanent meeting site with a clubhouse. A clubhouse committee was formed and Peter Brust served on it. A decision was made in 1910 to purchase the former Plankinton Mansion at North 15th Street and West Wisconsin Avenue.

John Plankinton built the mansion in 1890 as a wedding present for his daughter, Elizabeth. Elizabeth was engaged to an artist, but when the wedding failed to happen, she chose not to live in the mansion. It was said that Elizabeth walked through the house just once after it was built, never to return again. The mansion remained empty until 1897, at which time, it was sold to the Johnston family of the Johnston Confectionery & Cracker Company.

When the mansion was purchased in 1910, the Knights of Columbus formed the Columbus Institute. This corporation was formed to handle the purchase of the mansion and its upkeep, since the organization's bylaws prevented the club from taking on debt.

In 1915, the architectural firm of Brust & Philipp was commissioned to design an addition to the old mansion that would contain a ballroom, an auditorium, bowling alleys, a gymnasium, and a swimming pool. The addition measured 93 feet by 144 feet and cost $110,000. The firm also did some remodeling work on the old mansion in 1926. The address of the mansion was changed to 1492 West Wisconsin Avenue in honor of the organization's patron, Christopher Columbus, and his discovery of America in 1492. A newspaper article (*Catholic Citizen*, April 11, 1916) stated that the clubhouse was the best-equipped building of its kind in the West. "Wherever possible, the work in each line was awarded to a member of the council, and it speaks well of their respective firms for having taken the contract for same at a very reasonable figure." The article went on to describe the new addition. The new ballroom measured 66 feet by 84 feet and featured an interior finish of white and gold. An elabo-

The old Plankinton Mansion is on the left, and the Brust & Philipp additions, designed for the Knights of Columbus, are to the rear.

rately decorated ladies parlor and dressing room were located near the ballroom. There was a new barroom in the addition, but only soft drinks were served there, since no intoxicating beverages were allowed at the club. Membership at this time was nearly 1,500.

The Knights of Columbus occupied the mansion until 1978. The mansion was then razed for the expansion of Marquette University.

The City Club
Milwaukee, Wisconsin

The City Club, a private civic organization, was founded in January 1909 and was incorporated in May 1911. Its members were citizens who wanted to promote ways to better the economic, civic, and social conditions in the city of Milwaukee and Milwaukee County. The Club provided speakers who addressed city problems. Committees were formed to study concerns such as charter issues, public health, city planning, and the public utilities. The first meeting location for the City Club was at 91 Wisconsin Avenue, but by 1919, the growing organization needed larger accommodations. The group relocated to the third floor of the Merrill building at 211 Grand Avenue, now known as West Wisconsin Avenue. The architectural firm of Brust & Philipp was commissioned to remodel the suite; the remodel featured a lounge and restaurant area.

By 1922, the City Club grew to over 2,000 members. However, by the 1960s, enrollment was declining dramatically. The last meeting took place on December 12, 1975. Many of the members also belonged to the Citizen's Governmental Research Bureau, a separate private organization, founded in 1913. The Citizen's Governmental Research Bureau group is now known as the Public Policy Foundation, Inc.

The majority of the Merrill building was razed in 1931 and replaced with

Top left, the lounge area of the City Club featured a beamed ceiling, a medieval style fireplace, arched doorways, and leaded-glass windows.

Left, the restaurant area featured Arts and Crafts style furniture and leaded-glass skylights.

the Kresge building; however, the back section, which housed the City Club, is still in its original location. Recently, the building was incorporated into a newly constructed building at the southwest corner of North 2nd Street and West Wisconsin Avenue. The photographs on the next page show an historical photograph and a recent photograph of the exterior of the former City Club.

Above, the Gothic style vault-like ceilings gave the hallway a dramatic and more spacious look. The ceiling also features leaded glass skylights.

Left, another view of the lounge area

The City Club, Continued

Above left, an historical photograph taken in the 1920s shows the North 2nd Street side of the Merrill Block building between West Wisconsin Avenue and West Michigan Street. The marquee of a theater is visible at the bottom left portion of this picture. The City Club was headquartered on the top floor of this building where the three arched windows are located. A theater auditorium was probably located below the City Club quarters.

Right, this is a contemporary photograph of the above historical photograph. Alterations were made, but the arched windows where the City Club was located still remain. This building is all that is left of the Merrill Block building that was razed in 1931 to make way for the Kresge building. This section of the Merrill building that housed the City Club was incorporated into a newly constructed building at the southwest corner of North 2nd Street and West Wisconsin Avenue.

Theaters, 1906-1926

Saxe Park Theater
Waukesha, Wisconsin

The Milwaukee Movie Kings, Thomas and John Saxe, hired the architectural firm of Brust & Philipp to design the Saxe Park Theater at 717 Grand Avenue in Waukesha. The brothers opened almost 100 theaters between the years 1902 and 1927. A nickelodeon theater was their first in 1902. They opened the Princess Theater on North 3rd Street, and they went on to own several other theaters, including the Alhambra, Wisconsin, Oriental, Garfield, Plaza, Tower, and the Uptown. The Saxe brothers were originally in the sign painting business. Their company painted placards for a small nickelodeon on North 2nd Street and West Wisconsin Avenue; however, when the theater owner could not pay his advertising bill, the Saxe brothers agreed to take the theater as payment. Soon after, the brothers opened another theater, the Theater Delight, on Wisconsin Avenue.

The architectural firm of Brust & Philipp designed the Park Theater in the city of Waukesha in 1920. The total cost was $105,000. At the time, Waukesha boasted four other theaters that were competing for the film-viewing public, so it was surprising that another theater would be built. However, the Park Theater was much more grand in design and more modern than the others. The theater was also more discriminate in what they staged there; only the best of the theatrical and film productions were shown.

Later, L. F. Thurwachter attempted to organize three of the five theaters so that all three could survive. With the reorganization, the Park Theater was still Waukesha's most prestigious theater, being the most elegant and expensive. The Auditorium Theater was renamed the Avon, nicknamed the "Blood Bucket," and showed westerns and adventure movies. The Empire Theater was renamed the Pix and was considered a budget movie theater showing second-run movies at inexpensive prices.

The Park Theater closed in 1987 due to low attendance and was guttered by an arson fire the next year. It was not rebuilt.

Thomas Saxe

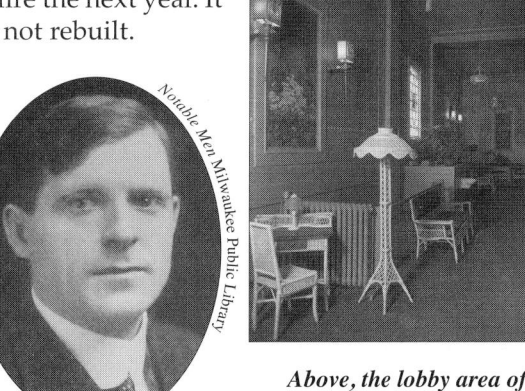

Above, the lobby area of the theater

Below, the theater interior

Tower Theater
Milwaukee, Wisconsin

The Saxe brothers, Thomas and John, sought architectural designs in 1924 for the new Tower Theater that they planned to build at 747 North 27th Street in Milwaukee. Four years earlier, the architectural firm of Brust & Philipp designed the Park Theater for the Saxe brothers in Waukesha. [See previous page.] The firm of Brust & Philipp submitted a drawing for the new Tower Theater; however, the Saxe brothers selected the architectural firm of Dick & Bauer to design the theater.

The new Tower Theater, completed in 1926, was a sister theater to the Oriental Theater on North Farwell Avenue. The Tower Theater was quite snazzy, with costumed ushers who showed customers to their seats and offered to brush their coats.

The drawing submitted by Brust & Philipp for the new Tower Theater on North 27th Street

Merrill Theater
Milwaukee, Wisconsin

The Merrill Theater was in the Merrill Block Building, located at 211 Grand Avenue, later known as West Wisconsin Avenue. In the early part of the twentieth century, Milwaukee's Grand Avenue was lined with movie theaters. Across the street from the Merrill Theater was the Butterfly Theater, and west of the Merrill Theater was the Majestic Theater.

In 1915, the architectural firm of Brust & Philipp designed the Merrill Theater, which was located on the lower floor of the ca. 1893 Merrill Building. The Merrill Theater seated 1,298 moviegoers. The theater was closed in 1930 due to competition from larger movie theaters and due to the fact that the Merrill Building was slated to be demolished. The Kresge building is now located on that site.

Chapter 6
Planned Communities Brust & Philipp, 1906-1926

Kohler Village: A Planned Community, Kohler, Wisconsin

John Michael Kohler immigrated to America in 1854 with his parents. After spending his youth in Minnesota, Kohler moved to Sheboygan, Wisconsin. Kohler partnered with Charles Silberzath and purchased the Union Iron and Steel Foundry from Jacob Vollrath in 1873. The business manufactured agricultural implements, ornamental iron pieces, hitching posts, cemetery crosses, urns, and settees. After selling the business, Vollrath went on to manufacture porcelain enamelware. [See Page 151 for the Vollrath Company commission.]

Kohler bought out Silberzath in 1879 and became sole owner of the business. Unfortunately, the foundry was destroyed by fire in 1880, but it was rebuilt. At this time, Kohler took on two new partners, Herman Hayssen and John Stehn, and the company became known as the Sheboygan Agricultural Works. The company employed thirty men, and by 1881, the company had grossed nearly $40,000 in sales. Along with his business interests, John Michael Kohler took an interest in civic affairs and served on the Sheboygan County Board of Supervisors from 1880 to 1881. He was also elected to the Sheboygan's City Council in 1882 and later became mayor of Sheboygan in 1892, serving one term.

In regards to his personal life, Kohler suffered a series of tragedies. The first was the death of his young wife, Lillie Vollrath Kohler, at the age of thirty-five in 1882. She left behind three children--Robert, Walter, and Carl--ranging in age from two to eleven years old. Lillie's sister, Mary Riess, along with her husband, John, and their daughter, Minnie, moved into the Kohler home to help with the children. Lillie's other sister, Millie, also helped with the children. On November 3, 1887, John Michael Kohler married Millie Vollrath. This union produced one son, Herbert, in 1891.

When his company was incorporated in 1888 as Kohler, Hayssen & Stehan Manufacturing Company, 125 men were employed at the company. Looking ahead to expansion, in 1897, the company purchased land southwest of Sheboygan in the village of Riverside. The first building was erected in 1898. When the old Sheboygan plant closed in 1899, part of the production unit was moved to the Riverside location.

John Michael Kohler died in November 1900, and in December of that same year, the new plant in Riverside was destroyed by fire. The business returned to its old site in Sheboygan while the factory was being rebuilt. John's son, Robert, became president and the company was renamed J.M. Kohler Sons Company.

Another tragedy struck the Kohler family when Robert's brother, Carl, accidentally drank carbolic acid and

The Kohler Company Administration Building

died within an hour. Then, in 1905, Millie found Robert dead in bed at the age of thirty-six. Robert's brother, thirty-year-old Walter, took over as company president. He held that position until his death in 1940. Walter's half-brother, Herbert, succeeded him as president.

When the village of Riverside was incorporated in 1912, residents voted to rename the village Kohler Village. By this time, Walter was president, and being a practical idealist, he envisioned the village as an attractive, well-organized village. He took seriously the job of creating such a city, a city that would give workers a chance of home ownership and a fine home life.

By definition, a company town is a town created around a single company. The company provides goods and services to employees such as housing, stores, medical services, and police and fire protection. When factories located in remote areas, it was necessary to create such a community environment in order to attract workers to the remote location. However, the term, company town, often conjured up visions of a dirty, unsightly looking town. Walter Kohler did not want such a town. Rather, he envisioned a planned community that would give his workers the best life possible.

Walter Kohler traveled to northern Europe in 1913 with architect Richard Philipp to study the planned communities there. Kohler and Philipp visited Berlin, Germany, to see the housing developments connected with the Krupp Steel Works, and they also visited the planned community of Port Sun-

In the background of this interior photograph the of Kohler Company Administration Building, one of the Arthur Covey murals can be seen. Also note the Gothic vaulted ceiling and Moravian tile floor.

The Kohler Engineering Building designed by Brust & Philipp in the 1920s

light in England that was developed in 1887. They met with Sir Ebenezer Howard who was known as the father of the European garden city movement. Sir Howard felt the congestion and slum conditions in the great cities would not have existed if the cities had planned for growth.

Upon his return home, Kohler hired the Olmstead Brothers of Boston to create a plan for the layout of the village, including the layout of the parks, streets, residential areas, and commercial buildings. This plan was to be a fifty-year plan that would shape the future growth of the village. The Olmstead Brothers were well known for their work on Central Park in New York City. The Olmstead's also designed Lake Park in Milwaukee. The architectural firm of Brust & Philipp was hired to design the Kohler Village commercial buildings, the school, and the individual homes.

Homes were started west of the Kohler factory in 1917, and in 1923, homes were developed south of the factory. The homes ranged from one-story bungalows to two-story colonials and split-levels. They were all in the New England and English Cottage style. There was a range of building materials including wood, brick, and stucco. The overall plan was to keep the green space that surrounded the village. Kohler sold lots and homes to employees with no profit going to the company. Town guidelines were set up to designate what materials and styles could be chosen. The Kohler Building & Loan Association was owned by employees, which allowed employees of Kohler to purchase homes at a reasonable cost.

Walter, like his father, was civic minded. Walter served as governor of Wisconsin from 1929 to 1931, but he lost a re-election bid in 1932, probably due to his support of Herbert Hoover in his presidential re-election bid. His son, Walter

Above, the Kohler Showroom building was also known as the "Stores Building." The Tudor Revival style exterior was done in red brick and stucco with peaked gables, arched doorways and a red tiled roof. The north end of this building presently houses the Kohler Design Center.

Below, two interior photographs of the Kohler Showroom building

Above and below, examples of Kohler Village homes

Jr., served as Wisconsin governor for three terms.

The centerpiece of Kohler Village was the American Club. This impressive Tudor Gothic style building, designed by the firm of Brust & Philipp, served as a dormitory for single male workers, mostly immigrants. The exterior was done in red brick, with a very steeply-pitched roof done in gray-green and purple Vermont slate. At the dedication of the American Club on June 23, 1918, Walter J. Kohler Jr. expressed hope that by naming the building the American Club, it would influence the immigrant workers to seek American citizenship. Indeed, immigrants were influenced. Due to the English language and citizenship classes offered by the Kohler Company, over 600 immigrants filed their first papers for citizenship between 1919 and 1930.

Located a short walk from the Kohler factory, the American Club offered room and board, which included a nice room, a bath with a shower, dining room privileges, and laundry services, all for a reasonable price of twenty-nine dollars to thirty-five dollars

A street scene showing homes designed by Brust & Philipp in Kohler Village

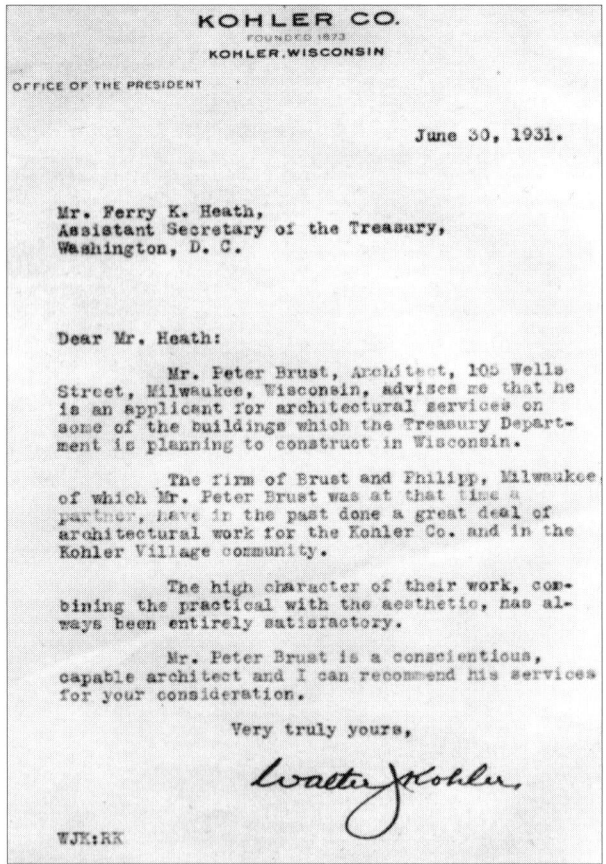

Walter J. Kohler wrote this letter of recommendation in 1931 on the behalf of Peter Brust. Brust was applying for a commission to design a U.S. Post Office building in Wisconsin. No records were found to show that Brust was awarded the commission. This letter came from the archives of the Zimmerman Design Group.

per month. By 1925, the club housed as many as 250 men and served more than 200 meals daily. The dining room, located in the south wing, was also open to the public. Bowling alleys provided recreation at fifteen cents a game.

In 1924, a north wing was added in a design complimentary of the original building. Soldiers returning from World War II found a temporary home at the American Club. Also, accommodations were made available on the first floor, in the east wing for single female teachers, secretaries, and switchboard operators.

As time went on, there were less immigrant workers, and more workers were buying homes in the village. As time went on, physical changes were made to the Club. The dining hall was renamed the Wisconsin Room, and it was used for Kohler Company functions. A large cafeteria replaced the original bowling alleys. By the 1970s, there were only seventy residents at the American Club.

The American Club was placed on the National Register of Historic Places in 1978. The American Club was featured in two periodicals. One feature was in the April 1925 issue of *Architecture,* and the second feature was in *American Architect* on October 2, 1982.

The Administration Building was also designed by the firm of Brust & Philipp and was completed in 1925 at a total cost of $332,218. The entrance vestibule measured 40 feet by 60 feet and contained seven large mural panels done by Arthur Covey of New York. Each panel depicted men working in the factory. One is called "Pouring a Mould" and another is "Tapping a Cupola." The floor was done in Moravian tiles surrounded by a border of blue Grueby tiles.

Chapter 6 – Brust & Philipp–Planned Communities 1906-1926

The American Club that housed immigrant male workers

This drawing was found in the Brust & Philipp records and it was labeled "north entrance to the Kohler Shops." According to other Brust & Philipp records, the firm designed a remodel for the building around 1917.

The Kohler public school, designed by the firm of Brust & Philipp, is still in use.

Combined Locks, Wisconsin: A Planned Community

The Combined Locks Village Hall and Fire Department designed by Brust & Philipp in 1924

The Van Nortwick family purchased a building site in 1889 on the south shore of the Fox River in Wisconsin. On this site they founded the Combined Locks Paper Company and the former farming community surrounding the new paper mill was then transformed into a mill town. The town and paper mill were named for the nearby boat locks along the Fox River. These boat locks were the highest of all the locks on the Fox River navigational system. On navigable waterways, a lock is a device for raising or lowering boats between stretches of water that are at different levels. A boat lock is a short section of a river or a canal with gates at each end and a mechanism for letting water flow in and out.

The new mill was the first on the Fox River to use ground up wood for pulp. Along with the new paper mill, the paper company built a dam. The company built small homes near the mill for workers, as well as a wooden boarding house that housed unmarried male workers. Most of the homes were located along the winding road on the east end of the current village boundaries.

The idea of incorporation for the town began in 1916. Incorporation would allow the village to keep the taxes paid by the mill within the village and to extinguish the attempts by other nearby communities to annex the village. Before the incorporation papers were filed, Albert E. McMahan did a land survey. The survey included the entire 810 acres---705 acres of land and 105 acres of water. A census was also done and showed 467 total residents in seventy-four families. On election day, there were fifty-four votes for incorporation and two against. With such overwhelming support, incorporation papers were officially submitted to the Secretary of

State in Madison on August 5, 1920. On August 16, 1920, another election was held in the old school house. This election would select the new village officers. Daniel J. Ryan, a farmer by profession, became the first village president and county board supervisor. Other elected officials were as follows: F.C. Schuler, a tavern keeper, as clerk; Herman Janssen, a mill pipe fitter, as treasurer; William Van Zeeland, real estate agent, as assessor; A.L. Beatz, a mill foreman, as constable; and Chris Kindler, a finishing room mill worker, as Justice of the Peace.

Soon after, the village board purchased four acres of land to be used for public buildings. The village board continued to hold their Tuesday monthly meetings at the old school house until 1924, at which time a new village hall was built. An ordinance created the fire department in 1922. The fire chief, appointed by the village board, served a term of one year. The fire chief, in turn, appointed volunteer firefighters. That same year, a fire truck was purchased for $11,250.

The architectural firm of Brust & Philipp was commissioned in 1924 to design a building that would house the fire department and the village hall. An historical photograph on the previous page shows the new fire department and village hall shortly after it was completed. The building is now used as a private home.

The firm of Brust & Philipp was hired in 1923 to design a store and office building for the Combined Locks Paper Company. The store and office building were later razed. No photographs or architectural plans could be located.

In 1923, three stock drawings were used for company houses that were built in the Combined Locks community near the Combined Locks Paper Company. As the paper company expanded, land was needed, and these houses were razed to make way for the expansion. The three stock drawings are pictured on this page and the following page.

The firm was also hired to design homes for the mill workers. Three stock plans were drawn up, and potential homeowners chose from one of the three plans. Unfortunately, as the mill expanded land was needed and these homes were razed to make way for the expansion.

The firm of Brust & Philipp was also involved in the establishment of the first Catholic church in Combined Locks. The first church was housed in the old fire-damaged school, which was purchased by the Combined Locks Paper Company from the school board for $5,000. The firm of Brust & Philipp remodeled the old school for St. Paul's Catholic Church. Along with designing the remodel of the church, the firm of Brust & Philipp designed a new rectory. [See Page 104 for the St. Paul's Catholic Church of Combined Locks commission.]

In 2002, the population of Combined Locks was 2,552 residents. The Combined Locks Paper Company is presently called Combined Paper Mills, Inc., and is still located at the original site.

Chapter 7
Peter Brust, Architect, 1927-1937

Residential Commissions, 1927-1937

Brumdner Building

The architectural firm of Brust & Philipp dissolved in 1926. There are probably a number of reasons for the ending of this partnership. One highly probable reason was that Peter Brust wanted to set up an independent practice in preparation for his sons joining him after they completed architectural school. For whatever reason, Peter Brust and Richard Philipp were practicing independently by 1927. Peter Brust renamed his company Peter Brust, Architect, and moved his practice to the Brumdner Building at 135 West Wells Street in downtown Milwaukee. Philipp remained at the old Broadway Street address for a time; he later moved to the Monroe Building at 756 North Milwaukee Streets. Peter Brust continued to accept religious, commercial, and public commissions. When his sons joined his firm on a full-time basis in 1938, the firm's name changed to Brust & Brust. The firm name Brust & Brust first appeared in the Milwaukee city directory in 1938.

Charles Billenness House
Shorewood, Wisconsin

Peter Brust designed the Charles Billenness house and garage in 1937. The Tudor Revival style home with a brown brick exterior is located at 4354 North Marlborough Avenue in Shorewood. Billenness was a purchase agent and building superintendent for Ed Schuster & Company.

Ecclesiastical Commissions 1927-1937

St. Mary of the Angels Chapel
St. John's for the Deaf
St. Francis, Wisconsin

Peter Brust was hired in 1930 to design an outdoor chapel on the grounds of St. John's for the Deaf Institute at 3680 South Kinnickinnic Avenue. The chapel was known by two names. St. Mary of the Angels Chapel was engraved on the facade, but the Sisters of St. Francis of Assisi, who worked at the school, called it the Portiuncula Chapel. The St. Mary of the Angels Chapel was a replica of the sixteenth century Portiuncula Chapel in Assisi, Italy. It was said that Saint Francis of Assisi used the Assisi chapel for prayer.

The St. Mary of the Angels Chapel was built at the edge of the woods behind St. John's for the Deaf. The exterior was covered in fieldstone gathered from the surrounding area. Tile trimmed the entrance and brick surrounded the windows. The Spanish tile roof, art-glass windows, and oak door made for a beautiful exterior. The altar and altar floor were from Venice. The stone floor in the nave was from Sweden. The four stained-glass windows of the chapel were from Munich and bore the likenesses of Saints Francis, Claire, Louis, and Elizabeth. The interior also featured recessed Stations of the Cross and oak pews. The chapel sat twelve people with a capacity of twenty. The total cost of the chapel was $1,991.

The chapel was built to commemorate the Golden Sacerdotal Jubilee of Monsignor Gerend who, beginning in 1895, headed St. John's for the Deaf Institute for many years.

Peter Brust won a design award, the First Medal in the Ecclesiastical Group, from the Wisconsin Association of Architects (WAA) in 1933. A bronze plaque recognizing this award was placed on the inside of the chapel on the back wall behind the door.

Sister Margaret Peters who taught many years at St. John's remembers well the 100th year anniversary of the school celebrated in 1976. A mass was said on the entrance steps of the St. Mary's Chapel. Neighbors were invited.

Unfortunately, the chapel was razed in the 1980s after St. John's for the Deaf was sold. Because of its poor condition, the chapel could not be moved. It is not known if the bronze plaque was salvaged during demolition. [See Page 132-133 for St. John's for the Deaf Institute commission.]

The award plaque

St. Florian's Catholic Church
West Milwaukee, Wisconsin

By August 1923, St. Florian's Congregation, located on South 45th Street in West Milwaukee, was growing and needed a new church building to replace the church/school/parish hall combination building. [See Pages 110-111 for St. Florian's combination church commission.] Money was tight so a long-term building plan was devised. In 1923, the architectural firm of Brust & Philipp was hired to design the new church. The first phase of the building plan was to build the church basement, which would serve as a church until the upper church could be built.

Peter Brust was commissioned in 1937 to design the upper church. The new church was completed in 1938 and was dedicated on January 26, 1939, with Archbishop Stritch officiating. The exterior was done in the Romanesque Revival style with a reddish-colored brick and Indiana limestone trim. A rose stained-glass window graced the main entrance, and two bell towers topped with gilded crosses flanked the entrance. St. Florian's is still an active parish and is located at 1233 South 45th Street.

The 1939 upper church was built upon the basement church that served the congregation from 1923 to 1938.

Chapter 7 – Peter Brust, Architect 1927-1937

St. Joseph's Convent Retirement Home Campbellsport, Wisconsin

The School Sisters of St. Francis of Layton Boulevard in Milwaukee commissioned the architectural firm of Brust & Philipp in 1932 to design St. Joseph's Convent Retirement Home. The building, located at 526 Mill Street in Campbellsport, was to become home to the old and infirm members of their religious order. The building is located on the property where the Sisters established their first residence in 1874, before establishing their Motherhouse in Milwaukee. [See Pages 115-121 for School Sisters of St. Francis commissions.]

Peter Brust donated two sanctuary windows for the chapel of the new retirement home. According to a letter to Peter Brust from Mother Stanislaus, the Sisters enrolled the Peter Brust family in the order's League of Perpetual Adoration. The Brust family was remembered in the hourly prayers of the Sisters.[See accompanying letter.]

Peter Brust returned to the Campbellsport convent to design a new barn and a chicken house in January 1941. The former barn and chicken house were destroyed in a fire in November 1940. Luckily, the fire didn't spread to the convent, considering that the barn and chicken house were very close to the convent buildings. After the fire, the farm animals were temporarily housed at nearby farms, and the old morgue was fixed up to house chickens.

The St. Joseph's Convent Retirement Home is still at its original location. The total cost of the building was $281,658. Many retired Sisters find the location a quiet place to reside.

The chapel in St. Joseph's Convent Retirement Home

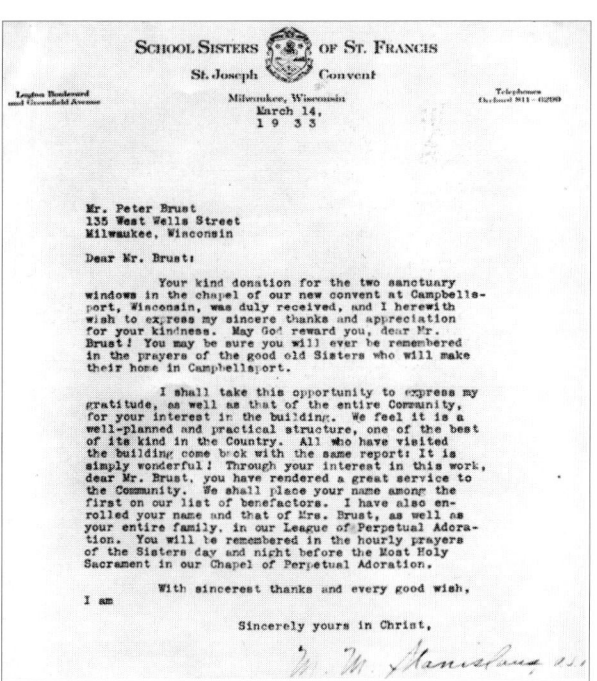

Mother Superior Stanislaus wrote this thank you letter in 1933 to Peter Brust. The letter is from the archives of the Zimmerman Design Group.

217

St. Joseph's Middle School Tsingtao, China

The Apostolic Vicar of Shantung, China, asked the order of the School Sisters of St. Francis in 1924 to staff a secondary school that would serve young women from affluent Chinese families. Milwaukee's Archbishop Messmer strongly disapproved of Mother Alfons' request to open such a school. The Archbishop's disapproval was based on his belief that the Sisters' religious order was not founded to take on foreign missions but rather to teach German immigrant children in America. Because of the archbishop's disapproval, Mother Alfons decided not to pursue the matter.

However, by 1929, due to Archbishop Messmer's advancing age, Bishop Weig was handling some of the Archbishop's work. Weig accepted the School Sisters second request to open the school in China. The first members of the School Sisters of St. Francis arrived in Tsingtao, China, in 1931. The School Sisters commissioned Peter Brust to design a new school for them. The school, St. Joseph Middle School, opened in September of that year with seventy-five students in grades seven, eight, and nine, with a high school opening the following year. The curriculum of the school was the same as any American high school. The chief purpose of the mission was an evangelical one. Over 75 percent of the students were Confucians and Buddhist.

Problems arose for the mission in 1937 when the Japanese invaded China. The U.S. Consul advised the Sisters to leave because their safety could not be guaranteed. The Sisters did not want to leave, and they requested permission from Mother Stanislaus to obey the bishop rather than the Consul. The Sisters did remain in Tsingtao; however, their schools did not reopen in fall of that year. In January of 1938, the Japanese took over Tsingtao, and they gave the Sisters permission to reopen the middle school.

When the United States declared war on Japan in 1942, the Japanese Navy took over the middle school, interned the Sisters, and reopened the school as a Japanese school. When the war ended, St. Joseph's reopened but under meager conditions. After the war, the Sisters tried to weather the conflict between the Nationalist and the Communist factions. Mother Superior Corona wanted the Sisters to return to America, but the Sisters wanted to remain in China.

By January 1949, the situation in China was grave for the missionaries. The Communists were winning the conflict. Mother Corona called all of the Sisters home except for Sister Adolph and Sister George who was of Chinese birth. Finally, these two Sisters were forced to flee the country. In June 1949, they left China on a troop ship; however, they needed to dress in Nationalist uniforms because the ship was only for soldiers. The St. Joseph Middle School for Girls fell into the hands of the communists and became a government school.

Above, St. Joseph's Middle School in Tsingtao, China

Below, a group photograph of boarding students

Ernest G. Miller Memorial Gymnasium, St. Francis Seminary
St. Francis, Wisconsin

The Ernest G. Miller Memorial Gymnasium, located on the grounds of the St. Francis Seminary on South Lake Drive, was named for the brewing mogul and philanthropist known for his support of a number of Catholic organizations. It was a bequest from the estate of Ernest G. Miller that made the building of the seminary gymnasium possible. Miller was the oldest son of Frederick J. Miller, founder of the Miller Brewing Company.

The Ernest G. Miller Gymnasium was built for the philosophical theological departments of the seminary. Done in the Colonial Revival style, the exterior was done in buff-colored brick with cut-stone trim. The building cost $147,249.

The basement housed four bowling alleys, a handball court, a smoking and card room, twelve showers, and a lavatory. The gym on the main floor measured 60 feet by 90 feet. The building also featured a billiard room, and the second floor contained living quarters for professors. The building was dedicated on February 2, 1927. The Ernest G. Miller Memorial Gymnasium is still part of the seminary complex.

An interior photograph of the gym area

The exterior of the Miller Gymnasium looks very similar to the drawing submitted by the firm of Brust & Philipp for the Salzmann Library built in 1907. [See Page 134 for the Salzmann Library commission.] The drawing was not used for the library, but was probably used for the gymnasium project.

Pio Nono/Salzmann Hall
St. Francis, Wisconsin

The interest in a Catholic normal school began in the 1850s when Archbishop Henni expressed interest in a teacher's seminary. In the 1860s, Joseph Salzmann was gathering funds from various fundraising endeavors, and by 1871, he raised enough money to build the Holy Family Normal School. A music program was added a few years later, as there was a need for trained organists and choirmasters.

Mother Caroline of the School Sisters of Notre Dame said the following about the Normal School:

> There were nineteen young men enrolled on the day of dedication. The purpose of the normal school was to train lay teachers for the Catholic parochial schools of the country, as there were at that time few Sisters who were permitted to teach boys beyond the age of ten or twelve years.

Pio Nono College was formed as a separate program and shared the Holy Family building. Mother Caroline goes on to say the following about Pio Nono:

> To the normal school, Father Salzmann added the Pio Nono College. The latter was to provide for such young men as wished to become neither priests nor teachers, but who desired to remain under Catholic influence and in a Catholic atmosphere, while fitting themselves for a business career. For the use of the students of Pio Nono College, Father Salzmann requisitioned part of the normal school building, which was sufficiently large to house both departments, at least for some years to come.[1]

The Holy Family Normal School closed in 1922. However, increasing high school enrollment at Pio Nono necessitated the building of Salzmann Hall in 1931. Salzmann Hall, designed by Peter Brust in the Tudor Gothic Revival style, housed administration offices, a chapel, a library, study halls, and dormitories.

With the growth of Pio Nono, it was necessary to separate the college-level major seminary from the minor seminary. In 1941, due to increased enrollment, the Pio Nono campus was turned into a minor seminary and renamed the St. Francis Minor Seminary. Salzmann Hall housed the four-year high school and the first two years of college. The minor seminary continued at this site until 1963, at which time De Sales Preparatory Seminary opened. [See Page 244 for the De Sales College commission.] In 1965, Salzmann Hall reopened as Pio Nono High School.

The firm of Brust & Brust went on to design an addition for Pio Nono in 1969. [See Page 239 for the Pio Nono High School addition.] Presently, the Salzmann Hall building is part of the Thomas More High School campus at 2601 East Morgan Avenue.

[1] *Mother Caroline and The School Sisters of Notre Dame in North America* (St. Louis: Woodward & Tiernan Company, 1928), 213-214.

Chapter 7 – Peter Brust, Architect 1927-1937

Business Commissions, 1927-1937

Pressed Steel Tank, West Allis, Wisconsin

The Pressed Steel Tank Company was incorporated in 1902, shortly after the owners of Pressed Steel Tank acquired the Seamless Structural Company of Milwaukee. The Pressed Steel Tank Company plant was located on South 3rd Street in Milwaukee. When the company needed to expand, it bought the Milwaukee Electric Company in West Allis at South 66th Street and West Greenfield Avenue. The Pressed Steel Tank Company moved to that site in 1906 and produced high-pressure and low-pressure cylinders and containers for the distribution of compressed gases, chemicals, and liquids. In 1936, Peter Brust designed an office building for the company at 1445 South 66th Street. The total cost of the building was $56,469. The company is still located at that site.

This drawing, done sometime between 1907 and 1917, is of the Pressed Steel Tank complex.

Wisconsin Telephone Company
Milwaukee, Wisconsin

The telephone was invented by Alexander Graham Bell in 1876 and was introduced to Milwaukee by Professor Charles H. Haskins in 1879. Haskins established the first central office in a rear room on the fourth floor of a building at 411 Broadway in downtown Milwaukee. The Haskins Company represented the American Bell Company in Milwaukee and was incorporated as the Wisconsin Telephone Company in 1882, establishing local exchanges throughout the state. Haskins served as president of the company until 1888. In 1890, Wisconsin Telephone Company acquired 5,972 subscribers and 4,223 miles of lines. The company obtained the exclusive license for Wisconsin from the American Bell Telephone Company for use of their telephonic apparatus and instruments.

The telephone was a luxury in the 1880s. Highly populated areas were first to receive phone service; many rural areas and small towns obtained no phone service at all. In 1893, with the expiration of the telephone patents held by American Bell, independent telephone companies sprung up across the state. These independent telephone companies were in competition with the Wisconsin Telephone Company and its parent company, American Bell. Drawbacks to subscribing with an independent telephone company were the inability to call people who subscribed to another telephone service and the lack of long-distance telephone service, since American Bell owned all the toll lines.

The Railroad Commission of Wisconsin was given in 1907 the right by state government to regulate the utility. As a result, American Bell and the independent telephone companies began to work together to connect the phone lines throughout the state. When the Wisconsin Telephone Company began buying up many of the smaller companies, they became dominant in larger towns and cities. By 1909, there were over 76,000 subscribers and over 30,000 miles of lines. However, the smaller towns and rural areas were still left to the smaller telephone companies.

During the years of 1930 to 1932, Peter Brust was commissioned by Wisconsin Telephone to design two buildings. One was located at 26th and West Lapham Street on Milwaukee's south side; it was called the Mitchell Building and cost a total of $146,525. The firm of Brust & Brust went on to design an addition in 1946 at a total cost of $251,986. The Mitchell Building is still being used by the phone company, now known as AT&T.

From 1931 to 1932, Peter Brust was commissioned to design the Hilltop Office at North 35th Street and West Wells Street at a total cost of $96,275. Brust & Brust later designed an addition in 1946 for the Hilltop office at a total cost of $235,761. The Hilltop office has since been razed.

The Mitchell Telephone Company Office

The Hilltop Telephone Company Office

Chapter 8
Brust & Brust, 1938-1946

> ## The architectural firm of Peter Brust, Architect becomes Brust & Brust when sons, Paul and John, join the firm.

Paul J. Brust was born on July 18, 1905, to Peter and Olga Brust and was raised with two siblings, John and Catherine, in the family home at 851 North 29th Street in Milwaukee. Paul attended Marquette University Engineering School from 1924 to 1925. From 1925 to 1928, he attended the University of Notre Dame and earned a Bachelor of Science degree in 1928. Paul attended Columbia University in New York in 1928 and 1929 and also toured Europe in 1929. He was registered by the State of Wisconsin as an architect in 1933.

During college summer vacations from 1924 to 1929, Paul worked in his father's architectural firm as a draftsman and designer. In 1929, after college graduation, he began working for his father full time. At times, Paul left his father's employment to work for government agencies. In 1933, Paul worked for the Federal Architectural Office at the Treasury Department in Washington, D.C., and in 1935, he worked as a Federal Housing Authority inspector.

Paul Brust and Mary McGinn married on May 18, 1936. They raised eight children: Barbara, Peter, Charlotte, Daniel, Richard, William, Janet, and Marian.

After his stint at the Federal Housing Authority, Paul returned to his father's architectural firm in 1936 and worked at the firm's office in the Brumdner Building at 135 West Wells Street in downtown Milwaukee. According to the Milwaukee city directories, the name of the firm changed from Peter Brust, Architect, to Brust & Brust, Architects, in 1938. Paul left his father's firm in 1943 to work for a government agency, spending the next two years in the United States Engineer's Office in Milwaukee's Federal Building.

It was in 1945 that Paul rejoined his father and brother, John, in the Brust & Brust firm. When Peter Brust died in 1946, his sons moved the business to a new location at 1212 West Wisconsin Avenue. Two other architects, William Schneider, AIA, and Charles Valentine, AIA, worked at the firm of Brust & Brust.

Many people thought of Paul as an authority on church design. In a newspaper article (*Milwaukee Journal*, March 17, 1964), Paul said the following about church design:

> All architecture is influenced by climate, social background, availability of materials and philosophy of the times. Church architecture should reflect the building's purpose, irrespective of the design and building material.
>
> Sometimes, new ideas are adopted that are startling and unusual and modern, but the result is disappointing because they don't reflect the use to which the building is being put. Churches are erected to the glory of God. Certainly, God would expect us to use good judgment in determining the cost. To achieve a perfect balance is difficult, because people do not think clearly about it.

By 1948, the firm of Brust & Brust employed the following staff positions: two principal architects, one additional architect, one engineer superintendent, two senior draftsmen, one junior draftsman, one secretary, and one stenographer. During the 1950s, the company was commissioned to design many Catholic Churches in the Milwaukee area.

Dave Zimmerman joined the firm in 1973, and the name was changed to Brust-Zimmerman, Architects. The firm relocated to 3333 North Mayfair Road in Wauwatosa, Wisconsin.

Paul retired in 1978. Paul's wife, Mary, had previously died in 1958, and he had remarried two years later to Ruth Gaunt. In retirement, he kept active by doing volunteer work such as helping to redesign the East Troy Library. He also gave architectural advice to the Lake Beulah Yacht Club and to St. James Catholic Church in Mukwonago, Wisconsin. Paul died at the age of eighty-eight of congestive heart failure. In Paul's obituary (*Milwaukee Journal*, April 3, 1994), his wife, Ruth, said the following about her husband: "He was deeply religious and just so kind. He was low key but just so highly respected by everybody."

John Joseph Brust was born to Peter and Olga Brust on April 21, 1912. John spent his childhood in the family home at 851 North 29th Street. After he graduating from Marquette University High School, he attended Notre Dame University. John did not do well in his first year at Notre Dame, and his father threatened to cut him off if he didn't buckle down and learn. John took heed, graduating with a degree in architectural engineering in 1934. John was awarded the Henry Adams award that allowed him to spend the next school year in graduate school at the Catholic University in Washington, D.C. During the summer of 1935, John traveled to Europe to study Italian architecture with a Notre Dame professor, John E. Miller, and three former classmates. The party sailed from New York to Porta Delgado, the Azores, and then on to Lisbon, Gibraltar, and Algiers, with Sicily and Naples next on their agenda. According to John, the highlight of his trip was an audience with the pope. The last port of call was France, with the party returning to New York at the end of August.

John went to work for the Quartermaster General's office of the Army in Washington, D.C., in September 1935, but in April 1936, he left the office to enter the Prix de Rome competition. The Prix de Rome, a scholarship for studying art in Italy, was awarded every four years to a talented young art student. John earned second place, Honorable Mention. He went on to win a scholarship to Yale University for the 1937 school year. This scholarship would have allowed him to finish his graduate work.

Courtesy of Patsy Brust Koenings

During school breaks, John worked for his father as a draftsman. Peter appeared to be somewhat impatient with John, expressing his wish that John would get down to work. In Peter's estimation, John had experienced enough book learning. Well, John appeared not to be ready to settle down to work just yet. In the summer of 1937, Father Coda, a historian from the Catholic University, asked John to accompany him to Mexico for two months. John ended up doing most of the driving but thoroughly enjoyed the experience.

When John returned home around Labor Day, he was greeted with a letter informing him that he was awarded the Langley Fellowship to study architecture in northern Europe. The American Institute of Architects was the sponsor of this award. John needed to make a decision: Would he attend graduate school on scholarship at Yale or take the Langley Fellowship? The Langley Fellowship won out and he was off to Europe. Upon his return from Europe on December 23, 1937, John joined his father in the architectural firm of Brust & Brust. According to John's son, David, his father never completed his master's degree. Apparently, John completed everything for his graduate degree except a speaking knowledge of the German language.

Sometime during 1937, probably in the months before his trip to Mexico, John was sent to Beaver Dam, Wisconsin, for fieldwork. At this time, his father's firm was working on St. Joseph's Hospital in Beaver Dam. The hospital was completed in 1938: [See Page 233 for St. Joseph's Hospital.]

After the competition of the Beaver Dam Hospital, John was sent to work at the Office of the State Architect in La Crosse, Wisconsin. He was to supervise the building of Morris Hall, a new Model School for the State Teachers' College designed by the firm of Brust & Brust. [See Page 234 for the La Crosse Teachers' College commission.] Upon his return from La Crosse in April 1940, John married Marjorie Twohig on May 4, 1940.

It was during 1939 that John was registered by the State of Wisconsin as an architect. He was made a member of the American Institute of Architects in 1940, and for a time, John served as director, vice president, and president of the Wisconsin chapter.

John worked at the A. O. Smith Company in 1940 as an air service inspector. The company made propellers for the Hurricane Fighter. He then worked in construction administration at the Great Lakes Naval Station. From 1944 to 1945, John was the architectural planner for the Milwaukee Redevelopment Commission Authority. The City of Milwaukee Common Council created the position in order to prepare a postwar planning program.

After leaving the Redevelopment Commission position, John returned to his father's architectural office. From 1945 to 1973, John was working exclusively with the firm of Brust & Brust. During those years, the firm was located on the eighth floor of the Brumdner Building in downtown Milwaukee. In 1946, the firm relocated to 1212 West Wisconsin Avenue.

John and several other architects were featured in a newspaper article (*Milwaukee Journal*, August 13, 1949) that explored the idea that old church architecture, with its tall spires and detailed ornamentation, was being cast aside for more modern designs. In the article, John expressed his belief that contemporary church design was a result of the economic conditions of the era. He felt that labor unions eliminated the "priceless craftsmen" and designs were now governed by the dollar. John said the following in regards to the economic factors governing modern church design:

> Modern church design has been forced on us with high priced labor and low priced materials, and we should make the most of it by design.
>
> There is a great deal of beauty in the styles of the past and on today's architects falls the responsibility of creating a beauty in the contemporary style. It is a challenge that can be met with clients who have courage and a conviction.

John and Marjorie raised eleven children: David, Robert, Catherine, Mary, Patricia, Elizabeth, Michael, James, Jane, Judith, and Ruth. John said that he was determined to accept whatever family the Lord would give them. For John it was important to provide for his children a good family life, religious training, and education. The couple bought a farm in Slinger in 1950 and later razed the old farmhouse to replace it with a home designed by John. Marjorie died on January 17, 1971.

The firm of Brust & Brust became Brust-Zimmerman when David Zimmerman became president of the company in 1973. Company officers were as follows: John Brust, board chairman; Paul Brust, principal; and David Brust, John's son, secretary-treasurer. The offices were relocated to 3333 North Mayfair Road in Wauwatosa. John retired from the firm in April 1976 and moved with his second wife, Betsy, to Naples, Florida. In Naples, John worked for the architectural firm of Forsythe Humphrey & Associates from 1984 to 1987. John died in Naples, Florida, on November 29, 1995.

Residences, 1938-1946

John Brust House
Wauwatosa, Wisconsin

John Brust designed a home for his family in 1946 at 2370 North 100th Street in Wauwatosa. The house was done in the International Modern Style. This style was introduced to America in the late 1920s and the early 1930s at the time that John and Paul Brust were attending architectural school. The International Modern Style, by definition, features clean lines and right angles. The style also features abundant glass for natural light and open spaces with living areas flowing into each other. The International Modern Style blends the house into its natural outdoor surroundings by having low-pitched gables or hip roofs, such as the one on the Brust house.

According to archival records, the total cost of the house was $35,000.

Frank J. Krehla
Fox Point, Wisconsin

Frank J. Krehla hired the architectural firm of Brust & Brust in 1943 to design a home at 8203 North Gray Log Lane in Fox Point. The exterior of the house was done in Lannon stone. The steep roof reflected the Tudor Revival style.

Frank's father, Frank A. Krehla founded the United American Fire Insurance Company of Milwaukee in 1900. His son, Frank J., was also a partner in the company, Krehla & Krehla. During World War I, Frank J. enlisted and served as a corporal in Battery A 120th Regiment of Artillery. He was discharged in 1919, and he then returned to Krehla & Krehla.

F. Edward Baldus
Whitefish Bay, Wisconsin

F. Edward Baldus hired the architectural firm of Brust & Brust in 1942 to design a Colonial style home at 5311 North Shoreland Avenue in Whitefish Bay. Baldus worked as a plumber for the Joseph Wittig Company.

Edward Conrad Schmitt House
Wauwatosa, Wisconsin

The architectural firm of Brust & Brust was hired in 1940 to design a house for Edward Schmitt in the Wauwatosa subdivision of Ravenwood. It is unclear if the house was ever built. The address given on the architectural drawings, 141 North 85th Street, does not exist in the Ravenwood subdivision.

Conrad Schmitt, the founder of Conrad Schmitt Studios, came to America in 1881. He was apprenticed as a church decorator to fresco painter, Louis Loeffler, and received instruction from muralist Jan Sukaczynski. In 1891, Conrad established a decorating business in Wausau, Wisconsin, but in 1895, he returned to Milwaukee to join Edmund H. Bodden and Conrad A. Brock-Mueller in the founding of Associated Artists. This firm specialized in providing murals for churches and concert houses. Around 1909, Conrad founded his own business, Conrad Schmitt Company, located at 223 North 2nd Avenue in Milwaukee. By 1914, Conrad designed a new studio at 1707 Grand Avenue, now known as Wisconsin Avenue. The studio's name was changed in 1925 to Conrad Schmitt Studio. In 1930, the studio moved to 1729 North Prospect Avenue on Milwaukee's northeast side.

All three sons, Rupert, Alphonse, and Edward, worked for the company. Rupert, the oldest, succeeded as president and moved the company to 1325 South 43rd in West Allis. In 1940, brother Edward, who worked for his father since 1922, became vice president. Around 1950, the company presidency passed to Bernard O. Gruenke. In the 1970s, the company was relocated to New Berlin, Wisconsin.

Wisconsin Architectural Archive

Ecclesiastical Commissions, 1938-1946

Christ King Congregation Chapel
Wauwatosa, Wisconsin

Christ King Congregation, located at 2604 North Swan Boulevard, was established on October 13, 1939. Before a church was built, masses were held at Mount Mary College. When the Christ King school was completed in April 1940, church services were held on the second floor of the school.

In 1945, $50,000 was raised to pay off the school building mortgage, thus enabling the church to finance an expansion. This expansion included a basement chapel that was designed by the architectural firm of Brust & Brust and was completed in June 1947. This long-term building plan was similar to the St. Florian's Catholic Church in West Milwaukee. [See Page 216 for the St. Florian's commission.] The basement church served the parish until enough money became available to build the upper church.

The firm of Brust & Brust drew up plans for the new upper church in 1953, and it was dedicated in December 1956. The total cost of the church was $111,000.

Above, the basement church is to the left of the school building.

Left, the upper church was dedicated in 1956.

Chile church

The architectural firm of Brust & Brust was hired in 1945 to design a church for Reverend Thomas Walsh in Temuco, Chile. Unfortunately, no information about this church or Reverend Walsh was located. However, the drawing of the church is located at the Wisconsin Architectural Archives.

St. John Evangelist Catholic Church
Kohler, Wisconsin

When the planned community of Kohler Village was in development, there were no provisions made for the establishment of churches. Walter Kohler, developed and nurtured the development of Kohler Village, and he definitely didn't want churches in the village. But as time went on, the number of Catholic residents increased, and with that increase came a demand for a church. Kohler decided that he had to relent and support the building of a church.

Money was raised by the usual church fundraising functions, with $23,000 raised by 1936. In order to make the church a reality, a loan for $40,000 was acquired. Kohler was willing to donate the land and all the plumbing and heating fixtures. He also assisted the parish in obtaining a low-interest loan, and he donated the landscaping services of the Olmstead Brothers. However, one big disagreement existed between the Archbishop Stritch and Kohler. The Archbishop wanted a school connected with the church, but Kohler didn't want one. After much discussion, Archbishop Stritch relented and no Catholic school was built.

Archbishop Stritch assigned Father John J. Carroll as the first pastor, and it was under Father Carroll that the new church was constructed. Known for their superior workmanship and honest use of materials, the architectural firm of Brust & Brust was given the commission to design the new church. The former firm of Brust & Philipp designed Kohler Village, so the firm was familiar with the village plan. It was very important to Kohler that the church blend into the village architecture, so the style selected was the English Rural Gothic style.

The church exterior, clad in variegated brick, featured a tower surrounding the east wing that held the sacristy and the acolytes' room. The church measured 115 feet by 45 feet and sat 400 parishioners. Interior architectural features included grillwork of ornamental iron that enclosed the area reserved for the choir and the organ console. The church also contained a side chapel with an altar over which was a mural designed by Milwaukee stained-glass artist, Carl Van Treeck. The central figure in the mural, the Virgin Mary, held baby Jesus and was surrounded by a modern day priest, nun, and children. In the background of the mural was the Kohler factory depicting men going home after work.

The church was dedicated on September 22, 1940. The final cost of the church and rectory was $67,748. The church is still located at 600 Green Tree Road.

Hospitals, 1938-1946

Sisters of St. Agnes
Fond du Lac, Wisconsin

When newly established parishes in Wisconsin completed their first church building, thoughts of a church school were not far behind. In 1845, Father Rehrl began establishing churches and church schools east of Lake Winnebago. Rehrl's slogan was: build a school and it will build a church. However, establishing a church school was difficult since religious teachers were scarce.

Father Rehrl returned to his native Austria in 1852 to recruit a religious order that would be willing to settle in Fond du Lac and teach in the Catholic schools. Unfortunately, he had no luck with the established orders. In 1855, during a visit to Rome, Father Rehrl prayed at the tomb of St. Agnes and was inspired to establish an American sisterhood by recruiting among his catechists in Wisconsin. After returning to Wisconsin that same year, Bishop Henni assigned Rehrl to the town of Barton on the west bend of the Milwaukee River. This area is now part of the city of West Bend, Wisconsin.

Gertrude Rehberg was recruited by Father Rehrl in 1858, and she took her vows as Sister Clara on August 12, 1858. The order was called Agnes Sisters, but the order's patron saint was the Virgin Mary. In 1863, the second Sister to join the order was Marie Hazotte who was from Detroit. She took the name of Sister Agnes. Father Rehrl sensed in Sister Agnes leadership ability, and she was elected Mother Superior in 1864 at the age of seventeen. She took her first vows the same day that she was elected Mother Superior.

By 1870, the convent at Barton proved too small for the growing order, Father Rehrl approved of purchasing property in Fond du Lac for a new convent. Mother Agnes and twenty-six Sisters moved to Fond du Lac. The remaining three Sisters arrived later on August 1, 1870, by lumber wagon with the baggage and the convent dog, Barney. The convent on East Division Street included a house, a stable, and a barn, with the barn eventually used as a dormitory annex. By 1880, the order grew to 100 Sisters with schools in Wisconsin, Ohio, Indiana, Michigan, Pennsylvania, Kansas, and Texas.

Sacred Heart Chapel
St. Agnes Hospital
Fond du Lac, Wisconsin

The order moved into hospital work in 1896 and erected St. Agnes Hospital. Mother Agnes purchased 410 acres of land east of Fond du Lac for $31,000. In 1901, John Boyle opened a sanitarium on part of this land and then later gave the building to the Sisters. The sanitarium was converted in 1909 to a school, St. Mary's Springs Academy, which still exists today.

In 1905, after Mother Agnes died, Antonia Schmitz became the Mother Superior. She opened St. Agnes School of Nursing in 1910, and it went on to educate hundreds of nurses. When Marian College of Fond du Lac was established, it took over from St. Agnes School of Nursing the role of educating nurses.

The firm of Brust & Brust was commissioned in 1942 to design a chapel addition for St. Agnes Hospital. According to Brust & Brust records, the chapel addition cost a total of $389,747. Wisconsin stained-glass artist, Carl Van Treeck, designed stained-glass windows for the Sacred Heart Chapel and four stained-glass windows for its two side chapels. The colors used for the chapel were light and iridescent. Archbishop Kiley dedicated the new chapel.

The chapel was razed in 2005. Two of the stained-glass windows from the sanctuary were re-installed in the new St. Agnes Convent build-

These two Van Treeck designed stained-glass windows were moved from the chapel to the new motherhouse.

ing at 320 County Road K in Fond du Lac. One window depicts St. Agnes and the other depicts St. Clare of Assisi. The other stained-glass windows were also removed during the demolition of the chapel and remain in storage. These stained-glass windows, according to order's archivist, Sister Jeremy Quinn, will be incorporated into the new hospital chapel that will be completed soon.

The hospital is now known as Agnesian Health Care, and it is still sponsored by the Congregation of the Sisters of St. Agnes. It is located at 430 East Division Street in Fond du Lac.

St. Clare Hospital
Monroe, Wisconsin

In 1937, physicians and surgeons were unhappy with what they felt were inadequate facilities at Deaconess Hospital in Monroe. Dr. William G. Bear and Dr. C.E. Baumle were instrumental in purchasing ten lots at the corner of 22nd Avenue and 5th Street on which to build a new hospital. Reverend Eugene McCollow of St. Victor's Church suggested that the two physicians ask the Congregation of St. Agnes in Fond du Lac to start a hospital in Monroe. The religious order was already operating several hospitals at the time. Archbishop Stritch gave Mother Aloysia of St. Agnes permission to build a hospital, and St. Clare Hospital was opened on August 1, 1939. The firm of Brust & Brust designed the new hospital. St. Clare Hospital, located at 515 22nd Avenue, opened with a staff of four Sisters, thirteen doctors, twenty-three registered nurses, and thirty other employees. The hospital contained sixty beds and eighteen bassinets.

Additions were soon needed, especially after Deaconess Hospital closed its doors. The original building designed by Brust & Brust is still part of the complex. Branch locations opened in seven communities in southern Wisconsin and northern Illinois. St. Clare Hospital and the Monroe Clinic merged in 1992, and an addition was built adjacent to the hospital to house a clinic. Today, the multi-specialty system offers the services of eighty providers, twenty-four-hour emergency services, home care, and hospice services.

The interior of the Sacred Heart Chapel addition

Top inset, a close-up photograph of the altar

St. Claire Hospital in Monroe, Wisconsin

St. Joseph's Hospital
Beaver Dam, Wisconsin

In the early 1900s, hospitals in many towns were located in houses. When many of these small-house hospitals closed, residents were forced to travel to other towns to seek medical care. Residents of Beaver Dam traveled to Columbus, Fond du Lac, and Milwaukee. To remedy the problem, the Beaver Dam community invited religious and hospital groups to consider building a hospital facility in their town.

For many years, Catholics in Beaver Dam dreamed of a Catholic hospital, so Father Rohner of St. Peter's Catholic Church in Beaver Dam formed a committee to encourage such a project. The parish of St. Peter's contributed $16,000 for a Catholic hospital. The School Sisters of St. Francis of Milwaukee agreed to build a hospital, and as a result, St. Joseph's Hospital on University Avenue opened in 1938.

The architectural firm of Brust & Brust designed the hospital, including the hospital chapel, at a total cost of $274,041. Father Rohner celebrated the first mass in the hospital chapel. There were sixty beds, with patient care provided by the Sisters who were experienced in the field of nursing. Fundraising efforts by the community were rewarded when the hospital was able to expand, providing more and improved services. In 1958, a new five-story addition was completed at a cost of $2 million.

Due to the need to improve medical care for the community of Beaver Dam, it was decided in 1972 to integrate medical services with the consolidation of St. Joseph's Hospital and Lutheran Deaconess Hospital of Beaver Dam. [See Page 176 for the Lutheran Deaconess Hospital commission.] The consolidation resulted in Beaver Dam Community Hospitals, a non-denominational institution.

Beaver Dam Community Hospital, at 707 South University Avenue, recently moved into a new $65 million building. Plans are to demolish the 1938 building designed by Brust & Brust.

The interior of the chapel designed by Brust & Brust for the St. Joseph's Hospital at Beaver Dam

Public Buildings, 1938-1946

La Crosse Teachers College
La Crosse, Wisconsin

Normal schools were first established in Wisconsin in the 1890s as a place to train teachers. The normal schools adopted the idea of a laboratory school in which student teachers would observe lessons being taught by master teachers. The student teacher would then conduct a lesson and be observed and evaluated by the master teacher. The Main Hall of the La Crosse Normal School housed the laboratory school and was completed in 1909. By the early 1930s, it was decided that a new building was needed to house just the laboratory school, also known as the Model School.

The architectural firm of Brust & Brust provided the design plans in 1938. John Brust was sent to supervise the work site and to keep peace among the many trades working on the building. The faculty and students moved into their new building at 1725 State Street in 1940. The total cost of the building was over $300,000.

The Art Deco style building was of reinforced concrete and fireproof brick construction. There were four entrances and collapsible security gates for when the auditorium was used after school. The floors in the corridors were terrazzo. The first floor of the building contained a gymnasium, a home economics room, a photography dark room, and an auditorium that sat 366 people. The second floor housed the classrooms, offices, library, and the music room. An unusual feature was a two-way sound system connecting the school director's office with classrooms. In 1953, the building was called the Campus School, but in 1973, it was renamed Thomas Morris Hall for the first regent of University of Wisconsin-La Crosse.

By the 1960s, enrollment in the teacher-training program was high, making it difficult to accommodate all of the practice teachers in the Model School. As a result, student teachers turned to the public schools for their observations and student teaching. Questions arose regarding the necessity of the Model School and the cost of such a program. As a result of these and other issues, the Model School was closed in 1973.

The building designed by Brust & Brust is still in use by the university. It was placed on the National Register of Historic Places.

Murphy Library, University of Wisconsin-La Crosse

Chapter 9
The Legacy, 1947-2006

Peter Brust dies at the age of 76

Peter Brust died on June 22, 1946, at Milwaukee's St. Luke's Hospital after a short illness. He was seventy-six years old. Peter was survived by his second wife, Charlotte; a daughter, Catherine Haboeck of Appleton; and two sons, John and Paul Brust of the Milwaukee area.

Peter's illustrious architectural career spanned over forty years, and he was recognized for his accomplishments in *Who Was Who in America 1943-1955*. As a member of a number of professional organizations, he often served in leadership roles. Peter was elected to the Wisconsin Chapter of the American Institute of Architects in 1911, and in 1923, he was made a Fellow in the American Institute of Architects. He was the fourth Wisconsin man to receive that honor in the state of Wisconsin. Peter went on to serve as the regional director of the American Institute of Architects, representing the districts of Illinois and Wisconsin. He served for two terms as president of the Wisconsin Chapter of the AIA and was president of the Milwaukee Chapter for two years.

Along with his interest in the professional architectural organizations, Peter's contemporaries knew him as a driven civic leader. It was said that for the last twenty years of his life, he was a member of virtually every important civic and state committee. Because of an aversion to publicity, Peter did not seek public office. Rather, he hoped that by serving on civic committees, he would make the city, the county, and the state a better place to live.

Peter was a member of the first County Park Commission established in 1906 and served on the Commission until 1940. The commission consisted of five appointed men, one member being Charles Whitnall for whom Whitnall Park was named.

Peter was also part of the committee that helped formulate the first Milwaukee building code, and from 1920 to 1938, he served as chairman of the Milwaukee Board of Appeals on Zoning. For twenty-nine years he served on the State Building Code Advisory Committee, serving as its chairman for sixteen years.

Other committees Peter served on were the following: the Art Commission, the Lakefront Planning Committee, Mayor Hoan's Advisory Council, and the Planning Committee of the City Club. Peter was also a member of the Allied Architects of Milwaukee, a group of Milwaukee architects who designed the Park Lawn Housing Project in 1935. Lastly, Peter served on the State Board of Examiners of Professional Architects and Engineers from 1938 until his death in 1946. Without doubt, Peter Brust, in his dedication to civic affairs, did leave the city, the county, and the state a better place to live.

Courtesy of Patsy Brust Koenings

Chapter 9 – The Legacy 1947-2006

Brust & Brust, Ecclesiastical Commissions, 1947 to 1972

A recent photograph of Kiley Hall

Heiss Hall, built as a student resident hall, is now Claire Hall, a residence for retired St. Francis of Assisi Sisters.

Heiss Hall, Ranier Hall and Kiley Hall
St. Francis, Wisconsin

As enrollment increased at St. Francis Major Seminary in the 1940s, the issue of expansion was being discussed at the Milwaukee Archdiocese. By 1949, Archbishop Kiley was planning new buildings for the St. Francis Seminary, located at 3257 South Lake Drive. A new power plant was first on the agenda, and the architectural firm of Brust & Brust was hired in 1949 to design it; the total cost was $206,000. Next, the architectural firm was hired in 1954 to draw up plans for a new residence hall with a chapel. Ground was broken on the Feast of St. Francis, January 29, 1955. The residence hall was christened Heiss Hall, named for the late Archbishop Michael Heiss and was dedicated on September 11, 1956. A new dining hall, Kiley Hall, named for Archbishop Kiley, was completed in 1958 and was located adjacent to Heiss Hall.

The firm of Brust & Brust was also commissioned in 1954 to remodel the old gymnasium building into an auditorium

237

The old Red Gym was built in 1910 and was remodeled in 1954 to house Rainer Hall. No records are available, but it is possible that Peter Brust designed the old Red Gym building.

Ranier Hall, the new drama and music facility, was located next to the old infirmary building. The site is now a parking lot.

The power plant designed by Brust & Brust in 1949

and music hall. Named for Monsignor Joseph Rainer, the remodel cost $341,000. The new drama music facility, Rainer Hall, was located between the new Heiss Hall and the old infirmary building. The music/drama building was later razed, and the site is now a parking lot.

To some observers, the architecture of Kiley, Heiss, and Ranier Halls were shockingly different from the other more Classical-style buildings on the seminary property. One highly vocal critic described the new residence hall as a four-story basement.

The total cost of the seminary expansion was almost $3 million. More than three decades later, due to low enrollment at the major seminary, the Heiss Hall building was transferred to the St. Francis of Assisi Convent. In 1988, the building was renamed Clare Hall and is now a residence for the retired Sisters.

Pio Nono High School
St. Francis, Wisconsin

Thomas More High School, located at 2601 East Morgan Avenue, is situated on the campus of the old Pio Nono College. The oldest building on the Thomas More campus is the red brick Salzmann Hall facing South Kinnickinnic Avenue. Peter Brust designed it in 1931, and it was named for Reverend Joseph Salzmann, a co-founder of the St. Francis Seminary. Brust attended school in the old Pio Nono College building in 1881. Salzmann Hall was built to accommodate the growing numbers of boys enrolling in the high school portion of Pio Nono College as either day students or boarding students. [See Page 220 for the Salzmann Hall commission.]

For the next ten years, Pio Nono College grew, and because of this growth, Archbishop Kiley decided in 1941 to make Pio Nono the minor seminary. The school was renamed St. Francis Minor Seminary, and it consisted of four years of high school and two years of college.

Due to an increasing enrollment at the minor seminary, the Milwaukee Archdiocese hired the firm of Brust & Brust in 1963 to design the new De Sales Preparatory Seminary to be located on South Lake Drive. [See Page 244 for the De Sales commission.] The Minor Seminary moved from Salzmann Hall to this new building, and the former St. Francis Minor Seminary building, Salzmann Hall, was reopened in 1965 as Pio Nono High School.

A new addition was planned for Pio Nono High School, and the architectural firm of Brust & Brust was hired to design the new building. It was completed on August 1, 1968. The cost of the new construction was $2,250,000. The operation of Pio Nono High School was turned over to the Catholic Archdiocese of Milwaukee.

The firm of Brust & Brust was honored with a merit award in the Educational Facilities Design Competition, which was sponsored by the National Catholic Educational Association. The firm also remodeled the old Salzmann Hall building. The old building and new building were connected to create a compact campus. The new addition, with a capacity of 1,000 students, was to be used for areas other than conventional classrooms. The new addition contained administrative offices, a 600-seat auditorium, a gymnasium seating 1,400 spectators, a library, and a cafeteria. Due to declining enrollment, it was decided in 1972 to merge Pio Nono High School and Don Bosco High School. Thomas More High School was the name chosen for the new school. In 1989, the school became co-ed. Enrollment as of 2005 was about 750 students.

A recent photograph of Thomas More High School shows the addition completed in 1968.

A 1968 photograph of the school addition

Holy Apostles Catholic Church and School
New Berlin, Wisconsin

The exterior of the ca. 1889 Holy Apostles Church before the 1907 fire

Top inset, the interior of 1907 church

Holy Apostles Catholic Church, located at 16010 West National Avenue in New Berlin, was known as St. Valerius when the congregation drew up its constitution in 1855. The first church was built in 1889, but it unfortunately sustained a devastating fire in 1907. It was rebuilt using the original brick walls. In all likelihood, the firm of Brust & Philipp was commissioned to rebuild the church. Brust & Philipp records are unclear, but the church is mentioned in records from that time period.

By the 1920s, the church was overflowing with parishioners, and plans were made to remodel and enlarge the church. In 1927, the architectural firm of Brust & Philipp was asked to submit a plan to accomplish this endeavor. Peter Brust's design plan placed an addition onto the rear of the church that would contain the sanctuary/sacristy area. Also, the church basement was converted to serve as a dining hall and kitchen. The total cost of the remodeling was $21,500.

The architectural firm of Brust & Brust was commissioned in 1958 to build the new school addition containing nine classrooms and a combination gym/auditorium. The total cost of this addition was $349,000.

The firm of Brust & Brust designed a new, larger church for the congregation in 1965. The first mass in the new church took place at midnight mass during the Christmas celebration of 1966. The new church sat 1,400 people. The tall bell tower with its carillon summoned all parishioners to mass.

The new church complex designed by the firm of Brust & Brust

Chapter 9 – The Legacy 1947-2006

St. John's School for the Deaf
St. Francis, Wisconsin

After St. John's School for the Deaf was destroyed by fire in 1907, the school was rebuilt. The firm of Brust & Philipp designed a new building in the Italianate style. [See Pages 132-133 for St. John's for the Deaf commission.]

As the years passed, a number of additions were built to accommodate increased enrollment. However, by the 1960s, St. John's was looking to raze the old building and build a new school. The old structure was beautiful but was considered a firetrap within. Also, more space was needed since the school was turning away potential students. Upon the death of Father Gehl in 1963, the building plan was taken over by Father Murphy. Fundraising was started in 1964 with eight different groups raising $50,000 each. The new school was built on the same property as the old school buildings. The architectural firm of Brust & Brust did the design work for the new school.

Construction of the elementary school at 3680 South Kinnickinnic Avenue began in the fall of 1965. There were ten classrooms, six dormitories, three playrooms, a library, and living quarters for full-time staff. It was completed in the fall of 1966 and was dedicated by Archbishop William Cousins on October 19, 1966. The high school north wing was completed in 1967.

St. John's closed in 1983 after 107 years of serving deaf children. The closing was due to two factors, the first being the lack of funds to support the school, and the second being the practice of mainstreaming deaf students into regular classrooms. Due to the closing, many students were transferred to the Wisconsin School for the Deaf in Delavan, Wisconsin. Between 1983 and 1992, the building was used for various archdiocesan programs. St. Francis School District purchased the St. John's building in the early 1990s, and in the fall of 1992, Deer Creek Elementary School opened.

A contemporary photograph of the former St. John's for the Deaf School building

An historical photograph of the former St. John's for the Deaf School building

St. Gregory the Great Catholic Church
Milwaukee, Wisconsin

Due to the rapid growth of Catholic parishioners on the southwest side of Milwaukee, the Archdiocese of Milwaukee founded the congregation of St. Gregory the Great at 3132 South 63rd Street. The church was named for the late Pope Gregory. In 1955, a decision was made by parish members that a church, parish hall, and gymnasium be built. The architectural firm of Brust & Brust was hired to design the new church.

The cornerstone was laid on March 23, 1957, and the first mass took place on May 19, 1957. The total cost of the church was $400,000. A school was needed, so the gymnasium was used as a school with moveable partitions. Again, the firm of Brust & Brust was hired to design the new school building. In September 1958, the school opened with 133 pupils. The New York-based Sisters of St. Ursula of the Blessed Virgin Mary accepted Pastor Mark Lyon's invitation to teach at the school.

St. John Kanty Catholic Church
Milwaukee, Wisconsin

Around the turn of the twentieth century, on Milwaukee's near south side, an increase in Polish immigration necessitated a need for more Catholic churches in that area. Father Louis Jurasinski, the pastor of SS Cyril and Methodius parish, urged the archdiocese to create a new church south of his parish.

Plans were made by the archdiocese in 1906 to build St. John Kanty on 966 West Dakota Street. The church was named for a Polish theologian who was canonized in 1767. The church was completed in 1907, and a school was built shortly after. As the parish grew, a new building was needed. The architectural firm of Brust & Brust designed the new church in 1953. And according to the firm's records, the total cost was $316,000. The church was built on a slant without steps and seated 800 people. The parish currently serves 1,200 families. The firm also designed a new school in 1959, and the total cost of the building was $174,000.

Chapter 9 – The Legacy 1947-2006

Immaculate Conception Catholic Church
Milwaukee, Wisconsin

On May 21, 1871, a group of men met at a Town of Lake public school to discuss the establishment of a Catholic church in their neighborhood. James Carmody, James McIver, John Kidney, Ambrose McGuigan, William Haney, and Christopher Brust, father of Peter Brust, were members of the building committee. The request for a parish was approved by the archdiocese, and Father Kundig dedicated the new church at 1023 East Russell Avenue on November 19, 1871. A fundraising contest was held to determine the name of the new parish. The parish men favored the name of St. Patrick's, while the parish women favored Immaculate Conception. Father Fagan was appointed as the temporary priest until a permanent priest became available. Brust family lore says that Frank Brust, the son of Christopher and the younger brother of Peter, was the first child baptized in the church. Family lore also says that Christopher, an accomplished carpenter, built the altar of the first church.

Three decades later, the church building proved too small for the growing parish, and a new church and rectory were subsequently built in 1907 at a total cost of $100,000.

It was decided by church members in 1958 to remodel the church in an effort to provide a greater seating capacity, better heating and ventilation, a crying room, a cloakroom, and a more convenient entrance. The new interior design blended well with the existing walls, windows, ornamental plaster, cornices, and arched ceiling. To create a more convenient entrance near the parking lot, an addition was erected to the rear of the church, and the entrance was moved from East Russell Avenue to South Kinnickinnic Avenue. The architectural firm of Brust & Brust was commissioned to do the church remodel. The total cost of the remodel was $365,075. The new church entrance was done in the Neo-Classical style with doorways, columns, panels, and cornice done in Indiana limestone, hand carved by an Old World artist, Adolph Roegner. The firm of Brust & Brust was later commissioned by the parish to do more design work for the church in 1966.

Top, the former entrance is now the rear of the church.

Below, the former rear of the church is now the entrance.

De Sales College Preparatory Seminary
St. Francis, Wisconsin

In the 1960s, the St. Francis Minor Seminary, located on South Kinnickinnic Avenue in St. Francis, found it necessary to expand because of increased enrollment. The Milwaukee Archdiocese decided to build a new minor seminary at 3501 South Lake Drive. The building site, comprised of fifty acres, was located southeast of the major seminary and overlooked Lake Michigan. This new building was intended to serve the spiritual, educational, living, and recreational needs of students studying for the priesthood. The new school accommodated 650 students, 32 faculty, and 28 housekeeping staff. Ground was broken on November 25, 1961. Albert Cardinal Meyer, the Archbishop of Chicago, dedicated De Sales College Preparatory Seminary on June 28, 1963. The complex contained twelve interconnected buildings and cost a total of $8 million.

Due to low enrollment, De Sales College Seminary closed in 1979. In 1983, the offices of the Milwaukee Catholic Archdiocese relocated to the former De Sales complex. The complex was renamed Cousin's Center for the late Archbishop Cousins. Due to financial difficulties, the Archdiocese decided in 2006 to put the complex up for sale.

School Sisters of Notre Dame of the Lake Mequon, Wisconsin

At the request of Bishop Henni, the School Sisters of Notre Dame established its order in Milwaukee in 1850. The Sisters originally traveled from Bavaria, Germany, to America in 1847 and settled in Baltimore, Maryland, to serve the educational needs of the Catholic schools. Sister Caroline Freiss was sent by her order to open a convent in Milwaukee.

Bishop Henni, in anticipation of the order's arrival in Milwaukee, purchased property for the Sisters. The property was comprised of a brick house on two lots at the corner of North Milwaukee Street and East Knapp Street in what is now downtown Milwaukee. Sister Caroline was appointed the first Vicar General and Motherhouse Superior.

The religious order's first school was at St. Mary's Catholic Church near the Motherhouse and enrollment was 130 students. Holy Trinity School was the second Milwaukee school staffed by the Sisters, and that school enrolled eighty-nine boys and girls. Since there was no convent at the Holy Trinity School, the Sisters were required to walk the two miles every day.

Later, in 1852, the Motherhouse moved into a new main building that faced Milwaukee Street. Additions were made over the years, and the building was finally completed in 1886. It measured 360 feet wide and took up an entire square block comprised of North Milwaukee Street, North Jefferson Street, East Ogden Street, and East Knapp Street.

After many decades as the order's Motherhouse, it was found in 1959 that major repairs were needed on the foundation of the convent buildings. It was decided that the wisest choice would be to demolish the old buildings.

The convent relocated to the city of Mequon in Ozaukee County at 12800 North Lake Shore Drive. The new convent was known as Notre Dame of the Lake and was situated on 155 acres on the shore of Lake Michigan. The architectural firm of Brust & Brust designed the majority of the new convent buildings in 1959. The firm designed the

The exterior of the chapel

The interior of the chapel

chapel, which is still used, as well as the dormitories, the gymnasium, and the language lab building, among other buildings. The Mequon Motherhouse housed almost 600 Sisters at its peak, and the complex also provided educational opportunities for the younger Sisters. The college wing was constructed as an extension of Mount Mary College in Milwaukee. The dormitories housed the young Sisters, the candidates, and the novices, with the older Sisters having small private rooms. Later, a high school was built for girls interested in becoming Sisters; these girls were also called aspirants. A good number of these girls did eventually enter the convent. The cost of this project, according to the Brust & Brust records, was almost $7 million.

Due to the declining number of Sisters and the number of aging Sisters, it was decided to sell the Mequon convent campus to Concordia College in 1982. The School Sisters of Notre Dame of the Lake relocated to their convent in Elm Grove, Wisconsin.

Concordia College took on university status in 1989. By 2004, enrollment climbed to 5,212 students. Around 2004, the School Sisters of Notre Dame sold Concordia University an additional thirty-seven acres of land south of the university on Highland Road. As of this writing, the university is beginning an $8 million bluff stabilization project.

At one time, this building on the Notre Dame campus housed the office of the Mother Superior.

This building is now the Luther Hall/Administration building for Concordia University. The entrance was remodeled.

Cardinal Stritch University
Glendale, Wisconsin

The Sisters of St. Francis of Assisi founded Cardinal Stritch University in 1937. The original name was St. Clare College, and it was housed at the Motherhouse at 3211 South Lake Drive in St. Francis, Wisconsin. St. Clare College began as a teacher training school for the Sisters. In 1946, laywomen were allowed to enroll, and the college was renamed Cardinal Stritch in honor of the late Samuel Stritch, a former archbishop of Milwaukee. A graduate school was established in 1956 with men being allowed to enroll. It wasn't until 1970 that men were allowed to enroll as undergraduates.

In 1962, the school moved to sixty acres of land in the village of Fox Point and the city of Glendale, both municipalities located just north of the city of Milwaukee. The college complex, located at 6801 North Yates Road, was dedicated in 1963. Covered passageways connected the five original buildings. Bonaventure Hall housed administration and the library, Duns Scotus Hall housed the language lab, the Roger Bacon Hall housed the science hall, the Serra Hall housed the dining hall, and Clare Hall was the Sisters' residence.

The nursing program was added in 1980, with a business school added in 1982. Off-campus classes were offered in 1983.

The school received university status in 1997. Four colleges make up Cardinal Stritch University: Arts and Sciences, Education, Business, and the College of Nursing. The First Doctoral program was established in 1998 in the College of Education.

At the present time, the college is expanding the campus. Zimmerman Design Group was commissioned to design the new college buildings.

Clare Hall

Serra Hall

Brust & Brust, Public Commissions, 1947-1972

Currie Park Clubhouse
Milwaukee, Wisconsin

Currie Park was named for James Currie. He was one of the original members of Park Commission and served from 1907 to 1922. Currie also served as president of the County Park Commission. The architectural firm of Brust & Brust designed the Currie Park Clubhouse in 1956. Located at 3535 North Mayfair Road in Wauwatosa, Currie Park is one of the largest parks in the Milwaukee County Park system. The Menomonee River Valley runs throughout the 217-acre park. In 1919, the area became the first county airport. The total cost of the clubhouse was $150,000.

Cooper Park Pavilion
Milwaukee, Wisconsin

The architectural firm of Brust & Brust designed the Cooper Park Pavilion in 1956, located at 8701 West Chambers Street, in Milwaukee. The eight-acre park was named for William Cooper, a member of the Milwaukee County Park Commission from 1948 to 1955. The pavilion can accommodate sixty people.

Clark Square Pavilion
Milwaukee, Wisconsin

There are only a handful of parks in the Milwaukee County Park System known as squares. As the word implies, the park was one block long and one block wide. The inception of public squares goes back to medieval days when land was set aside for public use, especially for market days. When Milwaukee was first being settled in the 1830s and 1840s, there was a lot of open space, but some civic-minded citizens were farsighted enough to donate or purchase land for public squares and parks.

The Clark Square Park, one of the oldest parks in the city of Milwaukee, is located at 2330 West Vieau Place. M. J. Brown and Norman and Lydia Clark donated the land for the park in 1837. The park was named for the Clark family. In 1937, the park was transferred to the Milwaukee County Park System from the City of Milwaukee. The architectural firm of Brust & Brust designed the park pavilion in 1956. The total cost was $47,667. The pavilion holds forty people.

Alexander Hamilton High School
Milwaukee, Wisconsin

The architectural firm of Brust & Brust designed Alexander Hamilton High School at 6215 West Warnimont Avenue in Milwaukee. In 1967, the design was selected by the National Council on Schoolhouse Construction as the School of the Month.

According to the council, the compactness of the school made it unique. In their design, Brust & Brust focused on the economical use of materials by using precast columns, beams, and slabs. Features included wide corridors enabling a smoother flow of traffic, music areas and business education areas grouped together, and a planetarium located within the school building. The planetarium was to serve the school and outside groups. The school accommodated 1,800 students. Construction costs were $4,656,755, excluding the cost of the land, landscaping, and furnishings. Hamilton High School is still serving high school students.

Brust & Brust, Business Commissions, 1947-1972

Bruce Publishing Company
Milwaukee, Wisconsin

William George Bruce was born in Milwaukee in 1857. He worked as a writer for the *Milwaukee Daily News* in 1874, and in 1885, as assistant business manager for the *Milwaukee Sentinel*.

William George Bruce

Two sons, William Conrad and Frank Milton, joined the business. After their father retired from the business in 1927, the Bruce sons transformed the business into a major Catholic book publishing company that dominated the Catholic schoolbook market.

By 1949, the company was the largest Catholic book publisher in the United States. With expansion in mind, Bruce Publishing puchased a building at 540 North Broadway Street, designed by the architectural firm of Schnetzky & Son in 1911. This nine-story building was the site of E. R. Godfrey and Sons, a wholesale grocery.

The Bruce Publishing Company hired the architectural firm of Brust & Brust in 1949 to renovate the building for a factory and office space. According to Brust & Brust records, the total cost of renovation was $433,000. By purchasing this building, the publishing company was able to centralize their various publishing operations under one roof.

William George died in 1949 at the age of ninety-three. Bruce Publishing reached its peak in the 1950s, but because of the changes brought on by Vatican II, the market for their materials declined drastically. The business was sold to Macmillan and Collier in 1968. The Godfrey and Sons/Bruce Publishing Company building now houses condominium units.

The firm of Brust & Brust did not design this building but rather designed a renovation in 1949.

Bruce formed the Bruce Publishing Company in 1891, and it was in 1920 that the company began publishing Catholic publications. Bruce was active in civic affairs, including the building of the Milwaukee Auditorium. The former Bruce Hall, now part of the Milwaukee Theater, was named for Bruce. Also, as a tribute to Bruce, a 1929 ordinance changed West Park Street to West Bruce Street.

Capital Court Shopping Center
Milwaukee, Wisconsin

Plans to build the Capital Court Shopping Center in Milwaukee began in 1953 when the Ed Schuster Company hired the architectural firm of Brust & Brust to submit design plans for the new shopping center. Two nationally known architectural firms were also hired to work in cooperation with Brust & Brust in the planning. Both these firms, John Graham & Company of Seattle and the Welton Becket & Associates of Los Angeles, were internationally known for their shopping center projects in Brazil, Honolulu, Singapore, and Manila. The Graham firm was known for the Seattle shopping center, Northgate, the first large regional retail center in the United States. The Becket firm was known for the Emporium-Capwell Company in the Stanestown center in San Francisco, as well as Macey's in the Hillsdale Center in San Mateo, California.

The Capital Court Shopping Center was a $15 million project located on sixty-five acres at 5500 West Capital Drive. The firm of Brust & Brust followed in the steps of Peter Brust's firm, Brust & Philipp, which was responsible for the Ed Schuster building projects from 1910 to 1947. [See Pages 153-155 for the Ed Schuster commissions.] The Ed Schuster store at Capital Court was completed at a total cost of $164,000. The Capital Court Shopping Center opened in 1956.

In 2001, the shopping center was razed and replaced with the Midtown Center. Walmart is the anchor store. A Pick 'n Save store is also part of the Midtown Center, along with 70,000 square feet of small retail space.

Aerial view of the Capital Court Shopping Center

A God-Given Talent: Peter Brust, Architect, His Work and Legacy 1906-2006

A Selected List of Other Brust & Brust Commissions

American Savings & Loan 640 Division Street, Stevens Point	1977
Burlington Memorial Hospital, Burlington	1957
Catholic Family Life Program Conference 2021 North 60th Street, Wauwatosa	1964
Dretzka's Department Store addition/alterations, Cudahy	1954, 1963
Fond du Lac Clinic Sheboygan Street, Fond du Lac	1948
Hamilton High School, Sussex	1962
Holy Family Infirmary, Elm Grove	1954
James Niedhoeffer Bomb Shelter Structure, Sussex	1961
John Marshall High School 4141 North 64th Street, Milwaukee	1958
Lake Beulah Yacht Club, East Troy	1965, 1966
Marquette University High School Addition, Milwaukee	1961
Matt Talbot Lodge 2612-19 West North Avenue, Milwaukee	1968
Mendota State Hospital Clinic, Madison	1951
Mercy Hospital Addition Oak Street and Parkway Avenue, Oshkosh	1966
Milwaukee County Hospital, 8700 West Wisconsin Avenue, Milwaukee	1956
Milwaukee County Hospital, Physician's Residence, Wauwatosa	1956
Misericordia Hospital North Wing, 1255 North 22nd Street, Milwaukee	1959
Newman Club Catholic Student Center UW-Milwaukee, 3001 North Downer Avenue, Milwaukee	1960
North 65th Street Elementary School 6600 West Melvina, Milwaukee	1955
Port View Medical Bldg., Port Washington	1972
Sacred Heart Congregation School 7963 South 116th Street, St. Martin (Franklin)	1954
Sacred Heart Congregation School, Allentown	1959
St. Aloyius Rectory 1414 South 93rd Street, West Allis	1948
St. Alphonsus Hospital Addition, Port Washington	1957
St. Andrew's Parish Rectory 714 Walworth Avenue, Delavan	1967
St. Ann's for the Elderly, Milwaukee	1966
St. Joan Antida, Sisters of Charity, Guardian Angel Nursery, 1323 North Cass Street, Milwaukee	1965
St. Joseph's Congregation School and Church, Big Bend	1953
St. Joseph's Hospital Addition, Beaver Dam	1957
St. Vincent de Paul Society Addition & Remodeling, 1862 West Fond du Lac, Milwaukee	1962
Templeton Middle School, Sussex	1969
Trinity Memorial Hospital Addition, Cudahy	1966
Wisconsin Telephone Company, Darlington Office Bldg., Darlington	1947
WITI-TV New offices and studios 9001 North Green Bay Road, Brown Deer	1976

Brust-Zimmerman Commissions, 1973 to 1980

Gary Zimmerman joined the architectural firm of Brust & Brust in 1961 and became the firm's lead designer. Zimmerman, a 1958 graduate of architecture from the University of Notre Dame, studied urban planning at Washington University in St. Louis, Missouri. In 1973, Zimmerman became the firm's president. With this change in leadership, there came a new name, Brust-Zimmerman, Inc. Other company officers included the following: John J. Brust as board chairman and vice president, Paul C. Brust as vice president, J. Thomas Maher III as vice president and director of design, Robert E. Lewcock as vice president and director of interior design, and David P. Brust as secretary-treasurer and director of business management.

In-house interior design services were offered to clients under the leadership of Gary Zimmerman. Robert Lewcock, considered one of the leading Midwest interior designers, was hired to lead this department. Another change occurred when the firm shifted its project focus from church and religious commissions to the designing of health care, industrial, educational, public, and corporate facilities.

Many important projects were commissioned during the period of 1973 to 1980, including the Blue Cross/Blue Shield Corporate Headquarters, Froedtert Hospital, the renovation of the Plankinton Arcade, the Bradley Center, and the Milwaukee County Jail.

John Brust retired from the firm of Brust-Zimmerman in 1976. Paul Brust retired in 1978.

Selected Commissions Designed by Brust-Zimmerman from 1973 to 1980

Blue Cross/Blue Shield of Wisconsin
Milwaukee, Wisconsin

Blue Cross/Blue Shield of Wisconsin was established in 1940 when six Milwaukee hospitals formed Associated Hospital Services. This was a prepayment insurance plan that provided hospital coverage to its 26,000 members. The architectural firm of Brust-Zimmerman was hired in 1973 to design their headquarters at 401 West Michigan Street in downtown Milwaukee. In 1979, the architectural firm was hired to provide additional design work. In 2005, the insurance company announced that the building on Michigan Street would be sold and the company would be relocating.

Noyes Pool
Milwaukee, Wisconsin

Noyes Pool, located at 8235 West Good Hope Road in Milwaukee, was built in 1978. This facility is a year-round public indoor pool facility with locker rooms, private showers, and concessions. The pool is part of the Milwaukee County Park System.

North Shore Savings and Loan
Brookfield, Wisconsin

In 1923, North Shore Bank was founded in the back room of Perkins Hardware Store in Shorewood. At that time, bank assets totaled $22,000. The corporate office, designed by Brust-Zimmerman in 1979 is located at 15700 West Bluemound Road in Brookfield. North Shore Savings currently has forty-one branch offices.

Mayfair Bank Tower
Wauwatosa, Wisconsin

The Mayfair Bank Tower, located at 2300 North Mayfair Road in Wauwatosa, was designed by Brust-Zimmerman in 1976.

Chapter 9 – The Legacy 1947-2006

Zimmerman Design Group Commissions, 1981 to 2006

In 1981, the firm of Brust-Zimmerman, Architects became the Zimmerman Design Group. The new name reflected the firm's growing diversification of design services that expanded services to include landscape design and complete engineering services. The firm expanded statewide and regionally, taking projects in Iowa, Michigan, Ohio, and Indiana. With his private sector experience, the firm's president, Gary Zimmerman, brought commercial and corporate clientele, which complemented the firm's previous commissions in the health care, residential, governmental, recreational, and educational areas. Gary Zimmerman was elected to the National College of Fellows and was named a fellow of the American Institute of Architects. He was awarded the WSA Golden Award, which is the highest award presented to a Wisconsin architect.

David Stroik, AIA, joined the firm of Brust-Zimmerman in 1975. He was named president of Zimmerman Design Group in 1999, with Gary Zimmerman remaining as CEO of the firm. Stroik managed many of Zimmerman Design Group's previous important commissions, including the S.C. Johnson Commercial Markets Headquarters, University of Wisconsin-Madison School of Business, and the Blood Center of Southeast Wisconsin.

As of 2004, Zimmerman Design Group received 120 professional, industrial, and community awards. According to *The Business Journal*, over the last ten years, the firm consistently ranked among the top four architectural firms in Milwaukee. Among their many awards were the following: the Commercial Building Achievement Award (1996), the Corporate Services and Facility Environmental Steward Award (1998), the Wisconsin AIA Merit Award (1998), and the International Masonry Institute Golden Trowel Award (1998). The firm was recently recognized by the Wisconsin Chapter of the American Institute of Architects with the 2000 Architectural Firm Award. This award is the highest honor that can be bestowed on an AIA member firm and recognizes significant contributions to architectural design.

In 2002, David Stroik said the following about Zimmerman Design Group:

> ZDG carries ninety-six years of experience and diversified practice into the twentieth century. The firm focuses on responding to client needs during changing economic, sociological, and technical conditions. Sustainable design, energy conservation, an increasing demand for greater cost control, new component technology, and construction methodology are key challenges facing the architectural profession. It is the ZDG's mission to meet these needs while continually striving to develop highly creative and functional design solutions and efficient methods of project delivery.

Zimmerman Design Group offices at 7707 Harwood Avenue, Wauwatosa, Wisconsin

Selected Commissions Designed by Zimmerman Design Group from 1981 to 2006

Amtrak Station, Mitchell International Airport
Milwaukee, Wisconsin

The Prairie style Amtrak Station, located at 5601 South 6th Street, was designed by Zimmerman Design Group in 2005. The 1,600-square-foot building includes restrooms and a seating area. In keeping with the Prairie style, the lawns are kept somewhat wild. Signs near the grassy areas read Do Not Mow. The station is located west of the Mitchell International Airport. Expectations are that the station will encourage northern Illinois residents to use Mitchell International Airport rather than O'Hare or Midway Airports in Illinois.

Sarah A. Scott Middle School
Milwaukee, Wisconsin

Sarah A. Scott Middle School, located at 1017 North 12th Street, was named for Sarah Scott who was the principal of Bay View High School. Scott died of cancer in 1979 at the age of fifty-eight years old. In designing the school, Zimmerman Design Group used a cluster design, in which there were three clusters, one for each grade level. The school was designed with three floors and a total of 150,000 square feet, all of which accommodated 600 students. Sarah Scott Middle School opened in 1991.

Brown Deer Fire Station
Brown Deer, Wisconsin

The Brown Deer Fire Department is located at 4401 West Brown Deer Lane in Brown Deer and was designed by Zimmerman Design Group in 1994. The station is the administrative office of the North Shore Fire Department and includes the communities of Bayside, Brown Deer, Fox Point, Glendale, River Hills, Shorewood, and Whitefish Bay. In 1994, these communities decided to consolidate firefighting services to save on costs and to improve the quality of service.

Chapter 9 – The Legacy 1947-2006

Pettit National Ice Center
Milwaukee, Wisconsin

The Pettit National Ice Center at 500 South 84th Street in Milwaukee opened for business in 1992. The cost of the center was $13.3 million, with a total of 172,800 square feet. Fashioned after the Calgary Olympic Ice Rink, the Pettit Center prided itself as the first indoor 400-meter racing oval in America. There are only six such centers in the world. Along with being an Olympic rink, the center is also open to the general public for recreational use. Zimmerman Design Group worked with the architectural firm of Kahler Slater on the building. Kahler Slater and Zimmerman Design Group formed Venture Architects in 1983. The two firms also collaborated on the Bradley Center in downtown Milwaukee.

Gaenslen Elementary School
Milwaukee, Wisconsin

Gaenslen School first opened in 1938. The school was established to serve polio victims and students with orthopedic disabilities. The school was named for Dr. Gaenslen, a professor of orthopedic surgery at University of Wisconsin-Madison School of Medicine during the 1920s. In 1988, a new school was designed by Zimmerman Design Group and built on the site of the old Gaenslen School. Gaenslen School and Fratney Street School merged at that time in order to allow for total integration of regular education students and exceptional education students.

Oak Creek Police Station
Oak Creek, Wisconsin

Zimmerman Design Group was hired in 2001 to design a new building for the Oak Creek Police Department at 301 West Ryan Road in Oak Creek. The facility also houses the Municipal Court.

257

Bartolotta's Lake Park Bistro
Milwaukee, Wisconsin

Bartolotta's Lake Park Bistro is located in Lake Park at 3133 East Newberry Boulevard on Milwaukee's northeast side. It is considered Milwaukee's premiere French restaurant. The restaurant resides in an historic building, the old Lake Park Pavilion. The famous Olstead Brothers, who designed Central Park in New York City, planned Lake Park from 1892 to 1895. In 1973, the City of Milwaukee designated Lake Park as a landmark. The plaque near the pavilion states that the park is recognized for its historical, aesthetic, environmental, and recreational significance to the community. Zimmerman Design Group did the remodeling of the building in 1995.

Bayside Village Hall/Police Station
Bayside, Wisconsin

The Bayside Village Hall and Police Department is located at 9075 North Regent Road in Bayside. Zimmerman Design Group designed the building in 1999.

The Metropolitan Condominiums
Milwaukee, Wisconsin

The Metropolitan Condominiums at 4485 North Oakland Avenue in Milwaukee is a twenty-two-unit condominium building. The two-bedroom/two-bath units are 1,200 square feet. The four-story Metropolitan Condominiums opened in 2004. Zimmerman Design Group designed the Metropolitan with 10,000 square feet of street-level retail commercial space.

Third District Police Station and Communications Operation Center
Milwaukee, Wisconsin

The 3rd District Police Station and Communications Operation Center is located at 2333 North 49th Street in Milwaukee. Completed in 2001, the 90,000 square foot Center is a neighborhood police station as well as the citywide technology and operation center. Zimmerman Design Group designed the interior and the landscaping. The $36 million project featured an exterior of buff-colored glass and two upper stories done in glass with a row of clerestory windows. The design took advantage of natural light, which illuminates the lobby and front desk area.

Franklin Police Station
Franklin, Wisconsin

The Franklin Police Station and the Municipal Court building are located at 9229 West Loomis Road in Franklin. Zimmerman Design Group designed the Franklin Police Station in 2001.

Johnson Controls Brengel Technology Building
Milwaukee, Wisconsin

Zimmerman Design Group designed the Johnson Controls Brengel Technology Building at 507 East Michigan Street in 1999. The building is attached to the old Johnson Controls building. The old Johnson Controls building was also known as the Johnson Service building. Herman Esser designed the 1902 building when Peter Brust was in his employ. [See Page 18 for the Johnson Service Building commission.]

The new Johnson Controls Brengel Technology Building is considered a "green" building because it makes use of recycled materials and takes advantage of natural light. It is thought that such environmentally sensitive environments can increase work productivity. The total number of workers at the Johnson Controls Brengel Technology building is 400. Johnson Controls is a $16 billion-a-year business that makes automotive systems and building controls. The building project costs were $130 a square foot, at a total cost of $16.9 million.

West Allis Police Station and Court Facility
West Allis, Wisconsin

The West Allis Police Station and Court Facility is located at 11301 West Lincoln Avenue in West Allis. Zimmerman Design Group designed the building in 1996.

We Energies Headquarters
Milwaukee, Wisconsin

Herman J. Esser was commissioned in 1903 by the Milwaukee Electric Railway and Light Company to design the Public Service Building. Peter Brust was working for Esser at the time. [See Page 19 for the Public Service Building commission.] In 1997, Zimmerman Design Group was commissioned to restore the building. The east and west train doors were replaced with replicas of the original doors, and the fifth floor, which was added during a previous renovation, was removed. The four-story building, located at 231 West Michigan Avenue, is now the home of We Energies. The building was placed on the National Register of Historic Places in 1998.

Van Buren City Lofts
Milwaukee, Wisconsin

In 1921, the firm of Brust & Philipp designed the Luick Ice Cream Garage building at 1325 North Van Buren Street. [See Page 164 for an original photograph of the Luick Ice Cream Garage commission.] In 2002, renovation began on the building to turn it into forty-two condominium units. The architectural firm of T-3 Group was selected to design the remodel, but they left the $6 million job before completion. Charges of mismanagement and construction errors were made against the company. Zimmerman Design Group was then hired to complete the project. The original windows and lentils of the ice cream factory building could not be saved, and the cornice was also lost when the additional story was added. The building now features a residential look with balconies on all four sides.

Cruisers Frozen Custard & Jumbo Burgers and Route 43 Harley Davidson
Sheboygan, Wisconsin

Crusiers Frozen Custard & Jumbo Burgers and the Route 43 Harley-Davidson dealership share a space off of Interstate 43 at 3740 South Taylor Drive in Sheboygan. The Crusiers building, designed by Zimmerman Design Group, was completed in 1998. It was designed in such a way to draw interstate drivers' attention to their restaurant.

Columbia-St. Mary's Family Health Center
Milwaukee, Wisconsin

Columbia St. Mary's Family Health Center is located in a building designed by Zimmerman Design Group at 1121 East North Avenue. The clinic is part of the Jewel-Osco complex and was completed in 1999. The building was added to the Jewel-Osco project after the Milwaukee Department of City Development suggested that shops along North Avenue would encourage commercial activity especially small local businesses. Unfortunately, it was difficult to find retailers for the space. Some prospective retailers claimed that the parking lot at the rear didn't allow for easy access to the shops. Because of the difficulty in renting the space to commercial businesses, Columbia St. Mary's was able to take over the space for their Family Health Center.

South Shore Medical Office Building (Lakeshore Medical Building)
St. Francis, Wisconsin

The South Shore Medical Office Building, designed by the Zimmerman Design Group, is located at 2000 East Layton Avenue in St. Francis. It is now the Lakeshore Medical Building.

Potawatomi Bingo Casino Expansion
Milwaukee, Wisconsin

*P*otawatomi Bingo Casino first opened in 1991. In 2000, the casino built a new $120 million casino adjacent to its old building at 313 North 13th Street in the Menomonee Valley. The new casino was five times the size of the old one with 1,000 slot machines, 25 blackjack tables, 5 new restaurants, and 2 concert rooms. A towering 120-foot torch dominates the entrance to the Casino. Zimmerman Design Group was commissioned to design the exterior of this new casino.

Johnson Wax Commercial Products Headquarters
Racine, Wisconsin

*Z*immerman Design Group was the architectural firm of record for the architecture and interiors of the Johnson Wax Commercial Products Headquarters in Racine. The 250,000-square-foot office building and laboratory facility was completed in 1998 and included a fitness center, conference center, and cafeteria. In the center of the building is an atrium that provides natural light to offices. This use of natural light is eco-sensitive, making this a "green" building. The Johnson Wax project was selected in 1998 by the American Institute of Architects as one of the top ten designs that enhance and protect the environment.

Marion Chester Read Center
Milwaukee, Wisconsin

*T*he Marion Chester Read Center, located at 131 South 69th Street, is the resource center for the Girl Scouts of Milwaukee Area. It was designed by Brust & Zimmerman and completed in 1987. The 18,000-square-foot building features seven meeting rooms, a large multi-purpose room, a Girl Scout Shop that sells scouting supplies and equipment, a resource center, and staff offices for forty employees.

Afterword

After spending the last 2 ½ years researching, writing, and editing this book on the architectural work of Peter Brust, the book is finally finished. Or is it really finished? Probably not. There will always be a burning desire on my part to continue to look for information on the Brust commissions that I was unable to locate.

For instance, who were F. W. Emerson, P. C. Owen, Mrs. A. Druecker, Mrs. J. Kersting, Leo Louis, and H. M. Graham? These commissions have so far eluded me. Why not just give up on finding these elusive commissions? I am a librarian by profession, and librarians love digging for information even after everyone else has given up and gone home.

Why did I choose to document the work of Peter Brust? That's a good question, since I never knew Peter Brust. He died in 1946, and I was born four years later. As I said in my introduction, I became intrigued with the thought of writing a book about him after I began locating architectural design work attributed to him.

When I began the book, I knew very little about Peter Brust as a person. Very little information was gleaned from family members who knew him. Those who did remember him described him as a very religious and pious man. He was a nice man, they said, who valued his family. Peter was known to visit his brother, Frank, every single Sunday. Most likely, Frank's home was full of relatives on Sunday afternoons. As Peter's son, John, said in his memoirs, getting together with family was very important.

Other than those pieces of memories provided by family members, I still know very little about Peter Brust the person. However, in researching and documenting his work, I have learned much about Peter Brust the architect. Basically, this book is a documentation of his work. In simple terms, the purpose of this book is to educate people about the architectural work of Peter Brust.

Also, I attempted to give the reader information about the people, the companies, and the organizations who commissioned Brust & Philipp, Brust, Philipp & Heimerl, Brust & Brust, Peter Brust-Architect, Brust & Zimmerman, and Zimmerman Design Group. It is said that a picture paints a thousand words, and perhaps, a picture also paints a thousand questions. Hopefully, the reader will find the information interesting and informative.

Every effort was made to be as complete and accurate as possible. However, there may be both typographical errors and errors in content. If such errors exist, I apologize. The errors were not intentional. My hope is that Peter Brust smiles down and is satisfied with my attempt to document his fifteen minutes of fame.

Appendix 1: Illinois Application

N.C.A.R.B. No. 134

CONTRIBUTIONS TO PROFESSIONAL LITERATURE, RESEARCH, DESIGN, PROFESSIONAL ETHICS, INVENTIONS, ETC.

Title of Article ___None___ Publication _____
Date of Publication ___None___ Publisher _____

I am the senior member of the firm of Brust & Philipp. This partnership was established in 1906 and our office is at present located at 405 Broadway. We now employ ten draughtsmen, two superintendents and three stenographers. Before establishing our office I spent twelve years in the office of Ferry & Clas where I had charge of the largest jobs going through the office.

Our practice has had a normal growth. We began with small buildings and have had larger and larger commissions from our earlier clients. To illustrate, - For St. Joseph's Convent we first enlarged a small house, then built an addition to their power house, then St. Mary's Hill, a hospital for mental cases, then we enlarged Sacred Heart Sanitarium three times and built a Nurses' Home for St. Mary's Hill, we then built the Convent Chapel, after that a home for student sisters at the Catholic University at Washington, D.C. We are now building a large Addition to the Convent costing $500,000 and are also preparing plans for them for a High School for Girls in Chicago. It is for this job we desire registration in the State of Illinois.

I have been President of the Wisconsin Architectural Club for two years and am now serving my second term as President of the Wisconsin Chapter of the A.I.A. I am a member of the Milwaukee Building Code Commission, also a member of the Board of Appeals, Milwaukee Zoning Law. I am also a member of the Board of Appeals, Wisconsin Industrial Commission, Building Code Division.

NOTE: Senior applicants are expected to use above space to give a brief statement concerning their record in practice for the ten years preceding the date of this application. This statement should include office locations, partnerships, and any other information which the applicant deems essential to a fair adjudication of his record in practice.

The undersigned, being duly sworn, upon his oath deposes and says that the foregoing statements are, to the best of his knowledge and belief, true and made in good faith.

NAME *Peter Brust*

STATE OF *Wisconsin*
County of *Milwaukee* } ss.

I, *Ray J. Rebhan*, a Notary Public in and for said County, in the State aforesaid, DO HEREBY CERTIFY that *Peter Brust*, personally known to me to be the same person whose name is subscribed to the foregoing instrument, appeared before me this day in person, and acknowledged that he signed, sealed and delivered the said Instrument as his free and voluntary act, for the uses and purposes therein set forth.

GIVEN under my hand and Notarial Seal this *27th* day of *November*, 1922.

(SEAL)

Ray J. Rebhan
Notary Public

My Commission Expires _____

(Form 3.)
Page 3

Appendix 2: Brust Family Memories

Author's note: When visiting with Patsy Koenings, the daughter of John Brust, she shared with me boxes of family history materials. It is from those materials that the following information was taken. I thank Patsy for sharing those documents with me and for giving me the opportunity to share these memories with other family members and interested parties.

The following reminiscences were taken from Christmas letters that John Brust wrote to his children during the 1980s and 1990s:

John Brust was asked by his children to include in his Christmas letters childhood memories and memories of family members. These memories included memories of his neighborhood, school, family trips, and other events.

John described his father, Peter, as a humble, honest person who was very well liked by all. John's parents, Peter and Olga, were married in 1902. Olga Greulich Brust was born to one of Wisconsin's founding families. Her grandfather, August Greulich, was elected a member of the first legislative assembly of the State of Wisconsin in 1848.

In 1906, Peter and Olga moved to a Queen Anne style house at 851 North 29th Street in Milwaukee; the house was built in 1894. In the 1920s, North 29th Street was known as North 28th Street and also as Queen Anne Place. This area of the city was considered country; the city limits went to North 35th Street. At that time, West Wisconsin Avenue was called Grand Avenue and Kilbourn Street was Cedar Street. John remembered a barn with a hayloft on their property that sheltered their horse up until World War I. The streets used gas for illumination, and John remembered the lamplighter lighting the gas streetlights on Queen Anne Place.

His mother, Olga, according to John, was very beautiful. Unfortunately, she died of a blood clot after minor surgery in 1915. John's maternal grandmother and his Aunt Charlotte helped to raise him and his sister, Catherine, and his brother, Paul, during what was surely a very difficult period. There were also maids that were hired to help with the housework and childcare. The three children, according to John, were spoiled by all of these caregivers. The maids were usually Polish immigrant girls who worked for room and board while looking for husbands. In 1921, Peter married Charlotte, known as Lottie, who was Olga's sister. Lottie, according to John, "was too good to me and spoiled me."

The elementary school was a good walking distance from home; the one-mile trip was made four times a day, as there was no lunchroom at the school. Part of the school curriculum was German script writing in first through third grade. John's maternal grandmother, Grandma Greulich, probably spoke German to him and helped him with his lessons.

Chores were part of John's daily routine when he was in the seventh grade. The messy job of banking the coal furnace and removing the ashes was his responsibility. The family owned no cow, so milk was delivered to the milk box at the back door. The top quarter of the bottle was cream, and in winter, if the milkman wasn't met at 5:30 a.m., the milk froze and

Charlotte "Lottie" Brust

the cream popped out of the top of the bottle. No one in the neighborhood gathered eggs in winter, since chickens needed light and heat in order to lay eggs. The only heat in the barn was generated by the cows, if the family owned one.

When John was in eighth grade, boys still wore knickers, which were short pants that were buttoned below the knee. Long pants were not worn until one entered high school. The schools that John attended were probably Catholic schools. He states in one of his letters that he was fortunate to be able to attend a private school. It was also during eighth grade that his father bought a superheterodyne radio that was three feet long and featured three dials for tuning. [Radio's premier inventor, Edwin H. Armstrong, invented the superheterodyne circuit in 1918. Armstrong adapted a technique called heterodyning found in early wireless but very seldom used. Armstrong designed a complex eight-tube receiver and named it the superheterodyne circuit. Today, the circuit is used in 98 percent of all television and radio receivers.] In order to get good reception, a tall aerial was needed, so his dad erected a steel pole in the backyard at their home on Queen Anne Place/North 29th Street. This pole was later moved to their Lake Beulah cottage and served as a flagpole. In the 1920s, when Milwaukee boasted a couple of its own radio stations, John built a crystal set that he listened to at bedtime. At first there were only four stations: Minneapolis, Chicago, St. Louis, and Pittsburgh.

John said that he was a loner as a child. Since his school was a mile away and he lived on the edge of the Irish district, he had few friends. Apparently, at that time children of the Irish and the Germans did not mix socially. However, the garage contained a lot of tools, so John spent most of his time making things or taking things apart to see how they worked.

During his childhood and early adulthood, John saw much change in the way people performed household tasks. Changes were also made in regard to safety issues, such as the safety razor that came out in the 1920s. John tried to shave himself with a straight edge in college, but he cut himself regularly. John remembered when candles illuminated Christmas trees, unfortunately causing many houses fires. With the advent of electricity, Christmas trees were more safely illuminated. Many inventions made life easier, especially for the lady of the house. Not only were these inventions laborsaving, but they also were safer than previous methods. A more efficient gas stove replaced the wood-burning kitchen stove used during John's childhood. The electric stove followed in the 1920s. Before the invention of the washing machine, soiled clothing was placed in an oblong copper tub that contained boiling water, and the tub was fitted over two gas burners to heat the water. The clothes were then rubbed on a corrugated scrub board to get out the dirt. In the 1920s, the washing machine was available, but the machine was open on the top, causing the water to spill and splash out. John recalled that the wringers also broke a lot of shirt buttons. Refrigerators took the place of iceboxes, and there were electric toasters, electric irons, and record players that took the place of hand-wound Victorolas. Telephones were no longer a rarity, but for long distance calls you needed to yell to be heard, John remembered.

After World War I ended, many things changed in America. Not only were there labor-saving appliances for homemakers, but it was also a time that ladies were introduced to cosmetics. American soldiers returning from France, brought home samples of cosmetics. But even with labor-saving devices to ease the household tasks and cosmetics to make them feel more glamorous, women were still required to spend a lot of time in the kitchen, according to John. They still needed to preserve food for the winter months, and like John's grandmother, they spent most of Saturday preparing for Sunday dinner. John recalled Grandma Greulich as being a very religious woman who was always praying, even while she made dinner.

Transportation changed dramatically during John's lifetime. Before 1920, everyone used streetcars or trains to travel to work or anywhere else, for that matter. It was said that in the 1920s, 98 percent of travel between cites was done by train and the other 2 percent by boat. It took his father a half-hour to get to work by streetcar from North 29th Street to downtown because the streetcar stopped at every corner. A horse and a wagon made deliveries of ice, coal, fruits, and vegetables. Even firemen fought fires with equipment pulled by horses. John remembered the boiler fire engines roaring pulled by four white horses and smoke sprewing from the smoke stack.

John's family was fortunate to be able to afford to rent a summer cottage on Pewaukee Lake for family vacations. In the 1920s, this meant a 1 ½ hour drive. The family used kerosene lamps to light the cottage, and since there was no indoor plumbing, they used outhouses that were surrounded by poison ivy. After installing their families at the cottage, the men folk came only on weekends by way of the interurban, which was a country streetcar. This streetcar picked up passengers at Bluemound Road between North 60th Street and North 70th Street. Later in 1922, Peter Brust bought an existing cottage on Lake Beulah. [Many years later, Peter's son, Paul, razed the old cottage on Lake Beulah and built a year-round home.]

Transportation to the cottage was often in the form of an automobile, especially after the state government began to pave the roads in the 1920s. According to John, new cars in the early 1920s were priced at about $300, and his father owned one of the first cars in the city. This was a Reo Touring Automobile with ininglass curtains. [See sidebar.] John recalled his father getting a speeding ticket for driving too fast at twenty-eight miles per hour.

One family trip that John clearly remembered was a trip to Crivitz, Wisconsin. They were traveling to see his mother's relative, Louie Ness, who owned a farm five miles outside of Crivitz. There was a two-car caravan for safety reasons, since tires were constantly in need of changing or repair every hundred miles or so. The caravan reached Green Bay in one day, but it took another day on sand roads to get to the farm. The Ness farm didn't have enough sleeping space for everyone, so John slept in the hayloft at the neighboring Gawerski family farm. John was surprised that the hayloft he shared with the Gawerski kids was their actual bedroom. John recalled that the Northern Lights up north were so bright that it actually scared him.

The Great Depression hit in 1929 when John was seventeen, and it lasted for seven years. Banks closed and food stamps bought you what food was available at that moment. Households turned to the backyard garden to supplement their meals. John speculated that every architect in Milwaukee was on welfare except for his father. John recalled that their meals were meager, but the meals probably were a lot better than what most other people subsisted on. Many people, according to John, kept on working at their jobs without pay, hoping to have a job when things got better.

John's memories of the Prohibition era that ran from 1918 to 1932 were quite vivid. The Prohibition Amendment made it illegal to buy alcoholic beverages. However, John's father hired a brew master from a closed brewery to make home-brewed beer in the family basement from ingredients that Peter purchased. In his memoirs, John stressed that this was legal. His father also stored a barrel of fermenting wine at all times. Like many families at the time, John and his siblings were brought up on beer and wine in moderation.

The importance of family is a constant theme in John's mem-

> **What was a Reo Touring Car?**
>
> In 1917, Ranson E. Olds, founder of the Oldsmobile automobile, designed the Reo Grand Touring Sedan. Olds' goal was to design a car much like an English luxury car. The automobile could seat seven passengers with a jump seat that folded down.
>
> **What were isinglass curtains?**
>
> The isinglass curtains, made of sheets of Mica, were stored under the automobile seats until they were hung up and rolled down during rain or cold weather. In the musical Oklahoma, the song "Surrey with the Fringe On the Top" mentions isinglass curtains:
>
> "The wheels are yellow, the upholstery's brown
> The dashboard's genuine leather
> With isinglass curtains y' can roll right down
> In case there's a change in the weather."

Above, a photograph of a Reo Touring Automobile

Below, a photograph of a car with isinglass curtains

oirs. Sunday afternoons and evenings were a time for family gatherings. Sometimes three or four families joined for inside picnics in winter and trips to nearby lakes in summer. It was a time for the children to play together and for the older folks to play cards, talk about old times, and politics. It saddened John that this tradition in families was slowly disappearing.

John Brust's children treasure the Christmas letters written by their father. Many people, including this author, wish that such family memoirs were theirs to cherish.

The following information was taken from a genealogy/family history document done on the Reiman branch of the Brust family. Patricia Raths Sherman, daughter of Louise Reiman Raths, sent the document to Paul Brust. Louise was the daughter of Anna Marie "Emma" Brust Reiman Dederich; Emma was the sister of Peter Brust. In 1970, Paul Brust hosted a family reunion at his Lake Beulah home, and at that time, family members were encouraged to share family memories.

Anna Marie Brust was Peter Brust's sister, and she was known as Emma. She met her first husband, John Reiman, when she was visiting her first cousin, Joe Thomas, in Iowa. John Reiman and the Thomas family had neighboring farms. Joe Thomas was the son of Mary Ann Brust Thomas, a sister of Peter and Emma.

Emma and John Reiman were married in 1900. Unfortunately, John Reiman died on March 7, 1905, while Emma was pregnant with their second child, John; their first child was Louise Catherine. After the death of her husband, Emma returned to Milwaukee and three years later married Nicholas Dederichs. The "s" on the end of Dederichs is the German spelling, and after coming to America, many Dederichs dropped the "s". Nicholas adopted Emma's two children, four-year-old Louise and three-year-old John, and raised them as his own. The couple went on to have child of their own, Marie.

Some of Louise's memories of her grandmother, Catherine Biever Brust, wife of Christopher, were somewhat humorous. Grandma Catherine, Louise recalled, was a stern and busy person. Grandma Catherine slept on a cornhusk mattress all her life, and every year new leaves would be dried and put into the big cloth bag she used as a mattress. Louise would sleep with Grandma Catherine when she stayed the night, and Louise remembered the mattress rattling every time she moved. One day, recalls Louise, Grandma Catherine was chopping wood, and a wood chip hit Grandma Catherine in the cheek. According to Louise, the injury turned cancerous and eventually killed her grandmother. The night before Grandma Catherine left for the hospital, never to return home, Catherine scrubbed the attic floor on her hands and knees.

There were memories of her grandfather, Christopher, who was known as fun and sociable. According to Louise's memoirs, there were few schools in the wilderness. Christopher acquired some private instruction and then was apprenticed to a carpenter, probably his father, Nicholas. In the 1880s, Christopher bought land in Town of Lake and established a truck garden.

Louise's memoirs also mention something that would shock people today. Louise learned how to drive when she was only thirteen years old! Her stepfather, Nicholas Dederichs, bought an Overland car in 1910 that was started by a hand crank. He later bought a self-starter which allowed Louise to drive all over town on her own without having to crank the car to start it.

The Reiman family history document also gave some brief details about other Brust family members, such as the following:

• Emma Brust possessed red hair and suffered from severe eczema all her life.

• A descendant of Louise Reiman, Robert Cards, who lived in Saginaw, Michigan, was said to have possession of a cowbell that belonged to Christopher Brust.

• Louise's Aunt Marie acquired a heavy white canvas bag that Christopher used to bring his belongings from Germany.

• Peter Brust's brother, Frank, constructed violins.

Appendix 2: Brust Family Memories

- Peter's brother, Monsignor Nicholas Brust, held an annual family reunion that took place between Christmas Day and New Years Eve.
- John Brust, another brother, was a CPA in Montana and died in 1930 of asthma. John was married to Margaret Tangney and raised two sons who became doctors. One son, Dr. William P. Brust, was a dentist in Everett, Washington, and the other son, Dr. Nicholas Brust, practiced medicine in Denver, Colorado.
- Peter's sister, Anna, died at the age of ten from lockjaw. She jumped off the porch steps onto the upright prongs of a garden rake that was lying in the grass. She contracted lockjaw. This took place at the family home on East St. Francis Avenue in St. Francis. The family history states, "She probably died at home because her sister, Emma, always had a terrible horror of both lockjaw and rakes lying with prongs up."
- Someone in the Reiman family is said to have the sunbonnet Grandma Catherine used for gardening.

The following information was taken from a family history done in 1977 by Rose Maller Braun. Rose was a daughter of Mary Jordan Maller and a granddaughter of Gertrude Brust Jordan, a sister of Christopher Brust.

Gertrude Brust married Casper Jordan who was twenty-four years her senior. The couple settled in Racine County on the western end of Caledonia Township on what is now Highway G. They purchased their forty-acre farm in 1858 from Peter Thelen for $1,200. Their first home was a log cabin

The Jordan family built this new, larger home in 1870, replacing the log cabin. From left to right are Gertrude Brust Jordan, Rose Jordan, Mary Jordan, Casper Jordan, and a woman who was a boarder at the Jordan home.

where sons Nicholas, Peter, Christopher, and Joseph were born.

Life was not easy for the settlers. According to Rose Maller Braun, land needed to be cleared and water hauled for the cattle when the dug wells went dry. Letters and newspapers were picked up at the railroad depot some distance away, and the telegraph was used to reach someone in a hurry. There were few farm implements, and most of the work was done by hand, but as time went on more machines became available.

Nature, at times, was not gentle to the settlers. The following passage is from the family history:

A cyclone passing through the town in 1903 damaged and destroyed valuable trees and buildings. Lightning later struck and burned the Jordan barn filled with hay and unthrashed grain. Neighbors brought water to help save the other buildings. A new barn was soon built with the help of neighbors, to house the cattle and feed.

According to Rose Maller Braun, Grandmother Gertrude worked in the home of Solomon Juneau as a young girl. Solomon Juneau later became the first mayor of Milwaukee. It was said that Mrs. Juneau was a kind, patient lady who taught Gertrude many useful things. Gertrude learned the ways of the Indians who came to trade at Juneau's general store, and her contact with the Indians at the trading post enabled her to trust Indian medicine. Years after her experience at the trading post, Gertrude's son, Christopher, was severely burned on his face when gunpowder was carelessly tossed into a fire and exploded. An Indian woman living nearby came to help care for Christopher, bringing with her salve made by the Indians. The salve was used to dress his wounds and accounted for his face healing nicely with few scars.

In 1870, the Jordan family built a new, larger, and more comfortable home. Their daughters, Mary and Rose, were born in this home. Life was hard and busy for Gertrude. Rose Maller Braun related the following about Gertrude:

Gertrude sewed clothes by hand for her children and even dyed some material by using walnut shells to make brown dye. Apples and pears were cut and dried for the winter. Some vegetables were stored in large crocks in a cool dry place. Meat was packed in salt or smoked in a smokehouse built for that purpose. They also made their own candles and soap.

The Jordan children attended St. Louis Catholic School, and the family attended mass in the wooden church building that was designed by Gertrude's brother, Christopher Brust. On August 25 of each year on the Feast Day of St. Louis, the parish community sponsored a picnic that was sometimes held in the Jordan's woods.

Rose Maller Braun relates an interesting story that showed a feisty Gertrude. Gertrude's son, Nicholas, owned a gun "but grandmother disliked having it in the house, so when she learned a neighbor wanted to buy a gun, she offered to trade it for a cow. It was a deal she did not regret."

After they married, sons Nicholas and Peter moved to California, while Christopher moved to South Dakota. Joseph remained in Caledonia working as a blacksmith, later moving to Milwaukee. Mary married Nicholas Maller and moved to Iowa but returned to Caledonia in 1902 to help with the farm work. Nicholas and Mary Maller bought the family farm in 1929, plus an additional twenty acres. Nicholas and Mary had three children, Francis, Rose and Helen. Francis continued to farm the land. Rose Maller Braun finished her memoir by saying the following:

New buildings were erected and a beautiful new home built in 1963. The farm has been in the family 100 years. Grandfather and Grandmother Jordan and Mary Jordan Maller remained at the farm as long as they lived.

[Casper Jordan lived to be ninety-eight years old, while Gertrude lived to be ninety-two years old.]

Rose Maller Braun (right), the author of the above article, is pictured her with her sister Helen (left). Helen is also pictured on Page 6 in Chapter 1 as one of Father Nicholas Brust's attendants.

The following information came from a letter that Paul Brust sent to Beverly Nicholas during the time she was doing some genealogy research on Gertrude Brust Jordan, sister of Christopher. Beverly was the mother-in-law of Pat Braun Nicholas; Pat was a descendent of Gertrude Brust Jordan.

According to Paul Brust, his grandfather, Christopher, farmed and resided on fifteen acres of land purchased around 1909 from R. Stewart near East Holt and South Indiana Avenues in Town of Lake. [See Page 27.] According to a 1876 plat map, the original Stewart farm ran from South Pennsylvania Avenue on the West, South Illinois Avenue on the east, East Morgan Avenue on the south, and East Holt Avenue on the north. Paul remembers his grandfather, Christopher, as having a large barn behind his house that housed farm implements on the first floor and a large woodworking shop on the upper level. Christopher was a cabinetmaker and a part-time farmer at this location.

Before Christopher Brust purchased the land on South Indiana Avenue, he owned property on St. Francis Avenue in St. Francis. [See Page 2.] In 1891, Christopher subdivided some of this land in St. Francis and named a street, South Brust Avenue, for himself. South Brust Avenue runs south from Oklahoma Avenue and is located east of Howell and west of Kinnickinnic Avenues. At one time, Brust Avenue ran south through the center of what is now the airport. Brust Avenue was discontinued south of East Layton Avenue after the airport extension.

Joseph Brust, son of Christopher and brother of Peter, built a home on the Vollmer property located at East Morgan Avenue in St. Francis. Christopher's son, Frank, built his family home on South Illinois Avenue, a stone throw from his father's house on South Indiana Avenue. [See Page 27.] Before the move to the South Illinois Avenue location, Frank Brust owned and lived on property where the Nash automobile plant was located, south of East Oklahoma Avenue. Many years later, Frank Brust lived at the northeast corner of East Layton and South Howell Avenues. When the airport was built, the county moved Frank's home farther south on Howell Avenue north of St. Stephen's Catholic Church. When the airport expanded again, his house was moved a mile south near College Avenue. The house is still located at the southwest corner of Howell and College Avenue, but it is on a back lot and not easily viewed from the road.

In the files of the St. Francis Historical Society is a letter written by Teresa Schmidling, the daughter of Mary Brust Schmidling and a niece of Peter Brust. Teresa was a secretary for Bishop Leo Brust. In the letter dated December 10, 1979, Teresa says the following about the Brust family:

My grandfather, Christopher Brust's home is located at 1738 East St. Francis Avenue, but I think he had land as far as American Motors on Clement Avenue.

The earlier settlers around here at first went to church at the seminary, later at Immaculate Conception. Christopher Brust built the first altar at Immaculate Conception and his son, Frank Brust (father of Bishop Brust), born on September 13, 1871, was the first baby baptized there. Later, of course, they attended Sacred Heart [of Jesus in St. Francis].

Monsignor Klein once told me most of the settlers were from a section of Germany called Alsace-Lorraine, I think, near the French border. Most of them were fed up with the continuous wars in Germany.

My uncle, Peter Brust (son of Christopher Brust), was the architect for the original St. John's School for the Deaf. [Authors note: The original St. John's School was built in 1878. Peter Brust designed the 1907 building after a fire destroyed the 1878 building.]

A God-Given Talent: Peter Brust, Architect, His Work and Legacy 1906-2006

Appendix 3: Family Tree

Brust/Brost/Prost Family Tree

Family Crest created for Bishop Leo Brust when he became an auxiliary bishop

Philbus BrostProst
born 1676, Alfen, Rheinland, Germany

Petri (John) Peter Prost
born 1733, Alflen, Rheinland, Germany
died 1809
married 1761 to Eva Roden
born 1733

Peter Joseph Prost
born 2-2-1766, Alflen, Rheinland, Germany
died 9-1844, Ulmen, Germany
married 5-5-1790 to Anna Margarethe Thomas
born 1-1-1774, Ulmen, Germany
died 1830, Ulmen, German

Nicholas Brust
born 12-19-1810 Ulmen, Germany
died 5-10-68 Town of Lake
married 2-5-1835 to Anna Margarethe Wallebohr
born 5-20-1808 Ulmen, died 6-8-1887

John Baptist Brost
born 5-23-1802 Ulmen, Daun, Germany
died 8-30-1886 Johnsburg, Wisconsin
married 10-16-1825 to Maria Eva Catherine Bell

Gertude Brust Jordan
born 1-10-1836, Ulmen
died 8-7-1928
married Casper Jordan
in 1856

Christopher Brust
born 3-28-1838, Ulmen
died 9-22-1913
married Catherine Biever
on 1-28-1869
born 10-27-1844
died 2-26-1925

Mary Ann Brust Thomas
born 6-18-1849
died 12-1-1894

Josephine Brust Link
born 10-28-1844
died 5-5-1887

Peter
b. 11-4-1869
d. 6-22-1946

Frank
b. 9-13-1871
d. 12-23-1952

Emma
b. 1-11-1873
d. 1-28-1930

Nicholas
b. 10-15-1874
d. 2-28-1957

Joseph
b. 4-13-1880
d. 6-12-1946

John
b. 2-17-1882
d. 5-18-1930

Anna
b. 4-19-1884
d. 10-5-1894

Mary
b. 8-14-1878
d. 8-20-1945

Appendix 4: Brust Ancestors: Where They Rest

For family members interested in locating the graves of their Brust ancestors, included here are photographs of the graves and their locations.

Left and top right, Nicholas Brust (born 12-19-1810 died 5-10-1868) is buried at St. Stephen's Cemetery on Howell Avenue south of St. Stephen's Catholic Church at 5880 South Howell Avenue.

Above, Anna W. Brust, wife of Nicholas Brust, (born 5-20-1808 died 6-8-1887) is buried next to her daughter Josephine at St. Stephen's Cemetery.

Left and far left, Josephine Brust Linck died in May 1887 at the age of 44. She is buried next to her mother, Anna, at St. Stephen's Cemetery.

The Christopher Brust family headstone is at the Sacred Heart of Jesus Cemetery at 3635 South Kinnickinnic Avenue in St. Francis, Wisconsin.

Top, Christopher Brust (born 3-28-1838 died 9-11-1913) is buried at Sacred Heart of Jesus Cemetery.

Above, Catherine Brust (born 10-27-1844 died 2-26-1925) is buried at Sacred Heart of Jesus.

Below, John Reiman, son-in-law of Christopher and Catherine, is buried in the Brust plot.

Anna Brust (born 4-19-1884 died 10-5-1894), daughter of Christopher and Catherine, died of lockjaw and is buried at Sacred Heart Cemetery.

Appendix 4: Brust Ancestors: Where They Rest

Top left and top right, Reverend Nicholas Brust (born 10-15-1874 died 2-28-1957) is buried at the St. Francis Seminary Cemetery located at 3257 South Lake Drive.

Casper and Gertrude (Brust) Jordan are buried at the St. Louis Catholic Church cemetery located at 13207 Hwy G in Caledonia, Wisconsin. Gertrude died in 1928. [See Page 265 for the Jordan family history.]

Joseph Brust (born 1889 died 1946), brother of Peter, is buried at the Sacred Heart Cemetery.

A God-Given Talent: Peter Brust, Architect, His Work and Legacy 1906-2006

Peter Brust (born 11-4-1869 died 6-22-1946) is buried at Holy Cross cemetery with his two wives, Olga and Lottie. The inscription on the stone reads, "Father Peter, Mother Olga and Aunt Lottie." Holy Cross Cemetery is located at 7301 West Nash Street in Milwaukee.

Frank and Matilda Brust are buried at St. Stephen's Cemetery. Frank died in 1952 and Matilda died in 1973.

Above, Paul Brust died in 1994 and is buried at Holy Cross cemetery with his first wife.

Left, John Brust died in 1995 and is buried at Holy Cross cemetery with his first wife and son, James. James died in a motorcycle accident at the age of twenty-four.

Appendix 5: Unknown Photographs

Appendix 5: Unknown photographs

Do you recognize these unidentified photographs from the Zimmerman Design Group Archives?

Unknown Residential Interiors

Note, all the photographs on this page and some on the next page are from the same home.

277

A God-Given Talent: Peter Brust, Architect, His Work and Legacy 1906-2006

Unknown Residential Interiors

Top left, middle left, and bottom left, all of these photographs and the photographs on the previous page are from the same home.

Appendix 5: Unknown Photographs

Unknown Residential Interiors

Above and below, both of these photographs are of the same house. The fireplace can be seen through the doorway in the top photograph.

Unknown Ecclesiastical Interiors

Unknown Auditorium Interiors

Bibliography

Aderman, Ralph M. ed. *Trading Post to Metropolis.* Milwaukee, Wisconsin: Milwaukee County Historical Society, 1987.

"AIA Fellows of the Past 30 Years." *Wisconsin Architect* (May 1963): 13.

"The American Club at Kohler, Wisconsin: Brust & Philipp, Architects." *American Architect* (2 October 1918): 401.

The American Club: A Heritage and History Remembered. Kohler, Wisconsin: Kohler Company, 1993.

American Country Houses of Today. New York: Architectural Book Publishing Company, Inc., 1912 & 1927.

Anderson, W. J. and Julius Bleyer, eds. *Milwaukee's Great Industries.* Milwaukee, Wisconsin: Association for the Advancement of Milwaukee, 1892.

Annual Report of the Park Commissioners of the City of Milwaukee. 16th and 17th ed. Milwaukee, Wisconsin: City of Milwaukee, 1906, 1907.

"Architecture: A Family Tradition." *Western Architect* (June 1963): 13-15.

Avella, Steven M. *In the Richness of the Earth: A History of the Archdiocese of Milwaukee, 1843-1958.* Milwaukee, Wisconsin: Marquette University Press, 2002.

Baehr, Carl. *Milwaukee Streets: The Stories Behind Their Names.* Milwaukee, Wisconsin: Cream City Press, 1995.

Barsantee, Harry. "The History and Development of the Telephone in Wisconsin." *Wisconsin Magazine of History* 10 (1926-1927): 150-163.

Bay View Neighborhood Historic Resources Survey. 2 vols. Milwaukee, Wisconsin: City of Milwaukee, [1990].

Better Hosiery: The Story of Holeproof. [Milwaukee, Wisconsin: Holeproof Hosiery Company], 1924.

Birr, Gordon. *The Shorewood Historical Society Presents a Guide to Shorewood's Architecture.* Shorewood, Wisconsin: The Society, 2001.

Blied, Benjamin. *A History of St. John the Baptist Congregation.* Johnsburg, Wisconsin: np, 1980.

Blodgett, Richard. *A Sense of Higher Design.* Lyme, Connecticut: Greenwich Publishing Group, Inc., 2003.

Bold Craftsmen. Kohler, Wisconsin: Kohler Company, 1973.

Bolton, Harry. *Centennial History of St. John's Cathedral 1847-1947.* Milwaukee, Wisconsin: n.p, 1947.

The Book of Milwaukee: Development, Resources, Enterprise and Beauty of the Peerless Cream City. Milwaukee, Wisconsin: Evening Wisconsin Company, 1901.

Bruce, William George. *History of Milwaukee, City and County.* Chicago: S. J. Clarke, 1922.

"Brust and Brust Collection." Wisconsin Architectural Archives.

"Brust and Philipp Collection." Wisconsin Architectural Archives.

Built in Milwaukee: An Architectural View of the City. ed. Randy Garber. Milwaukee, Wisconsin: Department of City Development, [1987].

Carmel of the Divine Heart of Jesus: 100 years, 1891-1991. Carmelite Sisters, 1991.

The Century Club of Business in Milwaukee. Milwaukee, Wisconsin: Milwaukee Sentinel, 1966.

City of Milwaukee. Department of Building Inspection. Building permits.

Columbia perspective [Milwaukee Wisconsin: Columbia Hospital], [1959?]

Combined Locks Golden Jubilee, 1920-1970. Combined Locks, Wisconsin: Jubilee Committee, 1970.

Commercial History of Wisconsin. Milwaukee, Wisconsin: Thompson H. Adams, 1910.

CommercialMilwaukee. Milwaukee, Wisconsin The Association, 1908-1919.

Conrad, Howard L., ed. *History of Milwaukee: From Its First Settlement to the Year 1895.* Chicago: American Biographical Publishing Co. n.d

Diamond Jubilee of St. Francis Seminary, 1856-1931. Milwaukee, Wisconsin: Husting Printing Co., [1931?].

Dictionary of Wisconsin Biography. Madison: State Historical Society of Wisconsin, 1960.

Dorr, James R. *Downtown Building Survey.* Milwaukee, Wisconsin: Redevelopment Corporation, 1977.

Environs: Kohler. Kohler, Wisconsin: Kohler Company, 1984.

Euper, Sister Jo Ann O.S.F. *1st Century of Service: the School Sisters of St. Francis.* Milwaukee, Wisconsin: Bulfin Printers, Inc., 1976.

Fanning, Ralph. "The Consideration of Materials in Architectural Design." *American Architecture.* 6 September 1916: 343+.

Farrow, Julaine. *Winnebago State Hospital, 1873-1973* [s.n.] [197?].

50 Years of Progress, 1901-1951. Milwaukee, Wisconsin: Allis (Louis) Company, 1951.

Flahive, Robert F. *Cardinal Stritch College: Yesterday, Today, and Tomorrow.* Marquette University, 1973.

Fleischmann, Sister Mary Plato. *A Century of Christian Love.* Milwaukee, Wisconsin: St. Joseph Convent, 1977.

Flower, Frank A. *History of Milwaukee.* Chicago: Western Historical Company, 1881.

Frank, Dr. Louis. *The Medical History of Milwaukee, 1834-1914.* Milwaukee, Wisconsin: Germania Publishing Company, [1915].

Friedlander, Ted. *The Story of Clothing Manufacturing in Milwaukee from 1843 to 2003.* [Milwaukee, Wisconsin]: Friedlander, 2003.

Gateway to the Pineries: An Architectural and Historical Guide to Downtown Stevens Point. Stevens Point, Wisconsin: City of Stevens Point Historic Preservation Design Review Commission, 1988.

Gauer, Paul. *The Gauer Story.* Milwaukee, Wisconsin: Paul Gauer, 1956.

German-American Artists in Early Milwaukee: A Biography Dictionary. Madison, Wisconsin: Friends of the Max Kade Institute for German American Studies, 1997.

Gilkey, George R. *The first seventy years: A History of the University of Wisconsin-La Crosse, 1909-1979.* La Crosse, Wisconsin: University of Wisconsin-La Crosse Foundation, 1981.

Golden Jubilee, 1896-1946. St. Nazianz, Wisconsin: Salvatorians, [1946].

Golden Jubilee of Saint Francis Seminary: 1856-1906. Milwaukee, Wisconsin: J.H. Yewdale & Sons, 1906.

The Grassroots History of Racine County. Racine, Wisconsin: Racine County Historical Museum Inc., 1978.

Gregory, John Goadby. *History of Milwaukee, Wisconsin.* Chicago: Clarke Publishing Company, 1931.

_____. *Southeastern Wisconsin,* 1932.

Gough, Marion. "Best Small Houses 1898 and 1986." *The House Beautiful.* November 1986: 60-61.

He Sent Two: The Story of the Beginning of the School Sisters of St. Francis. Milwaukee, Wisconsin: Bruce Publishing Co., 1965.

Headley, Robert Jr. *The Theatres of Milwaukee.* Washington, D.C.: Theatre Historical Society, 1971.

Hessel, Susan T. *Recollections, 1909-1973: Campus School of Wisconsin Lacrosse.* Lacrosse, Wisconsin: University of WI-La Crosse Foundation, 1992.

Hewitt, Mark Alan. "The Other Proper Style." *Old-House Journal.* March/April 1997: 30-37.

_____. "To Build a Tudor." *Old-House Journal.* January/February 1998: 50-55.

Hildebrand, Janice. *Sheboygan County: 150 years of Progress: An Illustrated History.* Northridge, California: Windsor Publications, 1988.

Hiller, Francis H. *The Juvenile Court and Detention Home.* Milwaukee, Wisconsin: Francis H. Hiller, 1946.

History of Milwaukee. Chicago: S. J. Clarke Publishing Company, 1922.

"History of Milwaukee." *Milwaukee Writer's Project.* 1946. [From the Wisconsin Architectural Archives files.]

History of Milwaukee Deluxe Supplement. Chicago: S. J. Clarke Publication Company, 1922.

The History of the Knights of Columbus in Wisconsin From Their Beginnings in the Year 1900. Oshkosh, Wisconsin: Curtis-Pierce, 1952.

Island of refuge : the Northern Wisconsin Center for the Developmentally Disabled, 1897-1997. Friendship, Wisconsin: New Past Press, 1997.

Johnson, Jean Lindsay. *When Midwest Millionaires Lived Like Kings.* Milwaukee, Wisconsin: n.p., 1981.

Johnson, Rt. Rev. Msgr. Peter Leo, D.D. *Halcyon Days: Story of the St. Francis Seminary Milwaukee: 1856-1956.* Milwaukee, Wisconsin: The Bruce Publishing Company, 1956.

Kelly, Tim. *Good as Gold: A History of Banking in Wisconsin.* Madison, Wisconsin: Straus Printing, 1992.

Kempsmith Machine Company: Celebrating a Century of Innovative Engineering. Milwaukee, Wisconsin: Kempsmith Machine Company, [1988?].

Kinsey, Virginia and Ed Schreiber. *Century of Life in a Door County Village.* Fish Creek, Wisconsin: John & Nancy Sargent, 1990.

"Kohler Company Ponders New Job For Family Mansion." *Milwaukee Journal Sentinel.* 7 June 1998.

Korn, Bernhard. *The Story of Bay View.* Milwaukee, Wisconsin: Milwaukee County Historical Society, 1980.

Korom, Joseph. *Milwaukee Architecture: A Guide to Notable Buildings.* Madison, Wisconsin: Prairie Oak Press, 1995.

Koyl, George S. ed. *American Architects Directory.* New York: R.R. Bowker, Co., 1962.

Kroll, Wayne L. *Badger Breweries.* Jefferson, Wisconsin: Kroll, 1976.

Langill, Ellen. *Powered by Our Past: 150 Years of Marshall & Ilsley Ban, 1847-1997.* Milwaukee, Wisconsin: M&I Corporation, 1997.

Layton Park, a Thriving Community of Milwaukee : A Book of Our Present Community Together With a History of Its Growth and Development. [Milwaukee, Wisconsin]: Layton Park Civic Association, 1927.

MacArthur, Shirley. *North Point South.* Milwaukee, Wisconsin: Land Ethics, Inc. and Water Tower Landmark Trust, Inc., 1978

_____. *North Point Historic Districts— Milwaukee.* Milwaukee, Wisconsin: North Point Historical Society, 1981.

Marrow, Robert. *Carrollville in Retrospect.* Oak Creek, Wisconsin: Robert Marrow, 1982.

Massey, James C. and Shirley Maxwell. "Early Colonial Revival" *Old-House Journal,* May/June 2004: 82-89.

Men of Milwaukee: A Biographical and Photographic Record of Business and Professional Men of Milwaukee. Milwaukee, Wisconsin: Associated Compliers, 1930.

Mendota Chronicle: A Short History of Mendota State Hospital: First One Hundred Years, 1860-1960. Madison, Wisconsin : Mendota State Hospital, 1960.

Messinger, Jean Goodwin. *A Closer Look at Beaver Dam.* Colorado Springs, Colorado: Cottonwood Press, 1981.

Meyer, Alfred J., Mrs. *History of Oak Creek Township.* [Oak Creek, Wisconsin]: n.p., [197?].

Milwaukee, a Half Century's Progress, 1846-1896. Milwaukee, Wisconsin: Consolidated Illustrating Co., [1896].

Milwaukee County Parks: Locations and Facilities. Milwaukee, Wisconsin: Park Commission, [1949].

Milwaukee Illustrated [Milwaukee, Wisconsin: s.n., 1918?]

Milwaukee Landmarks. Milwaukee, Wisconsin: Milwaukee Historic Preservation, [1982].

Milwaukee: A Picturesque and Descriptive Account of the Present Mercantile and Industrial Interests and Advantages of the Metropolis of Wisconsin. Milwaukee, Wisconsin: Merchants & Manufactures Association, 1903.

Moore, John M., ed. *Moore's Who is Who in Wisconsin*. Los Angeles: John Moore, 1960.

Mother Caroline and The School Sisters of Notre Dame in North America. St. Louis: Woodward & Tiernan Company, 1928.

"The Nation's School of the Month: Alexander Hamilton High School Wisconsin." *Nation's Schools*. May 1967: 97-99

A New Assisi: The First Hundred Years of the Sisters of St. Francis of Assisi, Milwaukee, Wisconsin, 1849-1949. Milwaukee, Wisconsin: Bruce Publishing Company, [1948].

Newcomb, Rexford. " The Continuity of Personal Influence as Sensed in the Work of Brust and Philipp of Milwaukee." *Western Architect*. August 1924: 87-88.

_____. "Craftsmanship in Architecture: An Appreciation of the Work of Brust and Philipp, Architects." *The Western Architect*. July 1925: 71-7.

Notable Men of Wisconsin. Milwaukee, Wisconsin: Williams Publishing Company, [2002].

Nuesse, George C. *Founding of the South Side Library*. Milwaukee, Wisconsin: Milwaukee Public Library, 1909.

O'Hearn, Reverend David J. *Fifty Years at Saint John's Cathedral*. Milwaukee, Wisconsin: St John's Cathedral, 1897.

One Hundred Years of Progress: Locks Mill Centennial Anniversary, 1889-1989. Appleton, Wisconsin: Appleton Papers, Inc., 1989.

Our Golden Years, 1884-1934. Milwaukee, Wisconsin: Edward Schuster & Co., 1934.

Parish History Files. Archives of the Archdiocese of Milwaukee, Wisconsin.

The Past in our Present: A Series of Articles From the Milwaukee Journal. Milwaukee, Wisconsin: Milwaukee Journal, 1974.

Perrin, Richard W. E. *The Architecture of Wisconsin*. Madison, Wisconsin: State Historical Society of Wisconsin, 1967.

_____. *Milwaukee Landmarks*. Milwaukee, Wisconsin: Milwaukee Public Museum, 1979.

"Peter Brust and Richard Philipp." *National Register of Historic Places*. United States Department of the Interior National Park Service. [1992?]

"Peter Brust, Architect, Dies at Age of 76." *Western Builder*. 27 June 1946.

"Peter Brust, FAIA" *National Architect*. September 1946: 13.

Portrait and Biographical Record of Sheboygan County, Wisconsin. Chicago: Excelsior Publishing Company, 1894.

"Prize Competition." *The House Beautiful*. August 1898.

Questions and Answers About the Milwaukee Public Library System Celebrate Its 75th Anniversary Year in 1953. [Milwaukee, Wisconsin: Board of Trustees of the Milwaukee Public Library], 1953.

Rummel, Leo. *History of the Catholic Church in Wisconsin*. Madison, Wisconsin: Wisconsin State Council, Knights of Columbus, 1976.

St. James Evangelical Lutheran Church: 50th Anniversary 1918-1968. [Marinette, Wisconsin: St. James, 1968.]

Schreiber, Edward and Lois Schreiber ed. *Fish Creek Voices*. Sister Bay, Wisconsin: Wm. Caxton Ltd, 1990.

"Shattuck Prize." *American Architect and Building News*. 5 Nov. 1898.

Soldier's and Citizens' Album of Biographical Record. Chicago, Illinois: Grand Army Publishing Company, 1890.

Souvenir Golden Jubilee. Sacred Heart of Jesus Congregation, 1868-1918. St. Francis, Wisconsin: Sacred Heart of Jesus Congregation, 1918.

Stark, William. *Pine Lake*. Sheboygan, Wisconsin: Zimmermann Press, 1984.

Still, Bayrd. *Milwaukee, the History of a City*. Madison, Wisconsin: Wisconsin State Historical Society, 1948.

"The Town of Kohler, Wisconsin: A Model Industrial Development."

Architecture. April 1925: 149-153.

Usher, Ellis Baker. *Wisconsin, Its Story and Biography, 1848-1913*. New York: The Lewis Publishing Company, 1914.

Waltrous, Jerome A., ed. *Memoirs of Milwaukee County*. Madison, Wisconsin: Western Historical, 1909.

West Side Neighborhood Historic Resources Survey: Final Report. Milwaukee, Wisconsin: The City of Milwaukee, Department of City Development, 1984.

Who's Who in America. Chicago: A.N. Marquis & Company, 1899.

Widen, Larry and Judi Anderson. *Milwaukee Movie Palaces*. Milwaukee, Wisconsin: Milwaukee County Historical Society, 1986.

Williams, Henry Lionel and Ottalie K. Williams. *Great Houses of America*. New York: Putnam, [1969]

Winkler, Ron. "Yesterday and Today: The Lenox St. Home Bakery." *Bay View Historian*. April 2003:5.

Wisconsin Architects. Madison, Wisconsin: State Historical Society of Wisconsin, [1968].

Wisconsin Men of Achievement. Milwaukee, Wisconsin: Hooper Publishing Company, 1975.

Wisconsin Necrology [microform]. Madison, Wisconsin: State Historical Society of Wisconsin, [198-?].

Wisconsin: Stability, Progress, Beauty. Chicago: Lewis, 1946.

Wisconsin State Historical Library Building: Memorial Volume 1901. Madison: Democrat Printing Company, 1901.

Withey, Henry F. and Elsie Rathburn Withey. *Biographical Dictionary of American Architects (Deceased)*. Los Angeles: Hennessey and Ingalls, 1970 [1956].

Wolkenheim, Stanley E. *Sylvester: The Story of Maynard*. Milwaukee, Wisconsin: Maynard Steel Casting Company, 1979.

Wright Directory Company. *City of Milwaukee Directory*. Milwaukee, Wisconsin: Wright Directory Company, 1880-?.

Zimmerman, J. Russell. *The Heritage Guidebook*. 2nd ed. Milwaukee, Wisconsin: H. W. Schwartz, 1989.

_____. *Magnificent Milwaukee*. Milwaukee, Wisconsin: Milwaukee Public Museum. 1987.

Index

A. R. Schmidt Electric Company, 59
A. F. Gallun & Sons, 161-162
Adler, David, 23
Adler, Emmanuel, 23, 93
Adler, Isaac, 23
Adler, Solomon, 23
Akin, William, 51
Albrecht, Dr. Edwin J., 74
Alexander Hamilton High School, 249
Allis, Louis, 22, 49
Alvernia Catholic High School, 121
American Club, 207-209
Amtrak Station, 256
Apple Green Lodge, 91
Argola Investment Co. Garage & Auditorium, 168
Babcock, Dr. Charles, 85
Baldus, F. Edward, 228
Bartolotta's Lake Park Bistro, 258
Battery Light & Power Company, 165
Bayside Village Hall/Police Station, 258
Beaver Dam Community Hospital, 176, 233
Billenness, Charles, 214
Blue Cross/Blue Shield, 253
Braun, Rose Maller, 269-270
Bresler, Frank H., 158-159
Brost, John Baptist, 2-3
Brown Deer Fire Station, 256
Bruce Publishing Company, 250
Brumdner Building, 214
Brust & Brust, 224-226
Brust & Philipp, 32-34
Brust, Anna (1884-1894), 2, 269, 274
Brust, Anna Margarethe Wallebohr
    (1808-1887), 3, 273
Brust, Anna Marie "Emma" (Reiman-Dedericks), 3, 268-269
Brust, Catherine Biever (1844-1923), 2, 3-4, 268, 274
Brust, Catherine (Haboeck), 7
Brust, Charlotte (Lottie) Greulich, 4, 7, 265, 276
Brust, Christopher, 3-4, 8, 24, 27, 271, 274
Brust, Frank, 3, 4, 27
Brust, Gertrude (Jordan), 3, 8, 269-270, 275
Brust, John (1882-1930), 3
Brust, John (1912-1995), 7, 225-226, 227, 265-268, 276
Brust, Joseph, 3, 275
Brust, Josephine (Linck), 3, 273
Brust, Leo, 4
Brust, Mary (Schmidling), 3, 24
Brust, Mary Ann (Thomas), 3

Brust, Nicholas (1810-1868), 2-3, 273
Brust, Reverend Nicholas (1874-1957), 3, 6, 275
Brust, Olga Greulich, 4, 7, 265, 276
Brust, Paul, 7, 224-225, 271, 276
Brust, Peter, 4-7, 8, 9, 32-34, 236, 276
Brust-Zimmerman, 253
Buick Motor Company, 170
Capital Court Shopping Center, 251
Cardinal Stritch University, 247
Carmelite Sisters of the Divine Heart of Jesus, 126
Casper, Stephan J., 55
Cathedral of St. John's the Evangelist, 12-13
Chile Church, 229
Christ King Catholic Church, 229
Citizen's Bank of Juneau, 146
City Club, 198-200
Clark Square Pavilion, 249
Clas, Alfred, 9, 10, 193
Cohen, Sanford M., 37
Columbia Hospital School of Nursing, 177-178
Columbia Hospital, 177-178
Columbia St. Mary's Family Health Center, 261
Combined Locks Paper Company, 104, 210-212
Concordia University, 245-246
Conlin, John, 11, 47
Cooper Park Pavilion, 248
Crane, Charles D., 17, 20
Cruisers Frozen Custard & Jumbo Burgers, 261
Currie Park Clubhouse, 248
Dankoler, Harry E., 77
David Adler and Sons, 23
De Sales College Preparatory Seminary, 244
Dederichs, Anna Marie "Emma"
    Brust Reiman, (See Brust, Anna Marie)
Deer Creek Elementary School, 241
Discalced Carmelite Monastery, Holy Hill, 110, 129
Discalced Carmelite Monastery,
    St. Florian's, West Allis, 129
Dominican Sisters of Racine, 128
Dominican Sisters of the Perpetual Rosary, 127
Donohue, Jerry, 81
E. A. Schroeter Warehouse, 169
Ed Schuster Stores, 153-155, 251
Emmerich, Herman L, 157
Ernest G. Miller Memorial Gymnasium, 219
Esser Gymnasium, 130
Esser, Herman, 18-19, 20
Esser, Reverend Lawrence, 130
Esser, T.C., 99, 130, 158

Evangelical Lutheran Church of East Milwaukee, 114
F. H. Bresler Galleries Showroom, 158-159
F. M. Prescott Steam Pump Company, 42, 152
F. M. Theisen Office and Flat, 157
F. Mann Store and Flat, 156
Ferry & Clas, 9, 10, 11-17, 32
Ferry, George, 9, 10
Filling Stations, 171-172
First Metal in the Ecclesiastical Group, 215
First National Bank of Stevens Point, 145
First Unitarian Church, 16
Flambeau Paper Company, 147, 150
Fond du Lac National Bank, 136-137
43 Harley Davidson, 261
Franciscans of Pulaski, Wisconsin, 128
Franklin Police Station, 259
Freschl, Carl, 148
Friedmann, Alfred, 90
Friedmann, Max E., 90
Friend, Julia, 54
Friend, Ralph, 54
Frisch, Abraham L., 42
Gaenslen Elementary School, 257
Gallun, Albert F., 46-47, 161-162
Gallun, August F., 161-162
George Heinemann & Company, 62-63
George Ziegler Candy Company, 55, 166-167
Gill, Thomas H., 39
Gimbels-Schusters, 154
Girl Scouts Milwaukee Area, 262
Goodrich, Hunter, 69
Graham, H.M., 94
Grau, August M. Jr., 59
Grau, Adelade, 47
Greulich, Andrew, 4
Greulich, August, 4, 265
Greulich, Charlotte (Lottie)--see Brust, Charlotte Greulich
Greulich, Olga--see Brust, Olga Greulich
Halcyon House, 35-36
Hall, Allan E., 68
Hansen Storage, 19
Hansen, Carl, 94
Hansen, Guido, 92-93
Hatch, Dr. W. Grant, 75, 76
Hays, Charles D., 38
Hayssen, Arthur, 78
Heimerl, Julius 9, 32, 41, 47, 49, 51, 55, 59, 60, 77, 86, 93, 165
Heinemann, Anna R., 62-63
Heinemann, George, 62

Heiss Hall, 237-238
Heller, Isidore, 86, 89
Heun, Henry, 69
Hodgson, Dr. Albert James, 74
Hoell, Sister Alexia, 115-119, 182-189
Holeproof Hosiery, 148
Holy Angels Catholic Church, 108
Holy Apostles Church, 240
Holy Family Normal School, 5, 220
Holy Redeemer Catholic Church, 96
Holy Rosary Academy, 128
Holy Trinity, Jericho, 105
Immaculate Conception, Juneau, Wisconsin, 25
Immaculate Conception Catholic Church, Milwaukee, 243
Johnson Controls' Brengel Technology Building, 259
Johnson Service Company, 18
Johnson, Caleb Elliot, 17
Johnson Wax, 262
Johnston, Harry S., 65
Kasten, Walter, 38
Kaumheimer, William, 64
Kempsmith Manufacturing Company, 149
Kieckhefer, Robert John, 57
Kilbourn Park World War I Memorial, 196
Kiley Hall, 237-238
Killen, William H., 85
Kneipp Method, 117, 182
Kneipp, Monsignor Sebastian, 117, 182
Knights of Columbus, 197
Knowlton Hospital, 177
Koch, Edward V., 9
Koch, H. C., 18, 21
Kohler Company, 204-209
Kohler Village, 204-209
Kohler, Charlotte, 82
Kohler, John Michael (1902-1968), 82-83, 88
Kohler, John Michael Jr., (1844-1901), 204
Kohler, Julilly, 82, 88
Kohler, Walter J. 81, 82-83, 204-209, 230
Krehla, Frank J., 227
La Crosse Teachers' College, 234
Lake Park Children's Pavilion, 194
Lakeside Distillery, 163
Lamoreux, D.P., 71-73, 176
Layton Park English Lutheran Church, 98
Lenox Street Home Bakery, 24
Linck, Josephine Brust, (See Brust, Josephine Linck)
Lochemes, Frederick, 142
Louis Allis Company, 22, 49
Luick Ice Cream Company, 44-45, 51, 164, 260
Luick, John, 164

Index

Luick, William Ferdinand, 44-45, 51, 164
Luther Memorial Chapel, 114
Lutheran Deaconess Hospital, 73, 176
Mack, Edwin S., 43
Mann, Frank J., 156
Marion Chester Read Center, 262
Marshall & Ilsley Bank, 140-141
Matthews Brothers, 16
Mayfair Bank Tower, 254
Maynard Steel Casing Company, 165
Mechanical Appliance Company, 22, 49
Mendota Hospital for the Insane (Mendota Mental Health Institute), 180
Mercy Catholic High School, 125
Merrill Theater, 202
Metropolitan Condominiums, 258
Miller, George Peckham, 52-53
Miller, Harry M., 66
Milwaukee Detention & Juvenile Court Building, 192
Milwaukee Public Library and Museum, 13-14
Milwaukee Sanitarium, 174-175
Milwaukee-Waukesha Brewery, 169
Mitchell Park Pavilion, 195
Munkwitz, William H., 61
Nadeau, Dr. Alexandre T., 87
North Avenue Bank, 144
North Point Historical District, 37-48
North Shore Savings and Loan, 254
Northern Hospital for the Insane, Winnebago, 181
Northern Wisconsin Center for the Developmentally Disabled (See Wisconsin Home for the Feeble-Minded)
Noyes Pool, 254
Nullmann, J., 48
O'Neil Oil and Paint Company, 171-172
Oak Creek Police Station, 257
Olmstead Brothers, 206, 230
Our Lady of Mercy Convent/Academy, 123
Pabst Mansion, 11
Packard Motor Car Company Garage, 171
Patek, Dr. Arthur, 65
Pettit National Ice Center, 257
Philipp, Richard, 9, 32-34, 35-36, 214
Pio Nono High School, 4, 5, 220, 239
Potawatomi Bingo Casino, 262
Prescott, F. M., 152
Pressed Steel Tank, 221
Public Service Building, 19
Puerner, Mrs. Amelia Heimerl, 86
Ranier Hall, 238
Raths, Louise Reiman, 268-269

Reiman, Anna Marie "Emma" Brust (See Brust, Anna Marie "Emma" Reiman-Dedericks)
Reiman, John, 268-269, 274
Richter, Oscar A., 75
Riesen, Frederick, 70
Riess, Mrs. J. R. (Mary), 79-80
Riverbend, 82-84
Roman Catholic Church of the Gesu, 18
Rusk Avenue Homes, 60
Sacred Heart Mortuary Chapel, 113
Sacred Heart of Jesus Parish School, 5
Sacred Heart Sanitarium, 182-188
St. Aemilian's Orphan Asylum, 131
St. Agnes Hospital, 231-232
St. Alphonsus Catholic Church, New Muster, 104
St. Anne's Catholic Church, 99
St. Anne's Home for the Elderly Ladies, 128
St. Anthony on the Lake Catholic Church, 100
St. Augustine of Hippo Catholic Church, 7, 100
St. Bonaventure, 128
St. Boniface Catholic Church, 109
St. Catherine's Home for Working Girls, 124
St. Clara's Home, 123
St. Clare Hospital, Monroe, Wisconsin, 232
St. Coletta's Institute, 122
St. Florian's Catholic Church, 110-111, 126, 129, 216
St. Florian's Catholic Church Convent, 126
St. Francis Bank, 142
St. Francis Building and Loan, 142
St. Francis House of Studies, 120
St. Francis Seminary, 29, 130, 131, 134, 219
St. Gregory the Great Catholic Church, 242
St. James' Evangelical Lutheran Church, 106
St. Joan of Arc Catholic Church, Delafield, 97
St. John Kanty, Milwaukee, 242
St. John's Evangelist Catholic Church, Kohler, 230
St. John's for the Deaf, 132-133, 215, 241
St. Joseph's Chapel, 118-120
St. Joseph's Convent Retirement Home, Campbellsport, 217
St. Joseph's Hospital, Beaver Dam, 233
St. Joseph's Middle School, Tsingtao, China, 218
St. Leo's Catholic Church, 109
St. Louis' Catholic Church, 8
St. Mary of the Angels Chapel, 215
St. Mary's Catholic Church, South Milwaukee, 97
St. Mary's Catholic Church, Juneau, 25
St. Mary's Catholic Church, (Dover) Kansasville, 107
St. Mary's Hill Hospital, 189
St. Mary's Institute (Academy), 28
St. Mary's Nativity of Mary Catholic, Lomira, 26

St. Mary's of the Visitation Catholic Church, Marytown, 107
St. Matthew's Catholic School, Campbellsport, 105
St. Michael's Catholic School and rectory, 101
St. Patrick's Catholic Church Convent, 124
St. Patrick's Catholic Church, 101
St. Paul's Combined Locks Catholic Church, 104, 212
St. Peter Claver Catholic Church, Sheboygan, 103
St. Rita's Catholic Church, 112
St. Rosa of Lima Catholic Church, Fredonia, 103
St. Stephen's Catholic Church, 102
Salvatorian Monastery, Mother of Good Counsel, 130
Salvatorians, Society of the Divine Savior, 130
Salzmann Hall, 220
Salzmann Library, 134
Sands, Sarah A., 92
Sarah A. Scott Middle School, 256
Saxe Park Theater, 201
Saxe, Thomas, 201, 202
Schmidling, Mary (See Brust, Mary Schmidling)
Schmidling, Teresa, 271
Schmidt, Albert R., 59
Schmid, Alfons, 115, 121
Schmitt, Edward Conrad, 228
School Sisters of Notre Dame of the Lake, 245-246
School Sisters of St. Francis, 105, 115-121, 233
Schroeter, E. A., 48, 169
Schuster, Edward, 90, 153-155, 251
Security National Bank, 138-139
Shattuck Prize, 30
Sherman, Mrs. Louis A., 70
Sherry, Avery, 147, 150
Sherry, Edward P., 147, 150
Sherry, Hugh, 147
Siegel, Phillip, 25
Sisters' House and Infirmary, 29
Sisters of Our Lady of Mercy, 123-125
Sisters of St. Agnes, Fond du Lac, 126, 231-232
Sisters of St. Francis of Assisi, 122, 247
Sleyster, Dr. Rock, 68, 174-175
Slocum Straw Works, 168
Smith, Charles F., 61
South Shore Medical Office, 261
South Side Library, 190-191
State Bank of Manitowoc, 143
Stein Studios, 160
Stein, Simon L., 160
Steinmeyer Building, 17
Stroik, David, 255
Sylvan Lodge, 77
T. C. Esser, 158

Theisen, F.M., 157
Third District Police Station, 259
Thomas, Mary Ann Brust (See Brust, Mary Ann Thomas)
Thomas More High School, 239
Tower Theater, 202
Town of Lake District #1 School, 5
Town of Lake, 3-4, 5
Tsingtao, China, 218
Van Buren City Lofts, 260
Van Treeck, Carl, 230, 231
Vaughn, Francis A., 58
Vollrath Company, 78, 151
Vollrath, Jean C., 78
Walsh, Reverend Thomas, 229
Warehouse # 1, 19
Washington Park Zoo, 193
We Energies Headquarters, 260
Wehr, William E., 40
Weil, Sarah Stern, 41
West Allis Police Station and Court Facility, 260
Winnebago Mental Health Institute (See Northern Hospital for the Insane)
Wisconsin Historical Society, Madison, 15
Wisconsin Home for the Feeble Minded, Chippewa Falls, 179
Wisconsin Realty Company, 147, 150
Wisconsin Telephone Company, 222
Wolff, Edwin, 66
Wollaeger, Edwin, 67
Wollaeger, Gustave Jr., 56
Worden, Euclid P., 42
Ziegler, Charles I, 55, 167
Ziegler, George, 166-167
Zimmerman Design Group, 255
Zimmerman, Gary, 253, 255
Zinn, Toni, 50, 91
Zinn, Walter, 50, 58, 91, 156

Quick Order Form

Postal Orders:

ElexDay Publications, Anna Passante
3207 South Indiana Avenue
Milwaukee, Wisconsin 53207
414-482-1781

Name:_____

Address:_____

City: _____ State:_____ Zip code:_____

Telephone:_____

email address:_____

Cost of book: $24.95 + $3.50 for postage

Send order and check or money order for $28.45 made out to ElexDay Publications to:

ElexDay Publications
C/O Anna Passante
3207 South Indiana Avenue
Milwaukee, WI 53207